Living Liturgy™

SUNDAY MISSAL

2010

CELEBRATING THE EUCHARIST

☩

LITURGICAL PRESS
Collegeville, Minnesota

www.litpress.org

Published with the approval of the
Committee on Divine Worship
United States Conference of Catholic Bishops

Nihil Obstat: Reverend Robert C. Harren, *Censor deputatus.*

Imprimatur: ✠ Most Reverend John F. Kinney, J.C.D., D.D., Bishop of St. Cloud,
Minnesota, June 17, 2009.

Excerpts from the English translation of *Lectionary for Mass* © 1969, 1981, 1997, International Committee on English in the Liturgy, Inc. (ICEL); excerpts from the English translation of *Rite of Baptism for Children* © 1969, ICEL; excerpts from the English translation of *The Roman Missal* © 1973, ICEL; the English translation of *Eucharistic Prayers for Masses of Reconciliation* © 1975, ICEL; excerpts from the English translation of *Rite of Confirmation (Second Edition)* © 1975, ICEL; excerpts from the English translation of *Rite of Christian Initiation of Adults* © 1985, ICEL. All rights reserved.

Scripture readings are taken from the *Lectionary for Mass for Use in the Dioceses of the United States of America, second typical edition* Copyright © 1970, 1986, 1997, 1998, 2001 Confraternity of Christian Doctrine, Inc., Washington, D.C. All rights reserved. No part of this book may be reproduced or transmitted in any form or by any means, electronic or mechanical, including photocopying, recording, or by any information storage and retrieval system, without permission in writing from the copyright owner.

Cover design by Ann Blattner. Art by Annika Nelson.

© 2009 by Order of Saint Benedict, Collegeville, Minnesota. All rights reserved. No part of this book may be reproduced in any form, by print, microfilm, microfiche, mechanical recording, photocopying, translation, or by any other means, known or yet unknown, for any purpose except brief quotations in reviews, without the previous written permission of Liturgical Press, Saint John's Abbey, P.O. Box 7500, Collegeville, Minnesota 56321-7500. Printed in the United States of America.

ISSN 1949-1166
ISBN 978-0-8146-3306-9

Contents

Aspects of the Nature of the Sacred Liturgy 5
The Order of Mass 9
Celebration of the Liturgy of the Word
[with Holy Communion] 37

November 29	First Sunday of Advent	40
December 6	Second Sunday of Advent	44
December 8	Immaculate Conception	48
December 13	Third Sunday of Advent	53
December 20	Fourth Sunday of Advent	58
December 24	The Vigil of Christmas	62
December 25	Christmas—Mass at Midnight	68
December 25	Christmas—Mass at Dawn	72
December 25	Christmas—Mass during the Day	76
December 27	Holy Family	80
January 1	Solemnity of Mary, Mother of God	85
January 3	Epiphany	89
January 10	Baptism of the Lord	94
January 17	Second Sunday in Ordinary Time	98
January 24	Third Sunday in Ordinary Time	103
January 31	Fourth Sunday in Ordinary Time	109
February 7	Fifth Sunday in Ordinary Time	114
February 14	Sixth Sunday in Ordinary Time	120
February 17	Ash Wednesday	124
February 21	First Sunday of Lent	130
February 28	Second Sunday of Lent	135
March 7	Third Sunday of Lent	140
March 14	Fourth Sunday of Lent	145
March 21	Fifth Sunday of Lent	151
March 28	Palm Sunday of the Lord's Passion	156
April 1	Holy Thursday	173
April 2	Good Friday	178
April 3	The Easter Vigil	197
April 4	Easter Sunday	233
April 11	Second Sunday of Easter	238
April 18	Third Sunday of Easter	244
April 25	Fourth Sunday of Easter	249
May 2	Fifth Sunday of Easter	254
May 9	Sixth Sunday of Easter	258
May 13	The Ascension of the Lord	263
May 16	Seventh Sunday of Easter	269
May 22	Vigil of Pentecost	273
May 23	Pentecost Sunday	277
May 30	Trinity Sunday	285
June 6	The Most Holy Body and Blood of Christ	289
June 13	Eleventh Sunday in Ordinary Time	295

June 20	Twelfth Sunday in Ordinary Time	301
June 27	Thirteenth Sunday in Ordinary Time	305
July 4	Fourteenth Sunday in Ordinary Time	309
July 11	Fifteenth Sunday in Ordinary Time	314
July 18	Sixteenth Sunday in Ordinary Time	320
July 25	Seventeenth Sunday in Ordinary Time	324
August 1	Eighteenth Sunday in Ordinary Time	330
August 8	Nineteenth Sunday in Ordinary Time	334
August 14	Vigil of the Assumption	340
August 15	Assumption of the Blessed Virgin Mary	344
August 22	Twenty-first Sunday in Ordinary Time	349
August 29	Twenty-second Sunday in Ordinary Time	353
September 5	Twenty-third Sunday in Ordinary Time	357
September 12	Twenty-fourth Sunday in Ordinary Time	362
September 19	Twenty-fifth Sunday in Ordinary Time	369
September 26	Twenty-sixth Sunday in Ordinary Time	374
October 3	Twenty-seventh Sunday in Ordinary Time	379
October 10	Twenty-eighth Sunday in Ordinary Time	383
October 17	Twenty-ninth Sunday in Ordinary Time	387
October 24	Thirtieth Sunday in Ordinary Time	391
October 31	Thirty-first Sunday in Ordinary Time	395
November 7	Thirty-second Sunday in Ordinary Time	400
November 14	Thirty-third Sunday in Ordinary Time	405
November 21	Christ the King	409

Aspects of the Nature of the Sacred Liturgy

Excerpts from The Constitution on the Sacred Liturgy, *Sacrosanctum Concilium* (SC), issued by The Second Vatican Council on December 4, 1963.

LITURGY

To accomplish so great a work [of redemption] Christ is always present in his church, especially in liturgical celebrations.

(SC 7)

Nevertheless, the liturgy is the summit toward which the activity of the church is directed; it is also the source from which all its power flows.

(SC 10)

Introductory Rites

But in order that the liturgy may be able to produce its full effects it is necessary that the faithful come to it with proper dispositions, that their minds be attuned to their voices, and that they cooperate with heavenly grace . . .

(SC 11)

. . . the principal manifestation of the church consists in the full, active participation of all God's holy people . . .

(SC 41)

Liturgy of the Word

The treasures of the Bible are to be opened up more lavishly so that a richer fare may be provided for the faithful at the table of God's word.

(SC 51)

Liturgy of the Eucharist

The more perfect form of participation in the Mass whereby the faithful, after the priest's communion, receive the Lord's body from the same sacrifice, is warmly recommended.

(SC 55)

Concluding Rites

Just as Christ was sent by the Father so also he sent the apostles, filled with the Holy Spirit. This he did so that they might preach the Gospel to every creature . . .
(SC 6)

The Order of Mass

INTRODUCTORY RITES

Options are indicated by A, B, C, D in the margin.

ENTRANCE SONG   STAND

After the entrance song, all make the sign of the cross:

Priest: In the name of the Father, and of the Son, and of the Holy Spirit.

People: Amen.

GREETING

A **Priest:** The grace of our Lord Jesus Christ and the love of God and the fellowship of the Holy Spirit be with you all.

People: And also with you.

B **Priest:** The grace and peace of God our Father and the Lord Jesus Christ be with you.

People: Blessed be God, the Father of our Lord Jesus Christ.

or: **And also with you.**

C **Priest:** The Lord be with you.

People: And also with you.

RITE OF BLESSING AND SPRINKLING OF HOLY WATER

This rite takes the place of the penitential rite. The Kyrie is also omitted. During the sprinkling of the people an antiphon or another appropriate song may be sung.

PENITENTIAL RITE

A As we prepare to celebrate the mystery of Christ's love,
let us acknowledge our failures
and ask the Lord for pardon and strength.

B Coming together as God's family,
with confidence let us ask the Father's forgiveness,
for he is full of gentleness and compassion.

C My brothers and sisters,
to prepare ourselves to celebrate the sacred mysteries,
let us call to mind our sins.

A Priest and people:

I confess to almighty God,
and to you, my brothers and sisters,
that I have sinned through my own fault

They strike their breast:

in my thoughts and in my words,
in what I have done,
and in what I have failed to do;
and I ask blessed Mary, ever virgin,
all the angels and saints,
and you, my brothers and sisters,
to pray for me to the Lord our God.

B Priest: Lord, we have sinned against you:
Lord, have mercy.

People: **Lord, have mercy.**

Priest: Lord, show us your mercy and love.

People: **And grant us your salvation.**

C Priest or other minister: *Invocation.*
Lord, have mercy.

People: **Lord, have mercy.**

Priest or other minister: *Invocation.*
Christ, have mercy.

People: **Christ, have mercy.**

Priest or other minister: *Invocation.*
Lord, have mercy.

People: **Lord, have mercy.**

The penitential rite always concludes:

Priest: May almighty God have mercy on us,
forgive us our sins,
and bring us to everlasting life.

People: **Amen.**

Kyrie

Unless included in the penitential rite, the Kyrie or Lord, have mercy is sung or said by all, with alternating parts for the choir or cantor and for the people.

℣. Lord, have mercy.   or: ℣. Kýrie, eleison.
℟. **Lord, have mercy.** or: ℟. **Kýrie, eleison.**

℣. Christ, have mercy.   or: ℣. Christe, eleison.
℟. **Christ, have mercy.** or: ℟. **Christe, eleison.**

℣. Lord, have mercy.   or: ℣. Kýrie, eleison.
℟. **Lord, have mercy.** or: ℟. **Kýrie, eleison.**

Gloria

Glory to God in the highest,
   and peace to his people on earth.
Lord God, heavenly King,
almighty God and Father,
   we worship you, we give you thanks,
   we praise you for your glory.
Lord Jesus Christ, only Son of the Father,
Lord God, Lamb of God,
you take away the sin of the world:
   have mercy on us;
you are seated at the right hand of the Father:
   receive our prayer.
For you alone are the Holy One,
you alone are the Lord,
you alone are the Most High, Jesus Christ,
   with the Holy Spirit,
   in the glory of God the Father. Amen.

Opening Prayer

Priest: **Let us pray.** Priest and people pray silently for a while. Then the priest says the opening prayer and concludes:
          for ever and ever.
People: **Amen.**

Liturgy of the Word

The proclamation of God's Word is always centered on Christ, present through his Word. Old Testament writings prepare for him; New Testament books speak of him directly. All of Scripture calls us to the faithful following of God's commandments. After the reading we reflect upon God's words and respond to them.

First Reading   SIT

Reader: The word of the Lord.
People: **Thanks be to God.**

Responsorial Psalm

Second Reading

Reader: The word of the Lord.
People: **Thanks be to God.**

Alleluia   STAND

The Alleluia is omitted if it is not sung.

Gospel

Deacon (or priest): The Lord be with you.
People: **And also with you.**

Deacon (or priest): A reading from the holy Gospel according to N.
People: **Glory to you, Lord.**

At the end:
Deacon (or priest): The Gospel of the Lord.
People: **Praise to you, Lord Jesus Christ.**

Homily   SIT

Profession of Faith   STAND

All say the profession of faith on Sundays and solemnities; the Apostles' Creed may be used with children. *See page 38.*

**We believe in one God,
   the Father, the Almighty,
   maker of heaven and earth,
   of all that is seen and unseen.**

We believe in one Lord, Jesus Christ,
>   the only Son of God, eternally begotten of the Father,
>   God from God, Light from Light,
>   true God from true God,
>   begotten, not made, one in Being with the Father.
> Through him all things were made.
> For us men and for our salvation
>   he came down from heaven:

All bow (on Christmas kneel) at the following words, up to: and became man.

> by the power of the Holy Spirit
>   he was born of the Virgin Mary, and became man.
> For our sake he was crucified under Pontius Pilate;
>   he suffered, died, and was buried.
>   On the third day he rose again
>   in fulfillment of the Scriptures;
>   he ascended into heaven
>   and is seated at the right hand of the Father.
> He will come again in glory to judge the living and the dead,
>   and his kingdom will have no end.

> We believe in the Holy Spirit, the Lord, the giver of life,
>   who proceeds from the Father and the Son.
>   With the Father and the Son he is worshiped and
>   glorified.
>   He has spoken through the Prophets.
> We believe in one holy catholic and apostolic Church.
> We acknowledge one baptism for the forgiveness of sins.
> We look for the resurrection of the dead,
>   and the life of the world to come. Amen.

General Intercessions (Prayer of the Faithful)

The priest celebrant invites the congregation to pray.

The cantor or reader continues with a number of petitions which should be offered: for the needs of the Church; for public authorities and the salvation of the world; for those oppressed by any need; for the local community; for particular celebrations to which the people respond: **Lord, hear our prayer** *or* **Lord, have mercy.**

Liturgy of the Eucharist

Preparation of the Gifts   SIT

While the gifts of the people are brought forward to the priest and are placed on the altar, the offertory song is sung. Before placing the bread on the altar, the priest says inaudibly:

Blessed are you, Lord, God of all creation.
Through your goodness we have this bread to offer,
which earth has given and human hands have made.
It will become for us the bread of life.

If there is no singing, the priest may say this prayer aloud, and the people may respond:

Blessed be God for ever.

Before placing the chalice on the altar, the priest says inaudibly:

Blessed are you, Lord, God of all creation.
Through your goodness we have this wine to offer,
fruit of the vine and work of human hands.
It will become our spiritual drink.

If there is no singing, the priest may say this prayer aloud, and the people may respond:

Blessed be God for ever.

Invitation to Prayer

Priest: Pray, brethren, that our sacrifice
         may be acceptable to God, the almighty Father.

                                                                STAND

People: **May the Lord accept the sacrifice at your hands**
         for the praise and glory of his name,
         for our good, and the good of all his Church.

Prayer over the Gifts

At the end:
People: **Amen.**

The Eucharistic Prayer

℣. The Lord be with you.   ℟. **And also with you.**
℣. Lift up your hearts.   ℟. **We lift them up to the Lord.**
℣. Let us give thanks to the Lord our God.
℟. **It is right to give him thanks and praise.**

Preface

The priest will select a preface for Eucharistic Prayer I (p. 15) and Eucharistic Prayer III (p. 22). For the prefaces proper to other Eucharistic prayers: *see* p. 19 for Eucharistic Prayer II; *see* p. 25 for Eucharistic Prayer IV; *see* p. 28 for Eucharistic Prayer for Reconciliation I; or *see* p. 31 for Eucharistic Prayer for Reconciliation II.

Sanctus

**Holy, holy, holy Lord, God of power and might,
heaven and earth are full of your glory.
Hosanna in the highest.
Blessed is he who comes in the name of the Lord.
Hosanna in the highest.**

The people kneel after the Sanctus is sung or said. **KNEEL**

Eucharistic Prayer I (The Roman Canon)

Praise to the Father

We come to you, Father,
with praise and thanksgiving,
through Jesus Christ your Son.

Through him we ask you to accept and bless ✢
these gifts we offer you in sacrifice.

Intercessions: for the Church

We offer them for your holy catholic Church,
watch over it, Lord, and guide it;
grant it peace and unity throughout the world.
We offer them for N., our Pope,
for N., our bishop,
and for all who hold and teach the catholic faith
that comes to us from the apostles.

Remember, Lord, your people,
especially those for whom we now pray, N. and N.
Remember all of us gathered here before you.
You know how firmly we believe in you
and dedicate ourselves to you.
We offer you this sacrifice of praise
for ourselves and those who are dear to us.
We pray to you, our living and true God,
for our well-being and redemption.

Order of Mass

In communion with the Saints

On Christmas and during the octave
In union with the whole Church
we celebrate that day (night)
when Mary without loss of her virginity
gave the world its Savior.
We honor Mary . . .

On Epiphany
In union with the whole Church
we celebrate that day
when your only Son,
sharing your eternal glory,
showed himself in a human body.
We honor Mary . . .

Holy Thursday
In union with the whole Church
we celebrate that day
when Jesus Christ, our Lord,
was betrayed for us.
We honor Mary . . .

From the Easter Vigil to the Second Sunday of Easter inclusive:
In union with the whole Church
we celebrate that day (night)
when Jesus Christ, our Lord,
rose from the dead in his human body.
We honor Mary . . .

Ascension
In union with the whole Church
we celebrate that day
when your only Son, our Lord,
took his place with you
and raised our frail human nature to glory.
We honor Mary . . .

Pentecost
In union with the whole Church
we celebrate the day of Pentecost
when the Holy Spirit appeared to the apostles
in the form of countless tongues.
We honor Mary . . .

In union with the whole Church
we honor Mary,
the ever-virgin mother of Jesus Christ our Lord and God.

We honor Joseph, her husband,
the apostles and martyrs
Peter and Paul, Andrew,
(James, John, Thomas, James, Philip,
Bartholomew, Matthew, Simon and Jude;
we honor Linus, Cletus, Clement, Sixtus,
Cornelius, Cyprian, Lawrence, Chrysogonus,
John and Paul, Cosmas and Damian)
and all the saints.
May their merits and prayers
gain us your constant help and protection.
(Through Christ our Lord. Amen.)

Father, accept this offering
from your whole family.
Grant us your peace in this life,
save us from final damnation,
and count us among those you have chosen.
(Through Christ our Lord. Amen.)

Bless and approve our offering;
make it acceptable to you,
an offering in spirit and in truth.
Let it become for us
the body and blood of Jesus Christ,
your only Son, our Lord.
(Through Christ our Lord. Amen.)

The Lord's Supper
The day before he suffered
he took bread in his sacred hands
and looking up to heaven,
to you, his almighty Father,
he gave you thanks and praise.
He broke the bread,
gave it to his disciples, and said:

**Take this, all of you, and eat it:
this is my body which will be given up for you.**

When supper was ended,
he took the cup.
Again he gave you thanks and praise,
gave the cup to his disciples, and said:

**Take this, all of you, and drink from it:
this is the cup of my blood,
the blood of the new and everlasting covenant.**

It will be shed for you and for all
so that sins may be forgiven.
Do this in memory of me.

Then he says:
Let us proclaim the mystery of faith:

A Christ has died,
Christ is risen,
Christ will come again.

B Dying you destroyed our death,
rising you restored our life.
Lord Jesus, come in glory.

C When we eat this bread and drink this cup,
we proclaim your death, Lord Jesus,
until you come in glory.

D Lord, by your cross and resurrection
you have set us free.
You are the Savior of the world.

The memorial prayer
Father, we celebrate the memory of Christ, your Son.
We, your people and your ministers,
recall his passion,
his resurrection from the dead,
and his ascension into glory;
and from the many gifts you have given us
we offer to you, God of glory and majesty,
this holy and perfect sacrifice:
the bread of life
and the cup of eternal salvation.

Look with favor on these offerings
and accept them as once you accepted
the gifts of your servant Abel,
the sacrifice of Abraham, our father in faith,
and the bread and wine offered by your priest Melchisedech.

Almighty God,
we pray that your angel may take this sacrifice
to your altar in heaven.
Then, as we receive from this altar
the sacred body and blood of your Son,
let us be filled with every grace and blessing.
(Through Christ our Lord. Amen.)

Order of Mass   19

For the dead
Remember, Lord, those who have died
and have gone before us marked with the sign of faith,
especially those for whom we now pray, N. and N.

May these, and all who sleep in Christ,
find in your presence
light, happiness, and peace.
(Through Christ our Lord. Amen.)

For ourselves, too, we ask
some share in the fellowship of your apostles and martyrs,
with John the Baptist, Stephen, Matthias, Barnabas,
(Ignatius, Alexander, Marcellinus, Peter,
Felicity, Perpetua, Agatha, Lucy,
Agnes, Cecilia, Anastasia)
and all the saints.

Though we are sinners,
we trust in your mercy and love.

Do not consider what we truly deserve,
but grant us your forgiveness.
Through Christ our Lord.

Through him you give us all these gifts.
You fill them with life and goodness,
you bless them and make them holy.

Concluding doxology
Through him,
with him,
in him,
in the unity of the Holy Spirit,
all glory and honor is yours,
almighty Father,
for ever and ever.

The people respond: **Amen.**
Turn to the Lord's Prayer, page 34.

EUCHARISTIC PRAYER II

Preface
Father, it is our duty and our salvation,
always and everywhere
to give you thanks
through your beloved Son, Jesus Christ.

He is the Word through whom you made the universe,
the Savior you sent to redeem us.

By the power of the Holy Spirit
he took flesh and was born of the Virgin Mary.

For our sake he opened his arms on the cross;
he put an end to death
and revealed the resurrection.
In this he fulfilled your will
and won for you a holy people.

And so we join the angels and the saints
in proclaiming your glory
as we sing (say):
**Holy, holy, holy Lord, God of power and might,
heaven and earth are full of your glory.
Hosanna in the highest.
Blessed is he who comes in the name of the Lord.
Hosanna in the highest.**

EUCHARISTIC PRAYER II

Invocation of the Holy Spirit
Lord, you are holy indeed,
the fountain of all holiness.

Let your Spirit come upon these gifts to make them holy,
so that they may become for us
the body ✠ and blood of our Lord, Jesus Christ.

The Lord's Supper
Before he was given up to death,
a death he freely accepted,
he took bread and gave you thanks.
He broke the bread,
gave it to his disciples, and said:

**Take this, all of you, and eat it:
this is my body which will be given up for you.**

When supper was ended, he took the cup.
Again he gave you thanks and praise,
gave the cup to his disciples, and said:

**Take this, all of you, and drink from it:
this is the cup of my blood,
the blood of the new and everlasting covenant.
It will be shed for you and for all
so that sins may be forgiven.
Do this in memory of me.**

Order of Mass 21

Priest: Let us proclaim the mystery of faith:

A Christ has died,
Christ is risen,
Christ will come again.

B Dying you destroyed our death,
rising you restored our life.
Lord Jesus, come in glory.

C When we eat this bread and drink this cup,
we proclaim your death, Lord Jesus,
until you come in glory.

D Lord, by your cross and resurrection
you have set us free.
You are the Savior of the world.

The memorial prayer
In memory of his death and resurrection,
we offer you, Father, this life-giving bread,
this saving cup.
We thank you for counting us worthy
to stand in your presence and serve you.

Invocation of the Holy Spirit
May all of us who share in the body and blood of Christ
be brought together in unity by the Holy Spirit.

Intercessions: for the Church
Lord, remember your Church throughout the world;
make us grow in love,
together with N., our Pope,
N., our bishop, and all the clergy.

> In Masses for the Dead the following may be added:
> Remember N., whom you have called from this life.
> In baptism he (she) died with Christ:
> may he (she) also share his resurrection.

For the dead
Remember our brothers and sisters
who have gone to their rest
in the hope of rising again;
bring them and all the departed
into the light of your presence.

In communion with the Saints
Have mercy on us all;
make us worthy to share eternal life
with Mary, the virgin Mother of God,

with the apostles, and with all the saints
who have done your will throughout the ages.
May we praise you in union with them,
and give you glory
through your Son, Jesus Christ.

Concluding doxology
Through him,
with him,
in him,
in the unity of the Holy Spirit,
all glory and honor is yours,
almighty Father,
for ever and ever.

The people respond: **Amen.**
Turn to the Lord's Prayer, page 34.

Eucharistic Prayer III

Praise to the Father
Father, you are holy indeed,
and all creation rightly gives you praise.
All life, all holiness comes from you
through your Son, Jesus Christ our Lord,
by the working of the Holy Spirit.
From age to age you gather a people to yourself,
so that from east to west
a perfect offering may be made
to the glory of your name.

Invocation of the Holy Spirit
And so, Father, we bring you these gifts.
We ask you to make them holy by the power of your Spirit,
that they may become the body ✛ and blood
of your Son, our Lord Jesus Christ,
at whose command we celebrate this eucharist.

The Lord's Supper
On the night he was betrayed,
he took bread and gave you thanks and praise.
He broke the bread, gave it to his disciples, and said:

Take this, all of you, and eat it:
this is my body which will be given up for you.

When supper was ended, he took the cup.
Again he gave you thanks and praise,
gave the cup to his disciples, and said:

Take this, all of you, and drink from it:
this is the cup of my blood,
the blood of the new and everlasting covenant.
It will be shed for you and for all
so that sins may be forgiven.
Do this in memory of me.

Priest: Let us proclaim the mystery of faith:

A Christ has died,
Christ is risen,
Christ will come again.

B Dying you destroyed our death,
rising you restored our life.
Lord Jesus, come in glory.

C When we eat this bread and drink this cup,
we proclaim your death, Lord Jesus,
until you come in glory.

D Lord, by your cross and resurrection
you have set us free.
You are the Savior of the world.

The memorial prayer
Father, calling to mind the death your Son endured for our salvation,
his glorious resurrection and ascension into heaven,
and ready to greet him when he comes again,
we offer you in thanksgiving this holy and living sacrifice.

Look with favor on your Church's offering,
and see the Victim whose death has reconciled us to yourself.

Invocation of the Holy Spirit
Grant that we, who are nourished by his body and blood,
may be filled with his Holy Spirit,
and become one body, one spirit in Christ.

Intercessions: in communion with the Saints
May he make us an everlasting gift to you
and enable us to share in the inheritance of your saints,
with Mary, the virgin Mother of God,
with the apostles, the martyrs,
(**Saint** N. —the saint of the day or the patron saint)
and all your saints,
on whose constant intercession we rely for help.

Order of Mass

For the Church

Lord, may this sacrifice,
which has made our peace with you,
advance the peace and salvation of all the world.
Strengthen in faith and love your pilgrim Church on earth;
your servant, Pope N., our bishop, N.,
and all the bishops,
with the clergy and the entire people your Son has gained for you.
Father, hear the prayers of the family you have gathered here before you.
In mercy and love unite all your children wherever they may be.*

For the dead

Welcome into your kingdom our departed brothers and sisters,
and all who have left this world in your friendship.

We hope to enjoy for ever the vision of your glory,
through Christ our Lord, from whom all good things come.

Concluding doxology

Through him,
with him,
in him,
in the unity of the Holy Spirit,
all glory and honor is yours,
almighty Father,
for ever and ever.

The people respond: **Amen.**
Turn to the Lord's Prayer, page 34.

---

*In Masses for the Dead the following may be said:
Remember N.
In baptism he (she) died with Christ:
may he (she) also share his resurrection,
when Christ will raise our mortal bodies
and make them like his own in glory.

Welcome into your kingdom our departed brothers and sisters,
and all who have left this world in your friendship.
There we hope to share in your glory
when every tear will be wiped away.
On that day we shall see you, our God, as you are.

We shall become like you
and praise you for ever through Christ our Lord,
from whom all good things come.

Concluding doxology as above.

Eucharistic Prayer IV

Preface
Father in heaven,
it is right that we should give you thanks and glory:
you are the one God, living and true.

Through all eternity you live in unapproachable light.
Source of life and goodness, you have created all things,
to fill your creatures with every blessing
and lead all men to the joyful vision of your light.
Countless hosts of angels stand before you to do your will;
they look upon your splendor
and praise you, night and day.
United with them,
and in the name of every creature under heaven,
we too praise your glory as we sing (say):
Holy, holy, holy Lord, God of power and might,
heaven and earth are full of your glory.
Hosanna in the highest.
Blessed is he who comes in the name of the Lord.
Hosanna in the highest.

EUCHARISTIC PRAYER IV

Praise to the Father
Father, we acknowledge your greatness:
all your actions show your wisdom and love.
You formed man in your own likeness
and set him over the whole world
to serve you, his creator,
and to rule over all creatures.
Even when he disobeyed you and lost your friendship
you did not abandon him to the power of death,
but helped all men to seek and find you.
Again and again you offered a covenant to man,
and through the prophets taught him to hope for salvation.
Father, you so loved the world
that in the fullness of time you sent your only Son to be our Savior.
He was conceived through the power of the Holy Spirit,
and born of the Virgin Mary,
a man like us in all things but sin.
To the poor he proclaimed the good news of salvation,
to prisoners, freedom,
and to those in sorrow, joy.
In fulfillment of your will
he gave himself up to death;

but by rising from the dead,
he destroyed death and restored life.
And that we might live no longer for ourselves but for him,
he sent the Holy Spirit from you, Father,
as his first gift to those who believe,
to complete his work on earth
and bring us the fullness of grace.

Invocation of the Holy Spirit
Father, may this Holy Spirit sanctify these offerings.
Let them become the body ✟ and blood of Jesus Christ our Lord
as we celebrate the great mystery
which he left us as an everlasting covenant.

The Lord's Supper
He always loved those who were his own in the world.
When the time came for him to be glorified by you, his heavenly Father,
he showed the depth of his love.

While they were at supper,
he took bread, said the blessing, broke the bread
and gave it to his disciples, saying:

Take this, all of you, and eat it:
this is my body which will be given up for you.

In the same way, he took the cup, filled with wine.
He gave you thanks, and giving the cup to his disciples, said:

Take this, all of you, and drink from it:
this is the cup of my blood,
the blood of the new and everlasting covenant.
It will be shed for you and for all
so that sins may be forgiven.
Do this in memory of me.

Priest: Let us proclaim the mystery of faith:

A Christ has died,
Christ is risen,
Christ will come again.

B Dying you destroyed our death,
rising you restored our life.
Lord Jesus, come in glory.

C When we eat this bread and drink this cup,
we proclaim your death, Lord Jesus,
until you come in glory.

D Lord, by your cross and resurrection
you have set us free.
You are the Savior of the world.

The memorial prayer
Father, we now celebrate this memorial of our redemption.
We recall Christ's death, his descent among the dead,
his resurrection, and his ascension to your right hand;
and, looking forward to his coming in glory,
we offer you his body and blood,
the acceptable sacrifice
which brings salvation to the whole world.

Lord, look upon this sacrifice which you have given to your Church;
and by your Holy Spirit, gather all who share this one bread and one cup
into the one body of Christ, a living sacrifice of praise.

Intercessions: for the Church
Lord, remember those for whom we offer this sacrifice,
especially N., our Pope,
N., our bishop, and bishops and clergy everywhere.
Remember those who take part in this offering,
those here present and all your people,
and all who seek you with a sincere heart.

For the dead
Remember those who have died in the peace of Christ
and all the dead whose faith is known to you alone.

In communion with the Saints
Father, in your mercy grant also to us, your children,
to enter into our heavenly inheritance
in the company of the Virgin Mary, the Mother of God,
and your apostles and saints.
Then, in your kingdom, freed from the corruption of sin and death,
we shall sing your glory with every creature through Christ our Lord,
through whom you give us everything that is good.

Concluding doxology
Through him,
with him,
in him,
in the unity of the Holy Spirit,
all glory and honor is yours,
almighty Father,
for ever and ever.

The people respond: **Amen.**
Turn to the Lord's Prayer, page 34.

Eucharistic Prayer for Masses of Reconciliation I
Preface

Father, all-powerful and ever-living God,
we do well always and everywhere to give you thanks and praise.
You never cease to call us
to a new and more abundant life.

God of love and mercy,
you are always ready to forgive;
we are sinners,
and you invite us
to trust in your mercy.

Time and time again
we broke your covenant,
but you did not abandon us.
Instead, through your Son, Jesus our Lord,
you bound yourself even more closely to the human family
by a bond that can never be broken.

Now is the time
for your people to turn back to you
and to be renewed in Christ your Son,
a time of grace and reconciliation.

You invite us
to serve the family of mankind
by opening our hearts to the fullness of your Holy Spirit.

In wonder and gratitude,
we join our voices with the choirs of heaven
to proclaim the power of your love
and to sing of our salvation in Christ:
Holy, holy, holy Lord, God of power and might,
heaven and earth are full of your glory.
Hosanna in the highest.
Blessed is he who comes in the name of the Lord.
Hosanna in the highest.

Father,
from the beginning of time
you have always done what is good for man
so that we may be holy as you are holy.

Look with kindness on your people
gathered here before you:
send forth the power of your Spirit
so that these gifts may become for us

the body ✠ and blood of your beloved Son, Jesus Christ,
in whom we have become your sons and daughters.

When we were lost
and could not find the way to you,
you loved us more than ever:
Jesus, your Son, innocent and without sin,
gave himself into our hands
and was nailed to a cross.
Yet before he stretched out his arms between heaven and earth
in the everlasting sign of your covenant,
he desired to celebrate the Paschal feast
in the company of his disciples.

While they were at supper,
he took bread and gave you thanks and praise.
He broke the bread, gave it to his disciples, and said:

Take this, all of you, and eat it:
this is my body which will be given up for you.

At the end of the meal,
knowing that he was to reconcile all things in himself
by the blood of his cross,
he took the cup, filled with wine.
Again he gave you thanks, handed the cup to his friends, and said:

Take this, all of you, and drink from it:
this is the cup of my blood,
the blood of the new and everlasting covenant.
It will be shed for you and for all
so that sins may be forgiven.
Do this in memory of me.

Priest: Let us proclaim the mystery of faith:

A Christ has died,
Christ is risen,
Christ will come again.

B Dying you destroyed our death,
rising you restored our life.
Lord Jesus, come in glory.

C When we eat this bread and drink this cup,
we proclaim your death, Lord Jesus,
until you come in glory.

D Lord, by your cross and resurrection
you have set us free.
You are the Savior of the world.

We do this in memory of Jesus Christ,
our Passover and our lasting peace.
We celebrate his death and resurrection
and look for the coming of that day
when he will return to give us the fullness of joy.
Therefore we offer you, God ever faithful and true,
the sacrifice which restores man to your friendship.

Father,
look with love
on those you have called
to share in the one sacrifice of Christ.
By the power of your Holy Spirit
make them one body,
healed of all division.

Keep us all
in communion of mind and heart
with N., our pope, and N., our bishop.
Help us to work together
for the coming of your kingdom,
until at last we stand in your presence
to share the life of the saints,
in the company of the Virgin Mary and the apostles,
and of our departed brothers and sisters
whom we commend to your mercy.

Then, freed from every shadow of death,
we shall take our place in the new creation
and give you thanks
with Christ, our risen Lord.

Concluding doxology
Through him,
with him,
in him,
in the unity of the Holy Spirit,
all glory and honor is yours,
almighty Father,
for ever and ever.

The people respond: **Amen.**
Turn to the Lord's Prayer, page 34.

Eucharistic Prayer for Masses of Reconciliation II

Preface

Father, all-powerful and ever-living God,
we praise and thank you through Jesus Christ our Lord
for your presence and action in the world.

In the midst of conflict and division,
we know it is you
who turn our minds to thoughts of peace.
Your Spirit changes our hearts:
enemies begin to speak to one another,
those who were estranged join hands in friendship,
and nations seek the way of peace together.

Your Spirit is at work
when understanding puts an end to strife,
when hatred is quenched by mercy,
and vengeance gives way to forgiveness.

For this we should never cease
to thank and praise you.
We join with all the choirs of heaven
as they sing for ever to your glory:

Holy, holy, holy Lord, God of power and might,
heaven and earth are full of your glory.
Hosanna in the highest.
Blessed is he who comes in the name of the Lord.
Hosanna in the highest.

God of power and might,
we praise you through your Son, Jesus Christ,
who comes in your name.
He is the Word that brings salvation.
He is the hand you stretch out to sinners.
He is the way that leads to your peace.

God our Father,
we had wandered far from you,
but through your Son you have brought us back.
You gave him up to death
so that we might turn again to you
and find our way to one another.

Therefore we celebrate the reconciliation
Christ has gained for us.

We ask you to sanctify these gifts
by the power of your Spirit,
as we now fulfill your Son's ✝ command.

While he was at supper
on the night before he died for us,
he took bread in his hands,
and gave you thanks and praise.
He broke the bread,
gave it to his disciples, and said:

Take this, all of you, and eat it:
this is my body which will be given up for you.

At the end of the meal he took the cup.
Again he praised you for your goodness,
gave the cup to his disciples, and said:

Take this, all of you, and drink from it:
this is the cup of my blood,
the blood of the new and everlasting covenant.
It will be shed for you and for all
so that sins may be forgiven.
Do this in memory of me.

Priest: Let us proclaim the mystery of faith:

A Christ has died,
Christ is risen,
Christ will come again.

B Dying you destroyed our death,
rising you restored our life.
Lord Jesus, come in glory.

C When we eat this bread and drink this cup,
we proclaim your death, Lord Jesus,
until you come in glory.

D Lord, by your cross and resurrection
you have set us free.
You are the Savior of the world.

Lord our God,
your Son has entrusted to us
this pledge of his love.
We celebrate the memory of his death and resurrection
and bring you the gift you have given us,
the sacrifice of reconciliation.
Therefore, we ask you, Father,
to accept us, together with your Son.

Fill us with his Spirit
through our sharing in this meal.
May he take away all that divides us.

May this Spirit keep us always in communion
with N., our pope, N., our bishop,
with all the bishops and all your people.
Father, make your Church throughout the world
a sign of unity and an instrument of your peace.

You have gathered us here
around the table of your Son,
in fellowship with the Virgin Mary, Mother of God, and all the saints.

In that new world where the fullness of your peace will be revealed,
gather people of every race, language, and way of life
to share in the one eternal banquet
with Jesus Christ the Lord.

Concluding doxology
Through him,
with him,
in him,
in the unity of the Holy Spirit,
all glory and honor is yours,
almighty Father,
for ever and ever.

The people respond: **Amen.**

Communion Rite

Lord's Prayer   STAND

Priest:

A Let us pray with confidence to the Father
in the words our Savior gave us.

B Jesus taught us to call God our Father,
and so we have the courage to say:

C Let us ask our Father to forgive our sins
and to bring us to forgive those who sin against us.

D Let us pray for the coming of the kingdom
as Jesus taught us.

People: **Our Father who art in heaven,
hallowed be thy name;
thy kingdom come;
thy will be done
on earth as it is in heaven.
Give us this day our daily bread,
and forgive us our trespasses
as we forgive those who trespass against us;
and lead us not into temptation,
but deliver us from evil.**

Priest: Deliver us, Lord, from every evil,
and grant us peace in our day.
In your mercy keep us free from sin
and protect us from all anxiety
as we wait in joyful hope
for the coming of our Savior, Jesus Christ.

People: **For the kingdom, the power, and the glory are yours, now and for ever.**

SIGN OF PEACE
The priest says the prayer for peace:

Lord Jesus Christ, you said to your apostles:
I leave you peace, my peace I give you.
Look not on our sins, but on the faith of your Church,
and grant us the peace and unity of your kingdom
where you live forever and ever. All: **Amen.**

Priest: The peace of the Lord be with you always.
People: **And also with you.**

Then the deacon (or the priest) may add:
Let us offer each other the sign of peace.

BREAKING OF THE BREAD
The priest breaks the host over the paten and places a small piece in the chalice, praying inaudibly. Meanwhile the people sing or say:

**Lamb of God, you take away the sins of the world:
have mercy on us.**

**Lamb of God, you take away the sins of the world:
have mercy on us.**

**Lamb of God, you take away the sins of the world:
grant us peace.**

Communion KNEEL

Priest: This is the Lamb of God
who takes away the sins of the world.
Happy are those who are called to his supper.

Priest and people (once only):
**Lord, I am not worthy to receive you,
but only say the word and I shall be healed.**

Priest: The body of Christ.
Communicant: **Amen.**

If there is no singing, the communion antiphon is recited.
When receiving Holy Communion. **STAND**
After communion, the priest and people may spend some time in silent prayer. (Sit or kneel) If desired, a hymn, psalm, or other song of praise may be sung.

Prayer after Communion STAND

Priest: Let us pray.

Priest and people pray silently for a while unless a period of silence has been observed. Then the priest says the prayer after communion. At the end: **Amen.**

Concluding Rite

Priest: The Lord be with you.
People: **And also with you.**

Blessing
Simple Blessing
Priest: May almighty God bless you,
the Father, and the Son, ✛ and the Holy Spirit.
People: **Amen.**

Solemn Blessing

Priest (or Deacon): Bow your heads and pray for God's blessing.
Priest: May almighty God bless you,
the Father, and the Son, ☩ and the Holy Spirit.
People: **Amen.**

Prayer over the People

Priest (or Deacon): Bow your heads and pray for God's blessing.
Priest: May almighty God bless you,
the Father, and the Son, ☩ and the Holy Spirit.
People: **Amen.**

Dismissal

Priest (or Deacon): Go in the peace of Christ.
People: **Thanks be to God.**
Priest: The Mass is ended, go in peace.
People: **Thanks be to God.**
Priest: Go in peace to love and serve the Lord.
People: **Thanks be to God.**

Celebration of the Liturgy of the Word
[With Holy Communion]

Introductory Rites

Introduction
Deacon or lay leader:
We gather here to celebrate the Lord's Day.
Sunday has been called the Lord's Day because
   it was on this day
that Jesus conquered sin and death and rose to new life.
Unfortunately, we are not able to celebrate the Mass today
because we do not have a priest.
Let us be united in the spirit of Christ with
   the Church around the world
and celebrate our redemption in Christ's suffering,
   death and resurrection.

Sign of the Cross   STAND
Deacon or lay leader:
In the name of the Father, and of the Son, and of the Holy Spirit.
All respond:
Amen.

Greeting
Deacon or lay leader:
Grace and peace to you from God our Father and from the Lord Jesus Christ.
All respond:
Blessed be God for ever.

Opening Prayer

Liturgy of the Word   SIT

First Reading

Responsorial Psalm

Celebration of the Liturgy of the Word

SECOND READING

GOSPEL ACCLAMATION — STAND

GOSPEL

HOMILY OR REFLECTION ON THE READINGS — SIT

PERIOD OF SILENCE

PROFESSION OF FAITH — STAND
[The Nicene Creed can be found on page 12]

Apostles' Creed

I believe in God the Father almighty,
  creator of heaven and earth.

I believe in Jesus Christ, his only Son, our Lord.
  He was conceived by the power of the Holy Spirit
    and born of the Virgin Mary.
  He suffered under Pontius Pilate,
    was crucified, died, and was buried.
  He descended to the dead.
  On the third day he rose again.
  He ascended into heaven,
    and is seated at the right hand of the Father.
  He will come again to judge the living and the dead.

I believe in the Holy Spirit,
  the holy catholic Church,
  the communion of saints,
  the forgiveness of sins,
  the resurrection of the body,
  and the life everlasting. Amen.

PRAYER OF THE FAITHFUL

COMMUNION RITE

LORD'S PRAYER
Deacon or lay leader:
The Father provides us with food for eternal life.
Let us pray for nourishment and strength.

All say:
**Our Father, who art in heaven,
hallowed be thy name;
thy kingdom come;
thy will be done on earth as it is in heaven.
Give us this day our daily bread;
and forgive us our trespasses
as we forgive those who trespass against us;
and lead us not into temptation,
but deliver us from evil.
Amen.**

INVITATION TO COMMUNION   KNEEL
Deacon or lay leader:
This is the Lamb of God
who takes away the sins of the world.
Happy are those who are called to his supper.

All say:
**Lord, I am not worthy to receive you
but only say the word and I shall be healed.**

COMMUNION

ACT OF THANKSGIVING   STAND

CONCLUDING RITE   SIT

INVITATION TO PRAY FOR VOCATIONS TO THE PRIESTHOOD
Deacon or lay leader:
Mindful of our Lord's word, "Ask the Master of the harvest to send out laborers for the harvest," let us pray for an increase of vocations to the priesthood. May our prayer hasten the day when we will be able to take part in the celebration of the Holy Eucharist every Sunday.

BLESSING   STAND

SIGN OF PEACE

First Sunday of Advent

November 29, 2009

Reflection on the Gospel

One sign of the Son of Man's presence and the redemption at hand promised in the gospel is that we are growing in love. Despite appearances to the contrary (disaster and destruction generated both by natural forces and human choices), God's plan and purpose are directed toward redemption and life. We need to read the right signs—new life in the midst of seeming destruction, the glory of the Son of Man coming into the darkness, the love of Christ growing in our hearts.

- *What helps me see the signs of God's redemption is . . . What distracts me from seeing the signs of God's redemption is . . .*

—Living Liturgy™, *First Sunday of Advent 2009*

Entrance Antiphon (Psalm 24:1-3)
To you, my God, I lift my soul, I trust in you; let me never come to shame. Do not let my enemies laugh at me. No one who waits for you is ever put to shame.

Opening Prayer
All-powerful God,
increase our strength of will for doing good
that Christ may find an eager welcome at his coming
and call us to his side in the kingdom of heaven,
where he lives and reigns with you and the Holy Spirit,
one God, for ever and ever. All: **Amen.**

Reading I (L 3) (Jeremiah 33:14-16)
A reading from the Book of the Prophet Jeremiah

I will raise up for David a just shoot.

**The days are coming, says the Lord,
    when I will fulfill the promise
    I made to the house of Israel and Judah.**

In those days, in that time,
    I will raise up for David a just shoot;
    he shall do what is right and just in the land.
In those days Judah shall be safe
    and Jerusalem shall dwell secure;
    this is what they shall call her:
"The Lord our justice."

The word of the Lord. All: Thanks be to God.

Responsorial Psalm 25

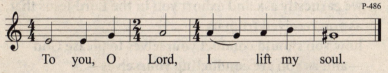

To you, O Lord, I lift my soul.

Music: Jay F. Hunstiger, © 1991, administered by Liturgical Press. All rights reserved.

Psalm 25:4-5, 8-9, 10, 14

℟. (1b) **To you, O Lord, I lift my soul.**

Your ways, O Lord, make known to me;
    teach me your paths,
guide me in your truth and teach me,
    for you are God my savior,
    and for you I wait all the day. ℟.

Good and upright is the Lord;
    thus he shows sinners the way.
He guides the humble to justice,
    and teaches the humble his way. ℟.

All the paths of the Lord are kindness and constancy
    toward those who keep his covenant and his decrees.
The friendship of the Lord is with those who fear him,
    and his covenant, for their instruction. ℟.

Reading II (1 Thessalonians 3:12—4:2)

A reading from the first Letter of Saint Paul to the Thessalonians

May the Lord strengthen your hearts at the coming of our Lord Jesus.

Brothers and sisters:
May the Lord make you increase and abound in love
    for one another and for all,
    just as we have for you,
    so as to strengthen your hearts,
    to be blameless in holiness before our God and Father
    at the coming of our Lord Jesus with all his holy ones.
        Amen.

Finally, brothers and sisters,
    we earnestly ask and exhort you in the Lord Jesus that,
    as you received from us
    how you should conduct yourselves to please God
    —and as you are conducting yourselves—
    you do so even more.
For you know what instructions we gave you through
    the Lord Jesus.

The word of the Lord. All: **Thanks be to God.**

GOSPEL (Luke 21:25-28, 34-36)
ALLELUIA (Psalm 85:8)
℣. Alleluia, alleluia. ℟. **Alleluia, alleluia.**
℣. Show us, Lord, your love;
    and grant us your salvation. ℟.

✠ **A reading from the holy Gospel according to Luke**

All: **Glory to you, Lord.**

Your redemption is at hand.

Jesus said to his disciples:
"There will be signs in the sun, the moon, and the stars,
    and on earth nations will be in dismay,
    perplexed by the roaring of the sea and the waves.
People will die of fright
    in anticipation of what is coming upon the world,
    for the powers of the heavens will be shaken.
And then they will see the Son of Man
    coming in a cloud with power and great glory.

But when these signs begin to happen,
> stand erect and raise your heads
> because your redemption is at hand.

"Beware that your hearts do not become drowsy
> from carousing and drunkenness
> and the anxieties of daily life,
> and that day catch you by surprise like a trap.

For that day will assault everyone
> who lives on the face of the earth.

Be vigilant at all times
> and pray that you have the strength
> to escape the tribulations that are imminent
> and to stand before the Son of Man."

The Gospel of the Lord. All: **Praise to you, Lord Jesus Christ.**

Prayer over the Gifts

Father,
from all you give us
we present this bread and wine.
As we serve you now,
accept our offering
and sustain us with your promise of eternal life.
Grant this through Christ our Lord. All: **Amen.**

Communion Antiphon (Psalm 84:13)

The Lord will shower his gifts, and our land will yield its fruit.

Prayer after Communion

Father,
may our communion
teach us to love heaven.
May its promise and hope
guide our way on earth.
We ask this through Christ our Lord. All: **Amen.**

Second Sunday of Advent

December 6, 2009

Reflection on the Gospel

The salvation of God is progressively revealed in repentance (our work) and forgiveness (God's work). To repent means to change one's mind, one's life. This is how we reach the fullness that is promised and our true home: by increasing our love for one another. Our work of repentance is a matter of turning ourselves toward the God who embraces us in mercy and forgiveness and welcomes us home.

• For me, salvation looks like . . . feels like . . . sounds like . . .

—Living Liturgy™, *Second Sunday of Advent 2009*

Entrance Antiphon (*See* Isaiah 30:19, 30)

People of Zion, the Lord will come to save all nations, and your hearts will exult to hear his majestic voice.

Opening Prayer

God of power and mercy,
open our hearts in welcome.
Remove the things that hinder us from receiving Christ with joy,
so that we may share his wisdom
and become one with him
when he comes in glory,
for he lives and reigns with you and the Holy Spirit,
one God, for ever and ever. **All: Amen.**

Reading I (L 6) (Baruch 5:1-9)

A reading from the Book of the Prophet Baruch

Jerusalem, God will show your splendor.

**Jerusalem, take off your robe of mourning and misery;
put on the splendor of glory from God forever:
wrapped in the cloak of justice from God,**

bear on your head the mitre
    that displays the glory of the eternal name.
For God will show all the earth your splendor:
    you will be named by God forever
    the peace of justice, the glory of God's worship.

Up, Jerusalem! stand upon the heights;
    look to the east and see your children
gathered from the east and the west
    at the word of the Holy One,
    rejoicing that they are remembered by God.
Led away on foot by their enemies they left you:
    but God will bring them back to you
    borne aloft in glory as on royal thrones.
For God has commanded
    that every lofty mountain be made low,
and that the age-old depths and gorges
    be filled to level ground,
    that Israel may advance secure in the glory of God.
The forests and every fragrant kind of tree
    have overshadowed Israel at God's command;
for God is leading Israel in joy
    by the light of his glory,
    with his mercy and justice for company.

The word of the Lord. All: Thanks be to God.

Responsorial Psalm 126

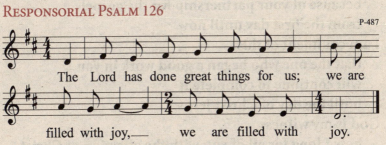

Music: Jay F. Hunstiger, © 1990, administered by Liturgical Press. All rights reserved.

Psalm 126:1-2, 2-3, 4-5, 6

℟. (3) **The Lord has done great things for us; we are filled with joy.**

When the LORD brought back the captives of Zion,
  we were like men dreaming.
Then our mouth was filled with laughter,
  and our tongue with rejoicing. ℟.

Then they said among the nations,
  "The LORD has done great things for them."
The LORD has done great things for us;
  we are glad indeed. ℟.

Restore our fortunes, O LORD,
  like the torrents in the southern desert.
Those who sow in tears
  shall reap rejoicing. ℟.

Although they go forth weeping,
  carrying the seed to be sown,
they shall come back rejoicing,
  carrying their sheaves. ℟.

READING II (Philippians 1:4-6, 8-11)

A reading from the Letter of Saint Paul to the Philippians

Show yourselves pure and blameless for the day of Christ.

**Brothers and sisters:
I pray always with joy in my every prayer for all of you,
  because of your partnership for the gospel
  from the first day until now.
I am confident of this,
  that the one who began a good work in you
  will continue to complete it
  until the day of Christ Jesus.
God is my witness,
  how I long for all of you with the affection of Christ Jesus.
And this is my prayer:
  that your love may increase ever more and more**

in knowledge and every kind of perception,
to discern what is of value,
so that you may be pure and blameless for the day
    of Christ,
filled with the fruit of righteousness
that comes through Jesus Christ
for the glory and praise of God.

The word of the Lord.   All: **Thanks be to God.**

G<small>OSPEL</small> (Luke 3:1-6)
A<small>LLELUIA</small> (Luke 3:4, 6)

℣. Alleluia, alleluia.   ℟. **Alleluia, alleluia.**
℣. Prepare the way of the Lord, make straight his paths:
all flesh shall see the salvation of God. ℟.

✠ A reading from the holy Gospel according to Luke

All: **Glory to you, Lord.**

All flesh shall see the salvation of God.

In the fifteenth year of the reign of Tiberius Caesar,
    when Pontius Pilate was governor of Judea,
    and Herod was tetrarch of Galilee,
    and his brother Philip tetrarch of the region
        of Ituraea and Trachonitis,
    and Lysanias was tetrarch of Abilene,
    during the high priesthood of Annas and Caiaphas,
    the word of God came to John the son of Zechariah in
        the desert.
John went throughout the whole region of the Jordan,
    proclaiming a baptism of repentance for the
        forgiveness of sins,
    as it is written in the book of the words of the prophet
        Isaiah:
      A voice of one crying out in the desert:
      "Prepare the way of the Lord,
        make straight his paths.
      Every valley shall be filled
        and every mountain and hill shall be made low.

> The winding roads shall be made straight,
> and the rough ways made smooth,
> and all flesh shall see the salvation of God."

The Gospel of the Lord. All: **Praise to you, Lord Jesus Christ.**

Prayer over the Gifts
Lord,
we are nothing without you.
As you sustain us with your mercy,
receive our prayers and offerings.
We ask this through Christ our Lord. All: **Amen.**

Communion Antiphon (Baruch 5:5; 4:36)
Rise up, Jerusalem, stand on the heights, and see the joy that is coming to you from God.

Prayer after Communion
Father,
you give us food from heaven.
By our sharing in this mystery,
teach us to judge wisely the things of earth
and to love the things of heaven.
Grant this through Christ our Lord. All: **Amen.**

Immaculate Conception

December 8, 2009

Reflection on the Gospel

This solemnity challenges us to say yes like Mary to whatever challenging word God sends our way. We, too, each have our "annunciation" by which the Spirit dwells within us, we bear Christ in the world today, and we are called to speak an ongoing yes to God. In these ways we, like Mary, participate in God's work of salvation.

• *One way I bear Christ in the world is . . .*

—*Living Liturgy*™, *Immaculate Conception 2009*

Entrance Antiphon (Isaiah 61:10)

I exult for joy in the Lord, my soul rejoices in my God; for he has clothed me in the garment of salvation and robed me in the cloak of justice, like a bride adorned with her jewels.

Opening Prayer

Father,
you prepared the Virgin Mary
to be the worthy mother of your Son.
You let her share beforehand
in the salvation Christ would bring by his death,
and kept her sinless from the first moment of her conception.
Help us by her prayers
to live in your presence without sin.
We ask this through our Lord Jesus Christ, your Son,
who lives and reigns with you and the Holy Spirit,
one God, for ever and ever. All: **Amen.**

Reading I (L 689) (Genesis 3:9-15, 20)

A reading from the Book of Genesis

I will put enmity between your offspring and hers.

**After the man, Adam, had eaten of the tree,
   the Lord God called to the man and asked him,
      "Where are you?"
He answered, "I heard you in the garden;
   but I was afraid, because I was naked,
   so I hid myself."
Then he asked, "Who told you that you were naked?
You have eaten, then,
   from the tree of which I had forbidden you to eat!"
The man replied, "The woman whom you put here
      with me—
   she gave me fruit from the tree, and so I ate it."
The Lord God then asked the woman,
   "Why did you do such a thing?"
The woman answered, "The serpent tricked me into it,
   so I ate it."**

Then the LORD God said to the serpent:
　"Because you have done this, you shall be banned
　　from all the animals
　　and from all the wild creatures;
　on your belly shall you crawl,
　　and dirt shall you eat
　　all the days of your life.
　I will put enmity between you and the woman,
　　and between your offspring and hers;
　he will strike at your head,
　　while you strike at his heel."
The man called his wife Eve,
　because she became the mother of all the living.

The word of the Lord. All: Thanks be to God.

RESPONSORIAL PSALM 98

Music: Jay F. Hunstiger, © 1990, administered by Liturgical Press. All rights reserved.

Psalm 98:1, 2-3ab, 3bc-4

℟. (1a) **Sing to the Lord a new song, for he has done marvelous deeds.**

Sing to the LORD a new song,
　for he has done wondrous deeds;
his right hand has won victory for him,
　his holy arm. ℟.

The LORD has made his salvation known:
　in the sight of the nations he has revealed his justice.
He has remembered his kindness and his faithfulness
　toward the house of Israel. ℟.

> All the ends of the earth have seen
>   the salvation by our God.
> Sing joyfully to the Lord, all you lands;
>   break into song; sing praise. ℟.

Reading II (Ephesians 1:3-6, 11-12)
A reading from the Letter of Saint Paul to the Ephesians

He chose us in Christ before the foundation of the world.

Brothers and sisters:
Blessed be the God and Father of our Lord Jesus Christ,
   who has blessed us in Christ
   with every spiritual blessing in the heavens,
   as he chose us in him, before the foundation of the world,
to be holy and without blemish before him.
In love he destined us for adoption to himself through Jesus Christ,
   in accord with the favor of his will,
   for the praise of the glory of his grace
   that he granted us in the beloved.

In him we were also chosen,
   destined in accord with the purpose of the One
   who accomplishes all things according to the intention of his will,
   so that we might exist for the praise of his glory,
   we who first hoped in Christ.

The word of the Lord. All: **Thanks be to God.**

Gospel (Luke 1:26-38)
Alleluia (*See* Luke 1:28)
℣. Alleluia, alleluia.   ℟. **Alleluia, alleluia.**
℣. Hail, Mary, full of grace, the Lord is with you;
   blessed are you among women. ℟.

✠ **A reading from the holy Gospel according to Luke**

All: **Glory to you, Lord.**

Hail, full of grace! The Lord is with you.

The angel Gabriel was sent from God
   to a town of Galilee called Nazareth,
   to a virgin betrothed to a man named Joseph,
   of the house of David,
   and the virgin's name was Mary.
And coming to her, he said,
   "Hail, full of grace! The Lord is with you."
But she was greatly troubled at what was said
   and pondered what sort of greeting this might be.
Then the angel said to her,
   "Do not be afraid, Mary,
   for you have found favor with God.
Behold, you will conceive in your womb and bear a son,
   and you shall name him Jesus.
He will be great and will be called Son of the Most High,
   and the Lord God will give him the throne of David
      his father,
   and he will rule over the house of Jacob forever,
   and of his kingdom there will be no end."
But Mary said to the angel,
   "How can this be,
   since I have no relations with a man?"
And the angel said to her in reply,
   "The Holy Spirit will come upon you,
   and the power of the Most High will overshadow you.
Therefore the child to be born
   will be called holy, the Son of God.
And behold, Elizabeth, your relative,
   has also conceived a son in her old age,
   and this is the sixth month for her who was called
      barren;
   for nothing will be impossible for God."
Mary said, "Behold, I am the handmaid of the Lord.
May it be done to me according to your word."
Then the angel departed from her.

The Gospel of the Lord. All: Praise to you, Lord Jesus Christ.

Prayer over the Gifts

Lord,
accept this sacrifice
on the feast of the sinless Virgin Mary.
You kept her free from sin
from the first moment of her life.
Help us by her prayers,
and free us from our sins.
We ask this in the name of Jesus the Lord. All: **Amen.**

Communion Antiphon

All honor to you, Mary! From you arose the sun of justice,
Christ our God.

Prayer after Communion

Lord our God,
in your love, you chose the Virgin Mary
and kept her free from sin.
May this sacrament of your love
free us from our sins.
Grant this through Christ our Lord. All: **Amen.**

Third Sunday of Advent

December 13, 2009

Reflection on the Gospel

In the gospel three groups of people ask the same question, "What should we do?" John exhorts them to define their obligations in right relation to others, just as John himself defines his role in relation to Jesus. The gospel, further, pivots on the people's "expectation." To whom were their expectations led? The Christ (the Messiah), yes, but also for another "who"—our neighbor. The "good news" is that our relationship with others makes visible our relation to Jesus. "What should we do?"

- *If I could ask John the Baptist, "What should I do?" he would say to me . . .*

—Living Liturgy™, *Third Sunday of Advent 2009*

Entrance Antiphon (Philippians 4:4, 5)

Rejoice in the Lord always; again I say, rejoice! The Lord is near.

Opening Prayer

Lord God,
may we, your people,
who look forward to the birthday of Christ
experience the joy of salvation
and celebrate that feast with love and thanksgiving.
We ask this through our Lord Jesus Christ, your Son,
who lives and reigns with you and the Holy Spirit,
one God, for ever and ever. All: **Amen.**

Reading I (L 9) (Zephaniah 3:14-18a)

A reading from the Book of the Prophet Zephaniah

The Lord will rejoice over you with gladness.

Shout for joy, O daughter Zion!
    Sing joyfully, O Israel!
Be glad and exult with all your heart,
    O daughter Jerusalem!
The Lord has removed the judgment against you,
    he has turned away your enemies;
the King of Israel, the Lord, is in your midst,
    you have no further misfortune to fear.
On that day, it shall be said to Jerusalem:
    Fear not, O Zion, be not discouraged!
The Lord, your God, is in your midst,
    a mighty savior;
he will rejoice over you with gladness,
    and renew you in his love,
he will sing joyfully because of you,
    as one sings at festivals.

The word of the Lord. All: **Thanks be to God.**

Responsorial Psalm

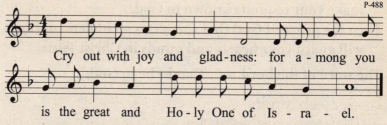

Cry out with joy and gladness: for among you is the great and Holy One of Israel.

Music: Jay F. Hunstiger, © 1991, administered by Liturgical Press. All rights reserved.

Isaiah 12:2-3, 4, 5-6

℟. (6) **Cry out with joy and gladness: for among you is the great and Holy One of Israel.**

God indeed is my savior;
  I am confident and unafraid.
My strength and my courage is the LORD,
  and he has been my savior.
With joy you will draw water
  at the fountain of salvation. ℟.

Give thanks to the LORD, acclaim his name;
  among the nations make known his deeds,
  proclaim how exalted is his name. ℟.

Sing praise to the LORD for his glorious achievement;
  let this be known throughout all the earth.
Shout with exultation, O city of Zion,
  for great in your midst
  is the Holy One of Israel! ℟.

Reading II (Philippians 4:4-7)
A reading from the Letter of Saint Paul to the Philippians

The Lord is near.

**Brothers and sisters:
Rejoice in the Lord always.
I shall say it again: rejoice!
Your kindness should be known to all.
The Lord is near.
Have no anxiety at all, but in everything,**

by prayer and petition, with thanksgiving,
make your requests known to God.
Then the peace of God that surpasses all understanding
will guard your hearts and minds in Christ Jesus.

The word of the Lord. All: **Thanks be to God.**

Gospel (Luke 3:10-18)

Alleluia (Isaiah 61:1; *see* Luke 4:18)

℣. Alleluia, alleluia. ℟. **Alleluia, alleluia.**
℣. The Spirit of the Lord is upon me,
because he has anointed me
to bring glad tidings to the poor. ℟.

✠ **A reading from the holy Gospel according to Luke**

All: **Glory to you, Lord.**

What should we do?

The crowds asked John the Baptist,
"What should we do?"
He said to them in reply,
"Whoever has two cloaks
should share with the person who has none.
And whoever has food should do likewise."
Even tax collectors came to be baptized and they said
to him,
"Teacher, what should we do?"
He answered them,
"Stop collecting more than what is prescribed."
Soldiers also asked him,
"And what is it that we should do?"
He told them,
"Do not practice extortion,
do not falsely accuse anyone,
and be satisfied with your wages."
Now the people were filled with expectation,
and all were asking in their hearts
whether John might be the Christ.

John answered them all, saying,
  "I am baptizing you with water,
  but one mightier than I is coming.
I am not worthy to loosen the thongs of his sandals.
He will baptize you with the Holy Spirit and fire.
His winnowing fan is in his hand to clear his threshing
    floor
  and to gather the wheat into his barn,
  but the chaff he will burn with unquenchable fire."
Exhorting them in many other ways,
  he preached good news to the people.

The Gospel of the Lord. All: **Praise to you, Lord Jesus Christ.**

Prayer over the Gifts
Lord,
may the gift we offer in faith and love
be a continual sacrifice in your honor
and truly become our eucharist and our salvation.
Grant this through Christ our Lord. All: **Amen.**

Communion Antiphon (*See* Isaiah 35:4)
Say to the anxious: be strong and fear not, our God will come to save us.

Prayer after Communion
God of mercy,
may this eucharist bring us your divine help,
free us from our sins,
and prepare us for the birthday of our Savior,
who is Lord for ever and ever. All: **Amen.**

Fourth Sunday of Advent

December 20, 2009

Reflection on the Gospel

The gospel really announces two "incarnations": Jesus in the womb of Mary, and the Holy Spirit who filled Elizabeth. Although Elizabeth extols Mary for her belief in what would happen to her, it was also Elizabeth's belief that enabled her to conceive John as well as recognize the presence of the Savior in her midst through Mary. Our own belief enables the "incarnation" within us of both the presence of the risen Christ and the Holy Spirit. Blessed are they, and blessed are we to whom God comes and within whom God dwells.

- I recognize Christ and the Holy Spirit "incarnated" in others when . . . in myself when . . .

—Living Liturgy™, *Fourth Sunday of Advent 2009*

ENTRANCE ANTIPHON (Isaiah 45:8)
Let the clouds rain down the Just One, and the earth bring forth a Savior.

OPENING PRAYER
Lord,
fill our hearts with your love,
and as you revealed to us by an angel
the coming of your Son as man,
so lead us through his suffering and death
to the glory of his resurrection,
for he lives and reigns with you and the Holy Spirit,
one God, for ever and ever. All: **Amen.**

READING I (L 12) (Micah 5:1-4a)
A reading from the Book of the Prophet Micah

From you shall come forth the ruler of Israel.

**Thus says the LORD:
You, Bethlehem-Ephrathah,
   too small to be among the clans of Judah,**

from you shall come forth for me
> one who is to be ruler in Israel;
whose origin is from of old,
> from ancient times.
Therefore the Lord will give them up, until the time
> when she who is to give birth has borne,
and the rest of his kindred shall return
> to the children of Israel.
He shall stand firm and shepherd his flock
> by the strength of the Lord,
> in the majestic name of the Lord, his God;
and they shall remain, for now his greatness
> shall reach to the ends of the earth;
> he shall be peace.

The word of the Lord. All: Thanks be to God.

Responsorial Psalm 80

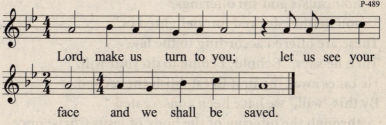

Music: Jay F. Hunstiger, © 1993, administered by Liturgical Press. All rights reserved.

Psalm 80:2-3, 15-16, 18-19

℟. (4) **Lord, make us turn to you; let us see your face and we shall be saved.**

O shepherd of Israel, hearken,
> from your throne upon the cherubim, shine forth.
Rouse your power,
> and come to save us. ℟.

Once again, O Lord of hosts,
> look down from heaven, and see;
take care of this vine,
> and protect what your right hand has planted,
> the son of man whom you yourself made strong. ℟.

(continued)

May your help be with the man of your right hand,
    with the son of man whom you yourself made strong.
Then we will no more withdraw from you;
    give us new life, and we will call upon your name. ℟.

Reading II (Hebrews 10:5-10)
A reading from the Letter to the Hebrews

Behold, I come to do your will.

**Brothers and sisters:
When Christ came into the world, he said:
    "Sacrifice and offering you did not desire,
        but a body you prepared for me;
    in holocausts and sin offerings you took no delight.
    Then I said, 'As is written of me in the scroll,
    behold, I come to do your will, O God.'"

First he says, "Sacrifices and offerings,
    holocausts and sin offerings,
    you neither desired nor delighted in."
These are offered according to the law.
Then he says, "Behold, I come to do your will."
He takes away the first to establish the second.
By this "will," we have been consecrated
    through the offering of the body of Jesus Christ once
        for all.**

The word of the Lord. All: **Thanks be to God.**

Gospel (Luke 1:39-45)
Alleluia (Luke 1:38)
℣. Alleluia, alleluia. ℟. **Alleluia, alleluia.**
℣. Behold, I am the handmaid of the Lord.
    May it be done to me according to your word. ℟.

✠ **A reading from the holy Gospel according to Luke**

All: **Glory to you, Lord.**

And how does this happen to me, that the mother of my Lord should come to me?

Mary set out
>   and traveled to the hill country in haste
>   to a town of Judah,
>   where she entered the house of Zechariah
>   and greeted Elizabeth.
> When Elizabeth heard Mary's greeting,
>   the infant leaped in her womb,
>   and Elizabeth, filled with the Holy Spirit,
>   cried out in a loud voice and said,
>   "Blessed are you among women,
>   and blessed is the fruit of your womb.
> And how does this happen to me,
>   that the mother of my Lord should come to me?
> For at the moment the sound of your greeting reached
>   my ears,
>   the infant in my womb leaped for joy.
> Blessed are you who believed
>   that what was spoken to you by the Lord
>   would be fulfilled."

The Gospel of the Lord. All: **Praise to you, Lord Jesus Christ.**

Prayer over the Gifts
Lord,
may the power of the Spirit,
which sanctified Mary the mother of your Son,
make holy the gifts we place upon this altar.
Grant this through Christ our Lord. All: **Amen.**

Communion Antiphon (Isaiah 7:14)
The Virgin is with child and shall bear a son, and she will call him Emmanuel.

Prayer after Communion
Lord,
in this sacrament
we receive the promise of salvation;
as Christmas draws near
make us grow in faith and love
to celebrate the coming of Christ our Savior,
who is Lord for ever and ever. All: **Amen.**

The Vigil of Christmas

December 24, 2009

The Mass of the Vigil of Christmas is to be used on Thursday evening in those places where the holy day of obligation may be fulfilled on Thursday evening.

Reflection on the Gospel
How much Joseph must have loved Mary, since he was "unwilling to expose her to shame"! How much Joseph must have loved God, since he did all that "the angel of the Lord commanded him." Joseph (and Mary) model for us the depths of love to which we humans are really capable: a love that is kind and merciful, gentle and compassionate, just and peaceful. How we long for this love! How fully we celebrate this love at Christmas! How fully we must live it throughout the year!

- *God's self-gift to us is the divine Son. My gift of self to others is . . .*

—Living Liturgy™, *Christmas 2009*

ENTRANCE ANTIPHON (See Exodus 16:6-7)
Today you will know that the Lord is coming to save us, and in the morning you will see his glory.

OPENING PRAYER
God our Father,
every year we rejoice
as we look forward to this feast of our salvation.
May we welcome Christ as our Redeemer,
and meet him with confidence when he comes to be our judge,
who lives and reigns with you and the Holy Spirit,
one God, for ever and ever. All: **Amen.**

READING I (L 13) (Isaiah 62:1-5)
A reading from the Book of the Prophet Isaiah

The Lord delights in you.

**For Zion's sake I will not be silent,
for Jerusalem's sake I will not be quiet,**

until her vindication shines forth like the dawn
 and her victory like a burning torch.

Nations shall behold your vindication,
 and all the kings your glory;
you shall be called by a new name
 pronounced by the mouth of the Lord.
You shall be a glorious crown in the hand of the Lord,
 a royal diadem held by your God.
No more shall people call you "Forsaken,"
 or your land "Desolate,"
but you shall be called "My Delight,"
 and your land "Espoused."
For the Lord delights in you
 and makes your land his spouse.
As a young man marries a virgin,
 your Builder shall marry you;
and as a bridegroom rejoices in his bride
 so shall your God rejoice in you.

The word of the Lord. All: **Thanks be to God.**

Responsional Psalm 89

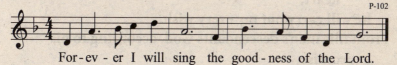

For-ev-er I will sing the good-ness of the Lord.

Music: Jay F. Hunstiger, © 1990, administered by Liturgical Press. All rights reserved.

Psalm 89:4-5, 16-17, 27, 29

℟. (2a) **Forever I will sing the goodness of the Lord.**

I have made a covenant with my chosen one,
 I have sworn to David my servant:
forever will I confirm your posterity
 and establish your throne for all generations. ℟.

Blessed the people who know the joyful shout;
 in the light of your countenance, O Lord, they walk.
At your name they rejoice all the day,
 and through your justice they are exalted. ℟.

(continued)

He shall say of me, "You are my father,
> my God, the Rock, my savior."
Forever I will maintain my kindness toward him,
> and my covenant with him stands firm. ℟.

Reading II (Acts of the Apostles 13:16-17, 22-25)
A reading from the Acts of the Apostles

Paul bears witness to Christ, the Son of David.

When Paul reached Antioch in Pisidia and entered the synagogue,
> he stood up, motioned with his hand, and said,
> "Fellow Israelites and you others who are God-fearing, listen.
The God of this people Israel chose our ancestors
> and exalted the people during their sojourn in the land of Egypt.
With uplifted arm he led them out of it.
Then he removed Saul and raised up David as king;
> of him he testified,
> 'I have found David, son of Jesse, a man after my own heart;
> he will carry out my every wish.'
From this man's descendants God, according to his promise,
> has brought to Israel a savior, Jesus.
John heralded his coming by proclaiming a baptism of repentance
> to all the people of Israel;
> and as John was completing his course, he would say,
> 'What do you suppose that I am? I am not he.
Behold, one is coming after me;
> I am not worthy to unfasten the sandals of his feet.'"

The word of the Lord. All: Thanks be to God.

GOSPEL (Matthew 1:1-25) *or* Shorter Form [ ] (Matthew 1:18-25)
ALLELUIA

℣. Alleluia, alleluia. ℟. **Alleluia, alleluia.**
℣. Tomorrow the wickedness of the earth will be destroyed: the Savior of the world will reign over us. ℟.

☩ **A reading from the beginning of the holy Gospel according to Matthew**

All: **Glory to you, Lord.**

The genealogy of Jesus Christ, the Son of David.

**The book of the genealogy of Jesus Christ,
   the son of David, the son of Abraham.**

**Abraham became the father of Isaac,
   Isaac the father of Jacob,
   Jacob the father of Judah and his brothers.
Judah became the father of Perez and Zerah,
   whose mother was Tamar.
Perez became the father of Hezron,
   Hezron the father of Ram,
   Ram the father of Amminadab.
Amminadab became the father of Nahshon,
   Nahshon the father of Salmon,
   Salmon the father of Boaz,
   whose mother was Rahab.
Boaz became the father of Obed,
   whose mother was Ruth.
Obed became the father of Jesse,
   Jesse the father of David the king.

David became the father of Solomon,
   whose mother had been the wife of Uriah.
Solomon became the father of Rehoboam,
   Rehoboam the father of Abijah,
   Abijah the father of Asaph.
Asaph became the father of Jehoshaphat,
   Jehoshaphat the father of Joram,
   Joram the father of Uzziah.**

Uzziah became the father of Jotham,
   Jotham the father of Ahaz,
   Ahaz the father of Hezekiah.
Hezekiah became the father of Manasseh,
   Manasseh the father of Amos,
   Amos the father of Josiah.
Josiah became the father of Jechoniah and his brothers
   at the time of the Babylonian exile.

After the Babylonian exile,
   Jechoniah became the father of Shealtiel,
   Shealtiel the father of Zerubbabel,
   Zerubbabel the father of Abiud.
Abiud became the father of Eliakim,
   Eliakim the father of Azor,
   Azor the father of Zadok.
Zadok became the father of Achim,
   Achim the father of Eliud,
   Eliud the father of Eleazar.
Eleazar became the father of Matthan,
   Matthan the father of Jacob,
   Jacob the father of Joseph, the husband of Mary.
Of her was born Jesus who is called the Christ.

Thus the total number of generations
   from Abraham to David
   is fourteen generations;
   from David to the Babylonian exile,
   fourteen generations;
   from the Babylonian exile to the Christ,
   fourteen generations.

Now [this is how the birth of Jesus Christ came about.
When his mother Mary was betrothed to Joseph,
   but before they lived together,
   she was found with child through the Holy Spirit.

Joseph her husband, since he was a righteous man,
  yet unwilling to expose her to shame,
  decided to divorce her quietly.
Such was his intention when, behold,
  the angel of the Lord appeared to him in a dream
      and said,
  "Joseph, son of David,
  do not be afraid to take Mary your wife into your home.
For it is through the Holy Spirit
  that this child has been conceived in her.
She will bear a son and you are to name him Jesus,
  because he will save his people from their sins."
All this took place to fulfill
  what the Lord had said through the prophet:
    Behold, the virgin shall conceive and bear a son,
      and they shall name him Emmanuel,
  which means "God is with us."
When Joseph awoke,
  he did as the angel of the Lord had commanded him
  and took his wife into his home.
He had no relations with her until she bore a son,
  and he named him Jesus.]

The Gospel of the Lord. All: **Praise to you, Lord Jesus Christ.**

Prayer over the Gifts
Lord,
as we keep tonight the vigil of Christmas,
may we celebrate this eucharist
with greater joy than ever
since it marks the beginning of our redemption.
We ask this in the name of Jesus the Lord. All: **Amen.**

Communion Antiphon (See Isaiah 40:5)
The glory of the Lord will be revealed, and all mankind
will see the saving power of God.

Prayer after Communion
Father,
we ask you to give us a new birth

as we celebrate the beginning
of your Son's life on earth.
Strengthen us in spirit
as we take your food and drink.
Grant this through Christ our Lord. **All: Amen.**

The Nativity of the Lord

MASS AT MIDNIGHT

December 25, 2009

Entrance Antiphon (Psalm 2:7)
The Lord said to me: You are my Son; this day have I begotten you.

Opening Prayer
Father,
you make this holy night radiant
with the splendor of Jesus Christ our light.
We welcome him as Lord, the true light of the world.
Bring us to eternal joy in the kingdom of heaven,
where he lives and reigns with you and the Holy Spirit,
one God, for ever and ever. **All: Amen.**

Reading I (L 14) (Isaiah 9:1-6)
A reading from the Book of the Prophet Isaiah

A son is given us.

**The people who walked in darkness
    have seen a great light;
upon those who dwelt in the land of gloom
    a light has shone.
You have brought them abundant joy
    and great rejoicing,**

as they rejoice before you as at the harvest,
  as people make merry when dividing spoils.
For the yoke that burdened them,
  the pole on their shoulder,
and the rod of their taskmaster
  you have smashed, as on the day of Midian.
For every boot that tramped in battle,
  every cloak rolled in blood,
  will be burned as fuel for flames.
For a child is born to us, a son is given us;
  upon his shoulder dominion rests.
They name him Wonder-Counselor, God-Hero,
  Father-Forever, Prince of Peace.
His dominion is vast
  and forever peaceful,
from David's throne, and over his kingdom,
  which he confirms and sustains
by judgment and justice,
  both now and forever.
The zeal of the LORD of hosts will do this!

The word of the Lord. All: **Thanks be to God.**

RESPONSORIAL PSALM 96

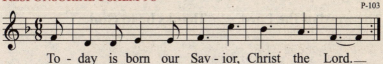

To - day is born our Sav - ior, Christ the Lord.

Music: Jay F. Hunstiger, © 1990, administered by Liturgical Press. All rights reserved.

Psalm 96:1-2, 2-3, 11-12, 13

℟. (Luke 2:11) **Today is born our Savior, Christ the Lord.**

Sing to the LORD a new song;
  sing to the LORD, all you lands.
Sing to the LORD; bless his name. ℟.

Announce his salvation, day after day.
  Tell his glory among the nations;
  among all peoples, his wondrous deeds. ℟.

(continued)

Let the heavens be glad and the earth rejoice;
    let the sea and what fills it resound;
    let the plains be joyful and all that is in them!
Then shall all the trees of the forest exult. ℟.

They shall exult before the Lord, for he comes;
    for he comes to rule the earth.
He shall rule the world with justice
    and the peoples with his constancy. ℟.

Reading II (Titus 2:11-14)
A reading from the Letter of Saint Paul to Titus

The grace of God has appeared to all.

**Beloved:
    The grace of God has appeared, saving all
    and training us to reject godless ways and worldly
        desires
    and to live temperately, justly, and devoutly in this age,
    as we await the blessed hope,
    the appearance of the glory of our great God
    and savior Jesus Christ,
    who gave himself for us to deliver us from all lawlessness
    and to cleanse for himself a people as his own,
    eager to do what is good.

The word of the Lord.** All: **Thanks be to God.**

Gospel (Luke 2:1-14)
Alleluia (Luke 2:10-11)
℣. Alleluia, alleluia. ℟. **Alleluia, alleluia.**
℣. I proclaim to you good news of great joy:
    today a Savior is born for us,
    Christ the Lord. ℟.

✠ **A reading from the holy Gospel according to Luke**

All: **Glory to you, Lord.**

Today a Savior has been born for you.

**In those days a decree went out from Caesar Augustus
    that the whole world should be enrolled.**

This was the first enrollment,
> when Quirinius was governor of Syria.

So all went to be enrolled, each to his own town.
And Joseph too went up from Galilee from the town of Nazareth
> to Judea, to the city of David that is called Bethlehem,
> because he was of the house and family of David,
> to be enrolled with Mary, his betrothed, who was with child.

While they were there,
> the time came for her to have her child,
> and she gave birth to her firstborn son.

She wrapped him in swaddling clothes and laid him in a manger,
> because there was no room for them in the inn.

Now there were shepherds in that region living in the fields
> and keeping the night watch over their flock.

The angel of the Lord appeared to them
> and the glory of the Lord shone around them,
> and they were struck with great fear.

The angel said to them,
> "Do not be afraid;
> for behold, I proclaim to you good news of great joy
> that will be for all the people.

For today in the city of David
> a savior has been born for you who is Christ and Lord.

And this will be a sign for you:
> you will find an infant wrapped in swaddling clothes
> and lying in a manger."

And suddenly there was a multitude of the heavenly host with the angel,
> praising God and saying:
>> "Glory to God in the highest
>>> and on earth peace to those on whom his favor rests."

The Gospel of the Lord. All: **Praise to you, Lord Jesus Christ.**

Prayer over the Gifts
Lord,
accept our gifts on this joyful feast of our salvation.
By our communion with God made man,
may we become more like him
who joins our lives to yours,
for he is Lord for ever and ever. All: **Amen.**

Communion Antiphon (John 1:14)
The Word of God became man; we have seen his glory.

Prayer after Communion
God our Father,
we rejoice in the birth of our Savior.
May we share his life completely
by living as he has taught.
We ask this in the name of Jesus the Lord. All: **Amen.**

MASS AT DAWN

Entrance Antiphon
(*See* Isaiah 9:2, 6; Luke 1:33)
A light will shine on us this day, the Lord is born for us: he shall be called Wonderful God, Prince of peace, Father of the world to come; and his kingship will never end.

Opening Prayer
Father,
we are filled with the new light
by the coming of your Word among us.
May the light of faith
shine in our words and actions.
Grant this through our Lord Jesus Christ, your Son,
who lives and reigns with you and the Holy Spirit,
one God, for ever and ever. All: **Amen.**

December 25

Reading I (L 15) (Isaiah 62:11-12)
A reading from the Book of the Prophet Isaiah

Behold, your Savior comes!

> See, the LORD proclaims
>   to the ends of the earth:
> say to daughter Zion,
>   your savior comes!
> Here is his reward with him,
>   his recompense before him.
> They shall be called the holy people,
>   the redeemed of the LORD,
> and you shall be called "Frequented,"
>   a city that is not forsaken.

The word of the Lord. All: Thanks be to God.

Responsorial Psalm 97

Music: Jay F. Hunstiger, © 1990, administered by Liturgical Press. All rights reserved.

Psalm 97:1, 6, 11-12

℟. **A light will shine on us this day: the Lord is born for us.**

> The LORD is king; let the earth rejoice;
>   let the many isles be glad.
> The heavens proclaim his justice,
>   and all peoples see his glory. ℟.
>
> Light dawns for the just;
>   and gladness, for the upright of heart.
> Be glad in the LORD, you just,
>   and give thanks to his holy name. ℟.

Reading II (Titus 3:4-7)
A reading from the Letter of Saint Paul to Titus
Because of his mercy, he saved us.

Beloved:
> When the kindness and generous love
>> of God our savior appeared,
>
> not because of any righteous deeds we had done
>> but because of his mercy,
>
> he saved us through the bath of rebirth
>> and renewal by the Holy Spirit,
>
> whom he richly poured out on us
>> through Jesus Christ our savior,
>
> so that we might be justified by his grace
>> and become heirs in hope of eternal life.

The word of the Lord. All: **Thanks be to God.**

Gospel (Luke 2:15-20)
Alleluia (Luke 2:14)
℣. Alleluia, alleluia. ℟. **Alleluia, alleluia.**
℣. Glory to God in the highest,
and on earth peace to those
on whom his favor rests. ℟.

✠ **A reading from the holy Gospel according to Luke**

All: **Glory to you, Lord.**

The shepherds found Mary and Joseph and the infant.

> When the angels went away from them to heaven,
>> the shepherds said to one another,
>> "Let us go, then, to Bethlehem
>> to see this thing that has taken place,
>> which the Lord has made known to us."
>
> So they went in haste and found Mary and Joseph,
>> and the infant lying in the manger.
>
> When they saw this,
>> they made known the message
>> that had been told them about this child.

All who heard it were amazed
   by what had been told them by the shepherds.
And Mary kept all these things,
   reflecting on them in her heart.
Then the shepherds returned,
   glorifying and praising God
   for all they had heard and seen,
   just as it had been told to them.

The Gospel of the Lord. All: **Praise to you, Lord Jesus Christ.**

Prayer over the Gifts
Father,
may we follow the example of your Son
who became man and lived among us.
May we receive the gift of divine life
through these offerings here on earth.
We ask this in the name of Jesus the Lord. All: **Amen.**

Communion Antiphon (*See* Zechariah 9:9)
Daughter of Zion, exult; shout aloud, daughter Jerusalem!
Your King is coming, the Holy One, the Savior of the world.

Prayer after Communion
Lord,
with faith and joy
we celebrate the birthday of your Son.
Increase our understanding and our love
of the riches you have revealed in him,
who is Lord for ever and ever. All: **Amen.**

MASS DURING THE DAY

ENTRANCE ANTIPHON (Isaiah 9:6)
A child is born for us, a son is given to us; dominion is laid on his shoulder, and he shall be called Wonderful-Counselor.

OPENING PRAYER
Lord God,
we praise you for creating man,
and still more for restoring him in Christ.
Your Son shared our weakness:
may we share his glory,
for he lives and reigns with you and the Holy Spirit,
one God, for ever and ever. All: Amen.

READING I (L 16) (Isaiah 52:7-10)
A reading from the Book of the Prophet Isaiah

All the ends of the earth will behold the salvation of our God.

> **How beautiful upon the mountains
>   are the feet of him who brings glad tidings,
> announcing peace, bearing good news,
>   announcing salvation, and saying to Zion,
>   "Your God is King!"
> Hark! Your sentinels raise a cry,
>   together they shout for joy,
> for they see directly, before their eyes,
>   the LORD restoring Zion.
> Break out together in song,
>   O ruins of Jerusalem!
> For the LORD comforts his people,
>   he redeems Jerusalem.
> The LORD has bared his holy arm
>   in the sight of all the nations;
> all the ends of the earth will behold
>   the salvation of our God.**

The word of the Lord. All: **Thanks be to God.**

Responsorial Psalm 98

All the ends of the earth have seen the saving pow'r of God. pow'r of God.

Music: Jay F. Hunstiger, © 1990, administered by Liturgical Press. All rights reserved.

Psalm 98:1, 2-3, 3-4, 5-6

℟. (3c) **All the ends of the earth have seen the saving power of God.**

Sing to the Lord a new song,
   for he has done wondrous deeds;
his right hand has won victory for him,
   his holy arm. ℟.

The Lord has made his salvation known:
   in the sight of the nations he has revealed his justice.
He has remembered his kindness and his faithfulness
   toward the house of Israel. ℟.

All the ends of the earth have seen
   the salvation by our God.
Sing joyfully to the Lord, all you lands;
   break into song; sing praise. ℟.

Sing praise to the Lord with the harp,
   with the harp and melodious song.
With trumpets and the sound of the horn
   sing joyfully before the King, the Lord. ℟.

Reading II (Hebrews 1:1-6)

A reading from the beginning of the Letter to the Hebrews

God has spoken to us through the Son.

Brothers and sisters:
In times past, God spoke in partial and various ways
   to our ancestors through the prophets;

in these last days, he has spoken to us through the Son,
>   whom he made heir of all things
>   and through whom he created the universe,
who is the refulgence of his glory,
>   the very imprint of his being,
>   and who sustains all things by his mighty word.
When he had accomplished purification from sins,
>   he took his seat at the right hand of the Majesty on high,
as far superior to the angels
>   as the name he has inherited is more excellent than theirs.

For to which of the angels did God ever say:
>   *You are my son; this day I have begotten you?*
Or again:
>   *I will be a father to him, and he shall be a son to me?*
And again, when he leads the firstborn into the world,
>   he says:
>   *Let all the angels of God worship him.*

The word of the Lord. All: Thanks be to God.

GOSPEL (John 1:1-18) *or* Shorter Form [ ] (John 1:1-5, 9-14)
ALLELUIA
℣. Alleluia, alleluia. ℟. **Alleluia, alleluia.**
℣. A holy day has dawned upon us.
>   Come, you nations, and adore the Lord.
>   For today a great light has come upon the earth. ℟.

✠ A reading from the holy Gospel according to John

All: **Glory to you, Lord.**

The Word became flesh and made his dwelling among us.

>   [In the beginning was the Word,
>   >   and the Word was with God,
>   >   and the Word was God.
>   He was in the beginning with God.
>   All things came to be through him,
>   >   and without him nothing came to be.

> What came to be through him was life,
> > and this life was the light of the human race;
> > the light shines in the darkness,
> > > and the darkness has not overcome it.]

A man named John was sent from God.
He came for testimony, to testify to the light,
> so that all might believe through him.
He was not the light,
> but came to testify to the light.
[The true light, which enlightens everyone,
> was coming into the world.

> He was in the world,
> > and the world came to be through him,
> > but the world did not know him.
> He came to what was his own,
> > but his own people did not accept him.

But to those who did accept him
he gave power to become children of God,
to those who believe in his name,
who were born not by natural generation
nor by human choice nor by a man's decision
but of God.

> And the Word became flesh
> > and made his dwelling among us,
> > and we saw his glory,
> > the glory as of the Father's only Son,
> > full of grace and truth.]

John testified to him and cried out, saying,
> "This was he of whom I said,
> 'The one who is coming after me ranks ahead of me
> because he existed before me.'"
From his fullness we have all received,
> grace in place of grace,
> because while the law was given through Moses,
> grace and truth came through Jesus Christ.

No one has ever seen God.
The only Son, God, who is at the Father's side,
  has revealed him.

The Gospel of the Lord. All: **Praise to you, Lord Jesus Christ.**

Prayer over the Gifts
Almighty God,
the saving work of Christ
made our peace with you.
May our offering today
renew that peace within us
and give you perfect praise.
We ask this in the name of Jesus the Lord. All: **Amen.**

Communion Antiphon (Psalm 98:3)
All the ends of the earth have seen the saving power of God.

Prayer after Communion
Father,
the child born today is the Savior of the world.
He made us your children.
May he welcome us into your kingdom
where he lives and reigns with you for ever and ever. All: **Amen.**

Holy Family

SUNDAY IN THE OCTAVE OF CHRISTMAS

December 27, 2009

Reflection on the Gospel

The familiarity of family life can sometimes blind us to see the goodness in each other. This feast reminds us to open our eyes and be "astonished" at the goodness of each other rather than anxious about our own concerns. Families grow in strength when each person in the family—from parents to the smallest child to anyone extended the hospitality of the family—is treated as a member of God's family and, therefore, holy.

- *My family calls me to holiness by . . . My family models holiness when . . .*

—Living Liturgy™, *Holy Family 2009*

Entrance Antiphon (Luke 2:16)
The shepherds hastened to Bethlehem, where they found Mary and Joseph, and the baby lying in a manger.

Opening Prayer
Father,
help us to live as the holy family,
united in respect and love.
Bring us to the joy and peace of your eternal home.
Grant this through our Lord Jesus Christ, your Son,
who lives and reigns with you and the Holy Spirit,
one God, for ever and ever. All: **Amen.**

Reading I (L 17) (Sirach 3:2-6, 12-14) *for this year additional options can be found in the Lectionary*

A reading from the Book of Sirach

Those who fear the Lord honor their parents.

God sets a father in honor over his children;
    a mother's authority he confirms over her sons.
Whoever honors his father atones for sins,
    and preserves himself from them.
When he prays, he is heard;
    he stores up riches who reveres his mother.
Whoever honors his father is gladdened by children,
    and, when he prays, is heard.
Whoever reveres his father will live a long life;
    he who obeys his father brings comfort to his mother.

My son, take care of your father when he is old;
    grieve him not as long as he lives.
Even if his mind fail, be considerate of him;
    revile him not all the days of his life;

kindness to a father will not be forgotten,
>firmly planted against the debt of your sins
>>—a house raised in justice to you.

The word of the Lord. All: Thanks be to God.

RESPONSORIAL PSALM 128

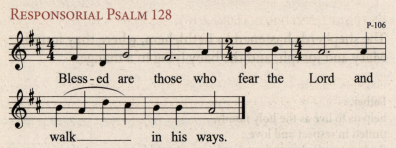

Music: Jay F. Hunstiger, © 1998, administered by Liturgical Press. All rights reserved.

Psalm 128:1-2, 3, 4-5

℟. (*See* 1) **Blessed are those who fear the Lord and walk in his ways.**

> Blessed is everyone who fears the LORD,
>> who walks in his ways!
> For you shall eat the fruit of your handiwork;
>> blessed shall you be, and favored. ℟.

> Your wife shall be like a fruitful vine
>> in the recesses of your home;
> your children like olive plants
>> around your table. ℟.

> Behold, thus is the man blessed
>> who fears the LORD.
> The LORD bless you from Zion:
>> may you see the prosperity of Jerusalem
>> all the days of your life. ℟.

READING II (Colossians 3:12-21) *or* Shorter Form [ ]
(Colossians 3:12-17) *for this year additional options can be found in the Lectionary*

A reading from the Letter of Saint Paul to the Colossians

Family life in the Lord.

[Brothers and sisters:
Put on, as God's chosen ones, holy and beloved,
    heartfelt compassion, kindness, humility, gentleness,
        and patience,
    bearing with one another and forgiving one another,
    if one has a grievance against another;
    as the Lord has forgiven you, so must you also do.
And over all these put on love,
    that is, the bond of perfection.
And let the peace of Christ control your hearts,
    the peace into which you were also called in one body.
And be thankful.
Let the word of Christ dwell in you richly,
    as in all wisdom you teach and admonish one another,
    singing psalms, hymns, and spiritual songs
    with gratitude in your hearts to God.
And whatever you do, in word or in deed,
    do everything in the name of the Lord Jesus,
    giving thanks to God the Father through him.]

Wives, be subordinate to your husbands,
    as is proper in the Lord.
Husbands, love your wives,
    and avoid any bitterness toward them.
Children, obey your parents in everything,
    for this is pleasing to the Lord.
Fathers, do not provoke your children,
    so they may not become discouraged.

The word of the Lord. All: **Thanks be to God.**

GOSPEL (Luke 2:41-52)
ALLELUIA (Colossians 3:15a, 16a)
℣. Alleluia, alleluia. ℟. **Alleluia, alleluia.**
℣. Let the peace of Christ control your hearts;
    let the word of Christ dwell in you richly. ℟.
or:

ALLELUIA (*See* Acts of the Apostles 16:14b)
℣. Alleluia, alleluia. ℟. **Alleluia, alleluia.**
℣. Open our hearts, O Lord,
   to listen to the words of your Son. ℟.

✠ **A reading from the holy Gospel according to Luke**

His parents found Jesus sitting in the midst of the teachers.

**Each year Jesus' parents went to Jerusalem for the feast
   of Passover,
   and when he was twelve years old,
   they went up according to festival custom.
After they had completed its days, as they were returning,
   the boy Jesus remained behind in Jerusalem,
   but his parents did not know it.
Thinking that he was in the caravan,
   they journeyed for a day
   and looked for him among their relatives and
      acquaintances,
   but not finding him,
   they returned to Jerusalem to look for him.
After three days they found him in the temple,
   sitting in the midst of the teachers,
   listening to them and asking them questions,
   and all who heard him were astounded
   at his understanding and his answers.
When his parents saw him,
   they were astonished,
   and his mother said to him,
   "Son, why have you done this to us?
Your father and I have been looking for you with great
   anxiety."
And he said to them,
   "Why were you looking for me?
Did you not know that I must be in my Father's house?"
But they did not understand what he said to them.**

He went down with them and came to Nazareth,
   and was obedient to them;
   and his mother kept all these things in her heart.
And Jesus advanced in wisdom and age and favor
   before God and man.

The Gospel of the Lord. All: **Praise to you, Lord Jesus Christ.**

Prayer over the Gifts
Lord,
accept this sacrifice
and through the prayers of Mary, the virgin Mother of God,
and of her husband, Joseph,
unite our families in peace and love.
We ask this in the name of Jesus the Lord. All: **Amen.**

Communion Antiphon (Baruch 3:38)
Our God has appeared on earth, and lived among men.

Prayer after Communion
Eternal Father,
we want to live as Jesus, Mary, and Joseph,
in peace with you and one another.
May this communion strengthen us
to face the troubles of life.
Grant this through Christ our Lord. All: **Amen.**

Solemnity of Mary, Mother of God

OCTAVE OF CHRISTMAS

January 1, 2010 (First Friday)

World Day of Peace

Reflection on the Gospel

The salvation events the incarnation unleashed are neither easy to understand nor to embrace. Mary heard the good news, took it into her heart, and reflected on it. Mary shows us the way: we, too, must adopt a contemplative stance before God and the mystery of salvation. Mary's ongoing yes to God wasn't really very easy at all. Yet she continued to be faithful because she took a contemplative stance: reflecting, pondering, praying.

- *If I am to imitate and develop Mary's reflective stance found in the gospel, I must . . .*

—*Living Liturgy*™, *Mary, Mother of God 2010*

Entrance Antiphon (*See* Isaiah 9:2, 6; Luke 1:33)

A light will shine on us this day, the Lord is born for us: he shall be called Wonderful God, Prince of peace, Father of the world to come; and his kingship will never end.

Opening Prayer

God our Father,
may we always profit by the prayers
of the Virgin Mother Mary,
for you bring us life and salvation
through Jesus Christ her Son
who lives and reigns with you and the Holy Spirit,
one God, for ever and ever. All: **Amen.**

Reading I (L 18) (Numbers 6:22-27)

A reading from the Book of Numbers

They shall invoke my name upon the Israelites, and I will bless them.

The Lord said to Moses:
　"Speak to Aaron and his sons and tell them:
　This is how you shall bless the Israelites.
Say to them:
　The Lord bless you and keep you!
　The Lord let his face shine upon
　　you, and be gracious to you!
　The Lord look upon you kindly and
　　give you peace!
So shall they invoke my name upon the Israelites,
　and I will bless them."

The word of the Lord. All: **Thanks be to God.**

Responsorial Psalm 67

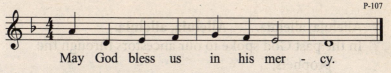

May God bless us in his mercy.

Music: Jay F. Hunstiger, © 1990, administered by Liturgical Press. All rights reserved.

Psalm 67:2-3, 5, 6, 8

℟. (2a) **May God bless us in his mercy.**

> May God have pity on us and bless us;
>> may he let his face shine upon us.
>
> So may your way be known upon earth;
>> among all nations, your salvation. ℟.
>
> May the nations be glad and exult
>> because you rule the peoples in equity;
>> the nations on the earth you guide. ℟.
>
> May the peoples praise you, O God;
>> may all the peoples praise you!
>
> May God bless us,
>> and may all the ends of the earth fear him! ℟.

Reading II (Galatians 4:4-7)

A reading from the Letter of Saint Paul to the Galatians

God sent his Son, born of a woman.

**Brothers and sisters:
When the fullness of time had come, God sent his Son,
  born of a woman, born under the law,
  to ransom those under the law,
  so that we might receive adoption as sons.
As proof that you are sons,
  God sent the Spirit of his Son into our hearts,
  crying out, "Abba, Father!"
So you are no longer a slave but a son,
  and if a son then also an heir, through God.
The word of the Lord.** All: **Thanks be to God.**

Gospel (Luke 2:16-21)

Alleluia (Hebrews 1:1-2)

℣. Alleluia, alleluia. ℟. **Alleluia, alleluia.**
℣. In the past God spoke to our ancestors through the prophets;
in these last days, he has spoken to us through the Son. ℟.

✠ **A reading from the holy Gospel according to Luke**

All: **Glory to you, Lord.**

They found Mary and Joseph and the infant. When the eight days were completed, he was named Jesus.

The shepherds went in haste to Bethlehem and found Mary and Joseph,
and the infant lying in the manger.
When they saw this,
they made known the message
that had been told them about this child.
All who heard it were amazed
by what had been told them by the shepherds.
And Mary kept all these things,
reflecting on them in her heart.
Then the shepherds returned,
glorifying and praising God
for all they had heard and seen,
just as it had been told to them.
When eight days were completed for his circumcision,
he was named Jesus, the name given him by the angel
before he was conceived in the womb.

The Gospel of the Lord. All: **Praise to you, Lord Jesus Christ.**

Prayer over the Gifts

God our Father,
we celebrate at this season
the beginning of our salvation.
On this feast of Mary, the Mother of God,
we ask that our salvation
will be brought to its fulfillment.
We ask this through Christ our Lord. All: **Amen.**

Communion Antiphon (Hebrews 13:8)
Jesus Christ is the same yesterday, today, and for ever.

Prayer after Communion
Father,
as we proclaim the Virgin Mary
to be the mother of Christ and the mother of the Church,
may our communion with her Son
bring us to salvation.
We ask this through Christ our Lord. All: **Amen.**

Epiphany

January 3, 2010

Reflection on the Gospel

The point to the gospel is even more amazing than the imaginative details it includes: God chooses to manifest the mystery of Christ Jesus to all the nations. This, of course, includes each of us today: we are both to search for the Christ as well as manifest his presence for others. Our task-response, note, is not only to search for the Christ among us but also to manifest that divine presence. In other words, we are to be the revelation of his presence in our daily living.

- *I search for Christ when . . . I am the revelation of Christ for others when . . .*

—Living Liturgy™, *Epiphany 2010*

Entrance Antiphon (See Malachi 3:1; 1 Chronicles 19:12)
The Lord and ruler is coming; kingship is his, and government and power.

Opening Prayer
Father,
you revealed your Son to the nations
by the guidance of a star.
Lead us to your glory in heaven
by the light of faith.

January 3

We ask this through our Lord Jesus Christ, your Son,
who lives and reigns with you and the Holy Spirit,
one God, for ever and ever. All: **Amen.**

Reading I (L 20) (Isaiah 60:1-6)
A reading from the Book of the Prophet Isaiah

The glory of the Lord shines upon you.

**Rise up in splendor, Jerusalem! Your light has come,
    the glory of the Lord shines upon you.
See, darkness covers the earth,
    and thick clouds cover the peoples;
but upon you the Lord shines,
    and over you appears his glory.
Nations shall walk by your light,
    and kings by your shining radiance.
Raise your eyes and look about;
    they all gather and come to you:
your sons come from afar,
    and your daughters in the arms of their nurses.**

**Then you shall be radiant at what you see,
    your heart shall throb and overflow,
for the riches of the sea shall be emptied out before you,
    the wealth of nations shall be brought to you.
Caravans of camels shall fill you,
    dromedaries from Midian and Ephah;
all from Sheba shall come
    bearing gold and frankincense,
    and proclaiming the praises of the Lord.**

The word of the Lord. All: **Thanks be to God.**

Responsorial Psalm 72

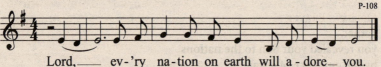

Lord, ev-'ry na-tion on earth will a-dore you.

Music: Jay F. Hunstiger, © 1990, administered by Liturgical Press. All rights reserved.

Psalm 72:1-2, 7-8, 10-11, 12-13

℟. *(See* 11) **Lord, every nation on earth will adore you.**

O God, with your judgment endow the king,
    and with your justice, the king's son;
he shall govern your people with justice
    and your afflicted ones with judgment. ℟.

Justice shall flower in his days,
    and profound peace, till the moon be no more.
May he rule from sea to sea,
    and from the River to the ends of the earth. ℟.

The kings of Tarshish and the Isles shall offer gifts;
    the kings of Arabia and Seba shall bring tribute.
All kings shall pay him homage,
    all nations shall serve him. ℟.

For he shall rescue the poor when he cries out,
    and the afflicted when he has no one to help him.
He shall have pity for the lowly and the poor;
    the lives of the poor he shall save. ℟.

Reading II (Ephesians 3:2-3a, 5-6)

A reading from the Letter of Saint Paul to the Ephesians

Now it has been revealed that the Gentiles are coheirs of the promise.

Brothers and sisters:
You have heard of the stewardship of God's grace
    that was given to me for your benefit,
        namely, that the mystery was made known to me by
            revelation.
It was not made known to people in other generations
    as it has now been revealed
    to his holy apostles and prophets by the Spirit:
    that the Gentiles are coheirs, members of the same body,
    and copartners in the promise in Christ Jesus through
        the gospel.
The word of the Lord. All: **Thanks be to God.**

January 3

GOSPEL (Matthew 2:1-12)
ALLELUIA (Matthew 2:2)

℣. Alleluia, alleluia. ℟. **Alleluia, alleluia.**
℣. We saw his star at its rising
and have come to do him homage. ℟.

✠ A reading from the holy Gospel according to Matthew

All: **Glory to you, Lord.**

We saw his star at its rising and have come to do him homage.

When Jesus was born in Bethlehem of Judea,
  in the days of King Herod,
    behold, magi from the east arrived in Jerusalem, saying,
    "Where is the newborn king of the Jews?
We saw his star at its rising
  and have come to do him homage."
When King Herod heard this,
  he was greatly troubled,
  and all Jerusalem with him.
Assembling all the chief priests and the scribes of the
    people,
  he inquired of them where the Christ was to be born.
They said to him, "In Bethlehem of Judea,
  for thus it has been written through the prophet:
    And you, Bethlehem, land of Judah,
      are by no means least among the rulers of Judah;
    since from you shall come a ruler,
      who is to shepherd my people Israel."
Then Herod called the magi secretly
  and ascertained from them the time of the star's
      appearance.
He sent them to Bethlehem and said,
  "Go and search diligently for the child.
When you have found him, bring me word,
  that I too may go and do him homage."
After their audience with the king they set out.

And behold, the star that they had seen at its rising
 preceded them,
 until it came and stopped over the place where the
  child was.
They were overjoyed at seeing the star,
 and on entering the house
 they saw the child with Mary his mother.
They prostrated themselves and did him homage.
Then they opened their treasures
 and offered him gifts of gold, frankincense, and myrrh.
And having been warned in a dream not to return to
 Herod,
 they departed for their country by another way.

The Gospel of the Lord. All: Praise to you, Lord Jesus Christ.

Prayer over the Gifts
Lord,
accept the offerings of your Church,
not gold, frankincense and myrrh,
but the sacrifice and food they symbolize:
Jesus Christ, who is Lord for ever and ever. All: **Amen.**

Communion Antiphon (See Matthew 2:2)
We have seen his star in the east, and have come with gifts to adore the Lord.

Prayer after Communion
Father,
guide us with your light.
Help us to recognize Christ in this eucharist
and welcome him with love,
for he is Lord for ever and ever. All: **Amen.**

Baptism of the Lord

January 10, 2010

Reflection on the Gospel

The gospel speaks of two baptisms. The first is the event this feast celebrates: the baptism Jesus received at the hands of John. The second is the baptism that we receive "with the Holy Spirit and fire." Jesus' baptism revealed him as "beloved Son"; our own baptism reveals us as ones who are saved, renewed, justified, and heirs of eternal life. This feast, then, is an epiphany not only of who Jesus is, but also of who we are.

- *Having been baptized "with the Holy Spirit and fire" means to me . . .*

—Living Liturgy™, *Baptism of the Lord, 2010*

ENTRANCE ANTIPHON (*See* Matthew 3:16-17)

When the Lord had been baptized, the heavens opened, and the Spirit came down like a dove to rest on him. Then the voice of the Father thundered: This is my beloved Son, with him I am well pleased.

OPENING PRAYER

Almighty, eternal God,
when the Spirit descended upon Jesus
at his baptism in the Jordan,
you revealed him as your own beloved Son.
Keep us, your children born of water and the Spirit,
faithful to our calling.
We ask this through our Lord Jesus Christ, your Son,
who lives and reigns with you and the Holy Spirit,
one God, for ever and ever. All: **Amen.**

READING I (L 21) (Isaiah 42:1-4, 6-7) *for this year additional options can be found in the Lectionary*

A reading from the Book of the Prophet Isaiah

Behold my servant with whom I am well pleased.

Thus says the LORD:
Here is my servant whom I uphold,
> my chosen one with whom I am pleased,
upon whom I have put my spirit;
> he shall bring forth justice to the nations,
not crying out, not shouting,
> not making his voice heard in the street.
A bruised reed he shall not break,
> and a smoldering wick he shall not quench,
until he establishes justice on the earth;
> the coastlands will wait for his teaching.

I, the LORD, have called you for the victory of justice,
> I have grasped you by the hand;
I formed you, and set you
> as a covenant of the people,
> a light for the nations,
to open the eyes of the blind,
> to bring out prisoners from confinement,
> and from the dungeon, those who live in darkness.

The word of the Lord. All: Thanks be to God.

RESPONSORIAL PSALM 29

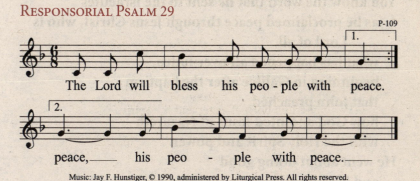

Music: Jay F. Hunstiger, © 1990, administered by Liturgical Press. All rights reserved.

Psalm 29:1-2, 3-4, 3, 9-10

℟. (11b) **The Lord will bless his people with peace.**

Give to the LORD, you sons of God,
> give to the LORD glory and praise,

(continued)

give to the Lord the glory due his name;
   adore the Lord in holy attire. ℟.

The voice of the Lord is over the waters,
   the Lord, over vast waters.
The voice of the Lord is mighty;
   the voice of the Lord is majestic. ℟.

The God of glory thunders,
   and in his temple all say, "Glory!"
The Lord is enthroned above the flood;
   the Lord is enthroned as king forever. ℟.

Reading II (Acts of the Apostles 10:34-38) *for this year additional options can be found in the Lectionary*

A reading from the Acts of the Apostles

God anointed him with the Holy Spirit.

**Peter proceeded to speak to those gathered
   in the house of Cornelius, saying:
"In truth, I see that God shows no partiality.
Rather, in every nation whoever fears him and acts
      uprightly
   is acceptable to him.
You know the word that he sent to the Israelites
   as he proclaimed peace through Jesus Christ, who is
      Lord of all,
   what has happened all over Judea,
   beginning in Galilee after the baptism
   that John preached,
   how God anointed Jesus of Nazareth
   with the Holy Spirit and power.
He went about doing good
   and healing all those oppressed by the devil,
   for God was with him."

The word of the Lord.** All: **Thanks be to God.**

Gospel (Luke 3:15-16, 21-22)
Alleluia (See Mark 9:7)
℣. Alleluia, alleluia. ℟. **Alleluia, alleluia.**
℣. The heavens were opened and the voice of the Father thundered:
 This is my beloved Son, listen to him. ℟.

or:

Alleluia (See Luke 3:16)
℣. Alleluia, alleluia. ℟. **Alleluia, alleluia.**
℣. John said: One mightier than I is coming;
 he will baptize you with the Holy Spirit and with fire. ℟.

✠ **A reading from the holy Gospel according to Luke**

All: **Glory to you, Lord.**

When Jesus had been baptized and was praying, heaven was opened.

**The people were filled with expectation,
 and all were asking in their hearts
 whether John might be the Christ.
John answered them all, saying,
 "I am baptizing you with water,
 but one mightier than I is coming.
I am not worthy to loosen the thongs of his sandals.
He will baptize you with the Holy Spirit and fire."**

**After all the people had been baptized
 and Jesus also had been baptized and was praying,
 heaven was opened and the Holy Spirit descended
  upon him
 in bodily form like a dove.
And a voice came from heaven,
 "You are my beloved Son;
 with you I am well pleased."**

The Gospel of the Lord. All: **Praise to you, Lord Jesus Christ.**

Prayer over the Gifts
Lord,
we celebrate the revelation of Christ your Son
who takes away the sins of the world.

Accept our gifts
and let them become one with his sacrifice,
for he is Lord for ever and ever. All: **Amen.**

COMMUNION ANTIPHON (John 1:32, 34)
This is he of whom John said: I have seen and have given witness that this is the Son of God.

PRAYER AFTER COMMUNION
Lord,
you feed us with bread from heaven.
May we hear your Son with faith
and become your children in name and in fact.
We ask this in the name of Jesus the Lord. All: **Amen.**

Second Sunday in Ordinary Time

January 17, 2010

Reflection on the Gospel

John uses this wedding occasion at the beginning of Jesus' public life to give us an overview of the meaning and purpose of Jesus' whole life. All Jesus' life and actions are directed toward his saving work culminating in his death and resurrection—and our response to this is "to believe in him." Our believing is expressed by our own action of entering into Jesus' saving work. The wedding feast was an opportunity for epiphany and belief.

• *Jesus reveals his glory to me in . . . by . . . through . . .*

—Living Liturgy™, *Second Sunday in Ordinary Time 2010*

ENTRANCE ANTIPHON (Psalm 65:4)
May all the earth give you worship and praise, and break into song to your name, O God, Most High.

Opening Prayer

Father of heaven and earth,
hear our prayers,
and show us the way to peace in the world.
Grant this through our Lord Jesus Christ, your Son,
who lives and reigns with you and the Holy Spirit,
one God, for ever and ever. All: **Amen.**

Reading I (L 66) (Isaiah 62:1-5)

A reading from the Book of the Prophet Isaiah

The bridegroom rejoices in his bride.

> **For Zion's sake I will not be silent,**
>   **for Jerusalem's sake I will not be quiet,**
> **until her vindication shines forth like the dawn**
>   **and her victory like a burning torch.**
>
> **Nations shall behold your vindication,**
>   **and all the kings your glory;**
> **you shall be called by a new name**
>   **pronounced by the mouth of the Lord.**
> **You shall be a glorious crown in the hand of the Lord,**
>   **a royal diadem held by your God.**
> **No more shall people call you "Forsaken,"**
>   **or your land "Desolate,"**
> **but you shall be called "My Delight,"**
>   **and your land "Espoused."**
> **For the Lord delights in you**
>   **and makes your land his spouse.**
> **As a young man marries a virgin,**
>   **your Builder shall marry you;**
> **and as a bridegroom rejoices in his bride**
>   **so shall your God rejoice in you.**

The word of the Lord. All: **Thanks be to God.**

Responsorial Psalm 96

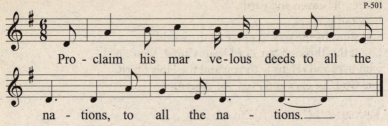

Music: Jay F. Hunstiger, © 1991, administered by Liturgical Press. All rights reserved.

Psalm 96:1-2, 2-3, 7-8, 9-10

℟. (3) **Proclaim his marvelous deeds to all the nations.**

Sing to the Lord a new song;
>sing to the Lord, all you lands.
Sing to the Lord; bless his name. ℟.

Announce his salvation, day after day.
Tell his glory among the nations;
>among all peoples, his wondrous deeds. ℟.

Give to the Lord, you families of nations,
>give to the Lord glory and praise;
>give to the Lord the glory due his name! ℟.

Worship the Lord in holy attire.
>Tremble before him, all the earth;
say among the nations: The Lord is king.
He governs the peoples with equity. ℟.

Reading II (1 Corinthians 12:4-11)

A reading from the first Letter of Saint Paul to the Corinthians

One and the same Spirit distributing them individually to each person as he wishes.

Brothers and sisters:
There are different kinds of spiritual gifts but the same Spirit;
>there are different forms of service but the same Lord;
>there are different workings but the same God
who produces all of them in everyone.

To each individual the manifestation of the Spirit
 is given for some benefit.
To one is given through the Spirit the expression of
 wisdom;
 to another, the expression of knowledge according to
  the same Spirit;
 to another, faith by the same Spirit;
 to another, gifts of healing by the one Spirit;
 to another, mighty deeds;
 to another, prophecy;
 to another, discernment of spirits;
 to another, varieties of tongues;
 to another, interpretation of tongues.
But one and the same Spirit produces all of these,
 distributing them individually to each person as he
  wishes.

The word of the Lord. All: Thanks be to God.

Gospel (John 2:1-11)
Alleluia (*See* 2 Thessalonians 2:14)
℣. Alleluia, alleluia. ℟. **Alleluia, alleluia.**
℣. God has called us through the Gospel
 to possess the glory of our Lord Jesus Christ. ℟.

✠ **A reading from the holy Gospel according to John**

All: **Glory to you, Lord.**

Jesus did this as the beginning of his signs at Cana in Galilee.

There was a wedding at Cana in Galilee,
 and the mother of Jesus was there.
Jesus and his disciples were also invited to the wedding.
When the wine ran short,
 the mother of Jesus said to him,
 "They have no wine."
And Jesus said to her,
 "Woman, how does your concern affect me?
My hour has not yet come."

His mother said to the servers,
   "Do whatever he tells you."
Now there were six stone water jars there for Jewish
      ceremonial washings,
   each holding twenty to thirty gallons.
Jesus told them,
   "Fill the jars with water."
So they filled them to the brim.
Then he told them,
   "Draw some out now and take it to the headwaiter."
So they took it.
And when the headwaiter tasted the water that had
      become wine,
   without knowing where it came from
   —although the servers who had drawn the water
         knew—,
   the headwaiter called the bridegroom and said to him,
   "Everyone serves good wine first,
   and then when people have drunk freely, an inferior
         one;
   but you have kept the good wine until now."
Jesus did this as the beginning of his signs at Cana in
      Galilee
   and so revealed his glory,
   and his disciples began to believe in him.

The Gospel of the Lord. All: **Praise to you, Lord Jesus Christ.**

Prayer over the Gifts
Father,
may we celebrate the eucharist
with reverence and love,
for when we proclaim the death of the Lord
you continue the work of his redemption,
who is Lord for ever and ever. All: **Amen.**

Communion Antiphon (1 John 4:16)
We know and believe in God's love for us.

Prayer after Communion

Lord,
you have nourished us with bread from heaven.
Fill us with your Spirit,
and make us one in peace and love.
We ask this through Christ our Lord. All: **Amen.**

Third Sunday in Ordinary Time

January 24, 2010

Reflection on the Gospel

After Jesus' proclamation in the synagogue, the hearers "looked intently at him." What were they expecting from Jesus? An explanation of what they had just heard, yes. But Jesus moves his hearers beyond receiving mere explanation of the word to encountering him as the Word made flesh. In this he also announces his saving mission: to meet the needs of the poor, the captives, the blind, the oppressed. Our hearing the Word today invites us to participate in these saving deeds as, through us, the Word continues to be made flesh.

- *I continue Jesus' mission to the poor, captives, blind, and oppressed whenever I . . .*

—Living Liturgy™, *Third Sunday in Ordinary Time 2010*

Entrance Antiphon (Psalm 94:1, 6)

Sing a new song to the Lord! Sing to the Lord, all the earth. Truth and beauty surround him, he lives in holiness and glory.

Opening Prayer

All-powerful and ever-living God,
direct your love that is within us,
that our efforts in the name of your Son
may bring mankind to unity and peace.
We ask this through our Lord Jesus Christ, your Son,
who lives and reigns with you and the Holy Spirit,
one God, for ever and ever. All: **Amen.**

Reading I (L 69) (Nehemiah 8:2-4a, 5-6, 8-10)
A reading from the Book of Nehemiah

They read from the book of the Law and they understood what was read.

Ezra the priest brought the law before the assembly,
   which consisted of men, women,
   and those children old enough to understand.
Standing at one end of the open place that was before
     the Water Gate,
   he read out of the book from daybreak till midday,
   in the presence of the men, the women,
   and those children old enough to understand;
   and all the people listened attentively to the book of
     the law.
Ezra the scribe stood on a wooden platform
   that had been made for the occasion.
He opened the scroll
   so that all the people might see it
     —for he was standing higher up than any of the
        people—;
   and, as he opened it, all the people rose.
Ezra blessed the Lord, the great God,
   and all the people, their hands raised high, answered,
   "Amen, amen!"
Then they bowed down and prostrated themselves before
     the Lord,
   their faces to the ground.
Ezra read plainly from the book of the law of God,
   interpreting it so that all could understand what was
     read.
Then Nehemiah, that is, His Excellency, and Ezra the
     priest-scribe
   and the Levites who were instructing the people
   said to all the people:
   "Today is holy to the Lord your God.

Do not be sad, and do not weep"—
> for all the people were weeping as they heard the words of the law.

He said further: "Go, eat rich foods and drink sweet drinks,
> and allot portions to those who had nothing prepared;
> for today is holy to our Lord.

Do not be saddened this day,
> for rejoicing in the Lord must be your strength!"

The word of the Lord. All: **Thanks be to God.**

RESPONSORIAL PSALM 19

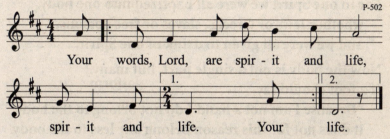

Music: Jay F. Hunstiger, © 1991, administered by Liturgical Press. All rights reserved.

Psalm 19:8, 9, 10, 15

℟. (*See* John 6:63c) **Your words, Lord, are Spirit and life.**

> The law of the Lord is perfect,
>> refreshing the soul;
>
> the decree of the Lord is trustworthy,
>> giving wisdom to the simple. ℟.
>
> The precepts of the Lord are right,
>> rejoicing the heart;
>
> the command of the Lord is clear,
>> enlightening the eye. ℟.
>
> The fear of the Lord is pure,
>> enduring forever;
>
> the ordinances of the Lord are true,
>> all of them just. ℟.
>
> Let the words of my mouth and the thought of my heart
>> find favor before you,
>
> O Lord, my rock and my redeemer. ℟.

READING II (1 Corinthians 12:12-30) *or* Shorter Form [ ]
(1 Corinthians 12:12-14, 27)

A reading from the first Letter of Saint Paul to the Corinthians

You are Christ's body and individually parts of it.

[Brothers and sisters:
As a body is one though it has many parts,
    and all the parts of the body, though many, are one body,
  so also Christ.
For in one Spirit we were all baptized into one body,
    whether Jews or Greeks, slaves or free persons,
    and we were all given to drink of one Spirit.
Now the body is not a single part, but many.]
If a foot should say,
    "Because I am not a hand I do not belong to the body,"
  it does not for this reason belong any less to the body.
Or if an ear should say,
    "Because I am not an eye I do not belong to the body,"
  it does not for this reason belong any less to the body.
If the whole body were an eye, where would the hearing be?
If the whole body were hearing, where would the sense of smell be?
But as it is, God placed the parts,
  each one of them, in the body as he intended.
If they were all one part, where would the body be?
But as it is, there are many parts, yet one body.
The eye cannot say to the hand, "I do not need you,"
  nor again the head to the feet, "I do not need you."
Indeed, the parts of the body that seem to be weaker
  are all the more necessary,
  and those parts of the body that we consider less honorable
  we surround with greater honor,

and our less presentable parts are treated with greater propriety,
whereas our more presentable parts do not need this.
But God has so constructed the body
as to give greater honor to a part that is without it,
so that there may be no division in the body,
but that the parts may have the same concern for one another.
If one part suffers, all the parts suffer with it;
if one part is honored, all the parts share its joy.

Now [you are Christ's body, and individually parts of it.]
Some people God has designated in the church
to be, first, apostles; second, prophets; third, teachers;
then, mighty deeds;
then gifts of healing, assistance, administration,
and varieties of tongues.
Are all apostles? Are all prophets? Are all teachers?
Do all work mighty deeds? Do all have gifts of healing?
Do all speak in tongues? Do all interpret?

The word of the Lord. All: Thanks be to God.

Gospel (Luke 1:1-4; 4:14-21)
Alleluia (*See* Luke 4:18)
℣. Alleluia, alleluia. ℟. **Alleluia, alleluia.**
℣. The Lord sent me to bring glad tidings to the poor,
and to proclaim liberty to captives. ℟.

✠ A reading from the holy Gospel according to Luke

All: **Glory to you, Lord.**

Today this Scripture passage is fulfilled.

**Since many have undertaken to compile a narrative of the events
that have been fulfilled among us,
just as those who were eyewitnesses from the beginning
and ministers of the word have handed them down to us,
I too have decided,**

after investigating everything accurately anew,
    to write it down in an orderly sequence for you,
    most excellent Theophilus,
    so that you may realize the certainty of the teachings
    you have received.

Jesus returned to Galilee in the power of the Spirit,
    and news of him spread throughout the whole region.
He taught in their synagogues and was praised by all.

He came to Nazareth, where he had grown up,
    and went according to his custom
    into the synagogue on the sabbath day.
He stood up to read and was handed a scroll of the
    prophet Isaiah.
He unrolled the scroll and found the passage where it
    was written:
The Spirit of the Lord is upon me,
    because he has anointed me
    to bring glad tidings to the poor.
He has sent me to proclaim liberty to captives
    and recovery of sight to the blind,
    to let the oppressed go free,
    and to proclaim a year acceptable to the Lord.
Rolling up the scroll, he handed it back to the attendant
    and sat down,
    and the eyes of all in the synagogue looked intently
    at him.
He said to them,
    "Today this Scripture passage is fulfilled in your
    hearing."

The Gospel of the Lord. All: **Praise to you, Lord Jesus Christ.**

Prayer over the Gifts
Lord,
receive our gifts.
Let our offerings make us holy
and bring us salvation.
Grant this through Christ our Lord. All: **Amen.**

Communion Antiphon (John 8:12)

I am the light of the world, says the Lord; the man who follows me will have the light of life.

Prayer after Communion

God, all-powerful Father,
may the new life you give us increase our love
and keep us in the joy of your kingdom.
We ask this in the name of Jesus the Lord. All: **Amen.**

Fourth Sunday in Ordinary Time

January 31, 2010

Reflection on the Gospel

This Sunday's gospel continues Jesus' teaching in the synagogue and he speaks words of truth. The gospel challenges us to stand pat on the truth of God's word, even to stake our life on it—as Jesus did. God is clear on the divine purpose: salvation for all at all costs, even if this means the life of the divine Son. While the gospel is always Good News, it is not always comfortable because it ever stretches us beyond where we are now.

- *My response to the gospel usually is . . .*

—Living Liturgy™, *Fourth Sunday in Ordinary Time 2010*

Entrance Antiphon (Psalm 106:47)

Save us, Lord our God, and gather us together from the nations, that we may proclaim your holy name and glory in your praise.

Opening Prayer

Lord our God,
help us to love you with all our hearts
and to love all men as you love them.
Grant this through our Lord Jesus Christ, your Son,
who lives and reigns with you and the Holy Spirit,
one God, for ever and ever. All: **Amen.**

January 31

Reading I (L 72) (Jeremiah 1:4-5, 17-19)
A reading from the Book of the Prophet Jeremiah

A prophet to the nations I appointed you.

The word of the L ORD came to me, saying:
> Before I formed you in the womb I knew you,
>> before you were born I dedicated you,
>> a prophet to the nations I appointed you.
>
> But do you gird your loins;
>> stand up and tell them
>> all that I command you.
>
> Be not crushed on their account,
>> as though I would leave you crushed before them;
>
> for it is I this day
>> who have made you a fortified city,
>
> a pillar of iron, a wall of brass,
>> against the whole land:
>
> against Judah's kings and princes,
>> against its priests and people.
>
> They will fight against you but not prevail over you,
>> for I am with you to deliver you, says the L ORD.

The word of the Lord. All: Thanks be to God.

Responsorial Psalm 71

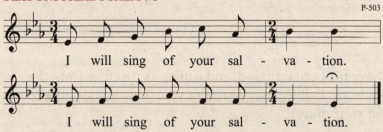

Music: Jay F. Hunstiger, © 1991, administered by Liturgical Press. All rights reserved.

Psalm 71:1-2, 3-4, 5-6, 15, 17

℟. (*See* 15ab) **I will sing of your salvation.**

> In you, O L ORD, I take refuge;
>> let me never be put to shame.

In your justice rescue me, and deliver me;
> incline your ear to me, and save me. ℟.

Be my rock of refuge,
> a stronghold to give me safety,
> for you are my rock and my fortress.

O my God, rescue me from the hand of the wicked. ℟.

For you are my hope, O Lord;
> my trust, O God, from my youth.

On you I depend from birth;
> from my mother's womb you are my strength. ℟.

My mouth shall declare your justice,
> day by day your salvation.

O God, you have taught me from my youth,
> and till the present I proclaim your wondrous deeds. ℟.

Reading II (1 Corinthians 12:31—13:13) *or* Shorter Form [ ]
(1 Corinthians 13:4-13)

A reading from the first Letter of Saint Paul to the Corinthians

So faith, hope, love remain, these three; but the greatest of these is love.

[Brothers and sisters:]
Strive eagerly for the greatest spiritual gifts.
But I shall show you a still more excellent way.

If I speak in human and angelic tongues,
> **but do not have love,**
> **I am a resounding gong or a clashing cymbal.**

And if I have the gift of prophecy,
> **and comprehend all mysteries and all knowledge;**
> **if I have all faith so as to move mountains,**
> **but do not have love, I am nothing.**

If I give away everything I own,
> **and if I hand my body over so that I may boast,**
> **but do not have love, I gain nothing.**

[Love is patient, love is kind.
It is not jealous, it is not pompous,
>it is not inflated, it is not rude,
>it does not seek its own interests,
>it is not quick-tempered, it does not brood over injury,
>>it does not rejoice over wrongdoing
>but rejoices with the truth.
It bears all things, believes all things,
>hopes all things, endures all things.

Love never fails.
If there are prophecies, they will be brought to nothing;
>if tongues, they will cease;
>if knowledge, it will be brought to nothing.
For we know partially and we prophesy partially,
>but when the perfect comes, the partial will pass away.
When I was a child, I used to talk as a child,
>think as a child, reason as a child;
>when I became a man, I put aside childish things.
At present we see indistinctly, as in a mirror,
>but then face to face.
At present I know partially;
>then I shall know fully, as I am fully known.
So faith, hope, love remain, these three;
>but the greatest of these is love.]

The word of the Lord. All: **Thanks be to God.**

GOSPEL (Luke 4:21-30)
ALLELUIA (Luke 4:18)

℣. Alleluia, alleluia. ℟. **Alleluia, alleluia.**
℣. The Lord sent me to bring glad tidings to the poor,
>to proclaim liberty to captives. ℟.

☩ **A reading from the holy Gospel according to Luke**

All: **Glory to you, Lord.**

Like Elijah and Elisha, Jesus was not sent only to the Jews.

Jesus began speaking in the synagogue, saying:
"Today this Scripture passage is fulfilled in your
hearing."
And all spoke highly of him
and were amazed at the gracious words that came
from his mouth.
They also asked, "Isn't this the son of Joseph?"
He said to them, "Surely you will quote me this proverb,
'Physician, cure yourself,' and say,
'Do here in your native place
the things that we heard were done in Capernaum.'"
And he said, "Amen, I say to you,
no prophet is accepted in his own native place.
Indeed, I tell you,
there were many widows in Israel in the days of Elijah
when the sky was closed for three and a half years
and a severe famine spread over the entire land.
It was to none of these that Elijah was sent,
but only to a widow in Zarephath in the land of Sidon.
Again, there were many lepers in Israel
during the time of Elisha the prophet;
yet not one of them was cleansed, but only Naaman
the Syrian."
When the people in the synagogue heard this,
they were all filled with fury.
They rose up, drove him out of the town,
and led him to the brow of the hill
on which their town had been built,
to hurl him down headlong.
But Jesus passed through the midst of them and went
away.

The Gospel of the Lord. All: **Praise to you, Lord Jesus Christ.**

Prayer over the Gifts

Lord,
be pleased with the gifts we bring to your altar,
and make them the sacrament of our salvation.
We ask this through Christ our Lord. All: **Amen.**

Communion Antiphon (Psalm 30:17-18)

Let your face shine on your servant, and save me by your love. Lord, keep me from shame, for I have called to you.

Prayer after Communion

Lord,
you invigorate us with this help to our salvation.
By this eucharist give the true faith continued growth
throughout the world.
We ask this in the name of Jesus the Lord. All: **Amen.**

Fifth Sunday in Ordinary Time

February 7, 2010

Reflection on the Gospel

What precipitated the radical response of the first disciples who "left everything and followed" Jesus? Clearly, Jesus' words and actions. To fishermen who had labored fruitlessly all night, Jesus says try again and leads them to a great catch. To a sinful Peter who considers himself unworthy of Jesus' company, Jesus says follow me and transforms his life's purpose. More than one miracle has occurred in this gospel. The miracle of the catch is the bridge to the second miracle: hearing the Good News and living it.

- *When I feel unworthy to be a follower of Jesus, the words of Jesus I hear are . . .*

—Living Liturgy™, *Fifth Sunday in Ordinary Time 2010*

Entrance Antiphon (Psalm 94:6-7)

Come, let us worship the Lord. Let us bow down in the presence of our maker, for he is the Lord our God.

Opening Prayer

Father,
watch over your family
and keep us safe in your care,
for all our hope is in you.
Grant this through our Lord Jesus Christ, your Son,
who lives and reigns with you and the Holy Spirit,
one God, for ever and ever. All: **Amen.**

Reading I (L 75) (Isaiah 6:1-2a, 3-8)

A reading from the Book of the Prophet Isaiah

Here I am! Send me.

In the year King Uzziah died,
    I saw the Lord seated on a high and lofty throne,
        with the train of his garment filling the temple.
Seraphim were stationed above.

They cried one to the other,
    "Holy, holy, holy is the Lord of hosts!
All the earth is filled with his glory!"
At the sound of that cry, the frame of the door shook
    and the house was filled with smoke.

Then I said, "Woe is me, I am doomed!
For I am a man of unclean lips,
    living among a people of unclean lips;
    yet my eyes have seen the King, the Lord of hosts!"
Then one of the seraphim flew to me,
    holding an ember that he had taken with tongs from
        the altar.
He touched my mouth with it, and said,
    "See, now that this has touched your lips,
    your wickedness is removed, your sin purged."

Then I heard the voice of the Lord saying,
    "Whom shall I send? Who will go for us?"
"Here I am," I said; "send me!"

The word of the Lord. All: **Thanks be to God.**

Responsorial Psalm 138

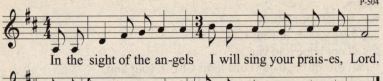

Music: Jay F. Hunstiger, © 1991, administered by Liturgical Press. All rights reserved.

Psalm 138:1-2, 2-3, 4-5, 7-8

℟. (1c) **In the sight of the angels I will sing your praises, Lord.**

I will give thanks to you, O Lord, with all my heart,
　for you have heard the words of my mouth;
　in the presence of the angels I will sing your praise;
I will worship at your holy temple
　and give thanks to your name. ℟.

Because of your kindness and your truth;
　for you have made great above all things
　your name and your promise.
When I called, you answered me;
　you built up strength within me. ℟.

All the kings of the earth shall give thanks to you, O Lord,
　when they hear the words of your mouth;
and they shall sing of the ways of the Lord:
　"Great is the glory of the Lord." ℟.

Your right hand saves me.
　The Lord will complete what he has done for me;
your kindness, O Lord, endures forever;
　forsake not the work of your hands. ℟.

Reading II (1 Corinthians 15:1-11) *or* Shorter Form [ ]
(1 Corinthians 15:3-8, 11)

A reading from the first Letter of Saint Paul to the Corinthians

So we preached and so you believe.

I am reminding you, [brothers and sisters,]
　　of the gospel I preached to you,
　　　which you indeed received and in which you also stand.
Through it you are also being saved,
　　if you hold fast to the word I preached to you,
　　unless you believed in vain.
For [I handed on to you as of first importance what I
　　　also received:
　　that Christ died for our sins
　　　in accordance with the Scriptures;
　　that he was buried;
　　that he was raised on the third day
　　　in accordance with the Scriptures;
　　that he appeared to Cephas, then to the Twelve.
After that, he appeared to more
　　　than five hundred brothers at once,
　　most of whom are still living,
　　though some have fallen asleep.
After that he appeared to James,
　　then to all the apostles.
Last of all, as to one born abnormally,
　　he appeared to me.]
For I am the least of the apostles,
　　not fit to be called an apostle,
　　because I persecuted the church of God.
But by the grace of God I am what I am,
　　and his grace to me has not been ineffective.
Indeed, I have toiled harder than all of them;
　　not I, however, but the grace of God that is with me.
[Therefore, whether it be I or they,
　　so we preach and so you believed.]

The word of the Lord. All: Thanks be to God.

Gospel (Luke 5:1-11)

Alleluia (Matthew 4:19)

℣. Alleluia, alleluia. ℟. **Alleluia, alleluia.**
℣. Come after me
and I will make you fishers of men. ℟.

✠ **A reading from the holy Gospel according to Luke**

All: **Glory to you, Lord.**

They left everything and followed Jesus.

**While the crowd was pressing in on Jesus and listening
 to the word of God,
 he was standing by the Lake of Gennesaret.
He saw two boats there alongside the lake;
 the fishermen had disembarked and were washing
  their nets.
Getting into one of the boats, the one belonging to Simon,
 he asked him to put out a short distance from the shore.
Then he sat down and taught the crowds from the boat.
After he had finished speaking, he said to Simon,
 "Put out into deep water and lower your nets for a
  catch."
Simon said in reply,
 "Master, we have worked hard all night and have
  caught nothing,
 but at your command I will lower the nets."
When they had done this, they caught a great number
  of fish
 and their nets were tearing.
They signaled to their partners in the other boat
 to come to help them.
They came and filled both boats
 so that the boats were in danger of sinking.
When Simon Peter saw this, he fell at the knees of Jesus
  and said,
 "Depart from me, Lord, for I am a sinful man."**

For astonishment at the catch of fish they had made
   seized him
   and all those with him,
   and likewise James and John, the sons of Zebedee,
   who were partners of Simon.
Jesus said to Simon, "Do not be afraid;
   from now on you will be catching men."
When they brought their boats to the shore,
   they left everything and followed him.

The Gospel of the Lord. All: **Praise to you, Lord Jesus Christ.**

Prayer over the Gifts
Lord our God,
may the bread and wine
you give us for our nourishment on earth
become the sacrament of our eternal life.
We ask this through Christ our Lord. All: **Amen.**

Communion Antiphon (Psalm 106:8-9)
Give praise to the Lord for his kindness, for his wonderful deeds toward men. He has filled the hungry with good things, he has satisfied the thirsty.

Prayer after Communion
God our Father,
you give us a share in the one bread and the one cup
and make us one in Christ.
Help us to bring your salvation and joy
to all the world.
We ask this through Christ our Lord. All: **Amen.**

Sixth Sunday in Ordinary Time

February 14, 2010

Reflection on the Gospel
Luke seems in this gospel to be exalting the downtrodden simply because they are downtrodden, and cursing the comfortable simply because they are comfortable. While it is true that God has special care for the poor and downtrodden, it is equally true that having possessions is not in itself cause for condemnation. What really is at the heart of this gospel is the manner of life that makes present the kingdom and assures us that our "reward will be great in heaven."

- *The manner of life to which the Beatitudes call me is . . . Those who model this for me are . . .*

—Living Liturgy™, *Sixth Sunday in Ordinary Time 2010*

Entrance Antiphon (Psalm 31:3-4)
Lord, be my rock of safety, the stronghold that saves me.
For the honor of your name, lead me and guide me.

Opening Prayer
God our Father,
you have promised to remain for ever
with those who do what is just and right.
Help us to live in your presence.
We ask this through our Lord Jesus Christ, your Son,
who lives and reigns with you and the Holy Spirit,
one God, for ever and ever. All: **Amen.**

Reading I (L 78) (Jeremiah 17:5-8)
A reading from the Book of the Prophet Jeremiah

Cursed is the one who trusts in human beings; blessed is the one who trusts in the Lord.

Thus says the Lord:
   Cursed is the one who trusts in human beings,
      who seeks his strength in flesh,
         whose heart turns away from the Lord.

He is like a barren bush in the desert
   that enjoys no change of season,
but stands in a lava waste,
   a salt and empty earth.
Blessed is the one who trusts in the LORD,
   whose hope is the LORD.
He is like a tree planted beside the waters
   that stretches out its roots to the stream:
it fears not the heat when it comes;
   its leaves stay green;
in the year of drought it shows no distress,
   but still bears fruit.

The word of the Lord.   All: **Thanks be to God.**

RESPONSORIAL PSALM 1

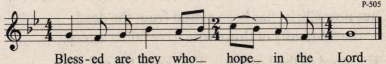

Music: Jay F. Hunstiger, © 1991, administered by Liturgical Press. All rights reserved.

Psalm 1:1-2, 3, 4 and 6

℟. (40:5a) **Blessed are they who hope in the Lord.**

Blessed the man who follows not
   the counsel of the wicked,
nor walks in the way of sinners,
   nor sits in the company of the insolent,
but delights in the law of the LORD
   and meditates on his law day and night. ℟.

He is like a tree
   planted near running water,
that yields its fruit in due season,
   and whose leaves never fade.
Whatever he does, prospers. ℟.

Not so the wicked, not so;
   they are like chaff which the wind drives away.
For the LORD watches over the way of the just,
   but the way of the wicked vanishes. ℟.

Reading II (1 Corinthians 15:12, 16-20)

A reading from the first Letter of Saint Paul to the Corinthians

If Christ has not been raised, your faith is vain.

Brothers and sisters:
If Christ is preached as raised from the dead,
    how can some among you say there is no resurrection
        of the dead?
If the dead are not raised, neither has Christ been raised,
    and if Christ has not been raised, your faith is vain;
    you are still in your sins.
Then those who have fallen asleep in Christ have perished.
If for this life only we have hoped in Christ,
    we are the most pitiable people of all.

But now Christ has been raised from the dead,
    the firstfruits of those who have fallen asleep.

The word of the Lord. All: **Thanks be to God.**

Gospel (Luke 6:17, 20-26)

Alleluia (Luke 6:23ab)
℣. Alleluia, alleluia. ℟. **Alleluia, alleluia.**
℣. Rejoice and be glad;
    your reward will be great in heaven. ℟.

✠ **A reading from the holy Gospel according to Luke**

All: **Glory to you, Lord.**

Blessed are the poor. Woe to you who are rich.

Jesus came down with the Twelve
    and stood on a stretch of level ground
    with a great crowd of his disciples
    and a large number of the people
    from all Judea and Jerusalem
    and the coastal region of Tyre and Sidon.
And raising his eyes toward his disciples he said:
    "Blessed are you who are poor,
        for the kingdom of God is yours.

> Blessed are you who are now hungry,
>> for you will be satisfied.
> Blessed are you who are now weeping,
>> for you will laugh.
> Blessed are you when people hate you,
>> and when they exclude and insult you,
>> and denounce your name as evil
>> on account of the Son of Man.
> Rejoice and leap for joy on that day!
> Behold, your reward will be great in heaven.
> For their ancestors treated the prophets in the same way.
>> But woe to you who are rich,
>>> for you have received your consolation.
>> Woe to you who are filled now,
>>> for you will be hungry.
>> Woe to you who laugh now,
>>> for you will grieve and weep.
>> Woe to you when all speak well of you,
>>> for their ancestors treated the false
>>> prophets in this way."

The Gospel of the Lord. All: **Praise to you, Lord Jesus Christ.**

Prayer over the Gifts
Lord,
we make this offering in obedience to your word.
May it cleanse and renew us,
and lead us to our eternal reward.
We ask this in the name of Jesus the Lord. All: **Amen.**

Communion Antiphon (John 3:16)
God loved the world so much, he gave his only Son, that all who believe in him might not perish, but might have eternal life.

Prayer after Communion
Lord,
you give us food from heaven.
May we always hunger
for the bread of life.
Grant this through Christ our Lord. All: **Amen.**

Ash Wednesday

February 17, 2010

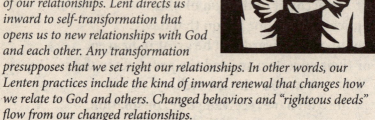

Reflection on the Gospel
Our strongest motivation for undertaking Lenten penance is the deepening of our relationships. Lent directs us inward to self-transformation that opens us to new relationships with God and each other. Any transformation presupposes that we set right our relationships. In other words, our Lenten practices include the kind of inward renewal that changes how we relate to God and others. Changed behaviors and "righteous deeds" flow from our changed relationships.

- *During this Lent the "righteous deeds" that I need to do for renewal of myself are . . .*

—Living Liturgy™, *Ash Wednesday 2010*

Entrance Antiphon (*See* Wisdom 11:24-25, 27)
Lord, you are merciful to all, and hate nothing you have created. You overlook the sins of men to bring them to repentance. You are the Lord our God.

Opening Prayer
Lord,
protect us in our struggle against evil.
As we begin the discipline of Lent,
make this season holy by our self-denial.
Grant this through our Lord Jesus Christ, your Son,
who lives and reigns with you and the Holy Spirit,
one God, for ever and ever. All: **Amen.**

Reading I (L 219) (Joel 2:12-18)
A reading from the book of the Prophet Joel

Rend your hearts, not your garments.

**Even now, says the LORD,
return to me with your whole heart,
with fasting, and weeping, and mourning;**

Rend your hearts, not your garments,
    and return to the Lord, your God.
For gracious and merciful is he,
    slow to anger, rich in kindness,
    and relenting in punishment.
Perhaps he will again relent
    and leave behind him a blessing,
Offerings and libations
    for the Lord, your God.

Blow the trumpet in Zion!
    proclaim a fast,
    call an assembly;
Gather the people,
    notify the congregation;
Assemble the elders,
    gather the children
    and the infants at the breast;
Let the bridegroom quit his room,
    and the bride her chamber.
Between the porch and the altar
    let the priests, the ministers of the Lord, weep,
And say, "Spare, O Lord, your people,
    and make not your heritage a reproach,
    with the nations ruling over them!
Why should they say among the peoples,
    'Where is their God?'"

Then the Lord was stirred to concern for his land
    and took pity on his people.

The word of the Lord.   **All:** Thanks be to God.

Responsorial Psalm 51

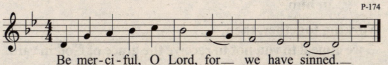

Be mer-ci-ful, O Lord, for we have sinned.

Music: Jay F. Hunstiger, © 1990, administered by Liturgical Press. All rights reserved.

Psalm 51:3-4, 5-6ab, 12-13, 14 and 17

℟. *(See* 3a) **Be merciful, O Lord, for we have sinned.**

Have mercy on me, O God, in your goodness;
>in the greatness of your compassion wipe out my offense.

Thoroughly wash me from my guilt
>and of my sin cleanse me. ℟.

For I acknowledge my offense,
>and my sin is before me always:
"Against you only have I sinned,
>and done what is evil in your sight." ℟.

A clean heart create for me, O God,
>and a steadfast spirit renew within me.
Cast me not out from your presence,
>and your Holy Spirit take not from me. ℟.

Give me back the joy of your salvation,
>and a willing spirit sustain in me.
O Lord, open my lips,
>and my mouth shall proclaim your praise. ℟.

READING II (2 Corinthians 5:20—6:2)

A reading from the second Letter of Saint Paul to the Corinthians

Be reconciled to God. Behold, now is the acceptable time.

**Brothers and sisters:
We are ambassadors for Christ,
>as if God were appealing through us.
We implore you on behalf of Christ,
>be reconciled to God.
For our sake he made him to be sin who did not know sin,
>so that we might become the righteousness of God
>>in him.

Working together, then,
>we appeal to you not to receive the grace of God in vain.
For he says:**

> *In an acceptable time I heard you,*
>> *and on the day of salvation I helped you.*

Behold, now is a very acceptable time;
>> **behold, now is the day of salvation.**

The word of the Lord. All: **Thanks be to God.**

GOSPEL (Matthew 6:1-6, 16-18)
VERSE BEFORE THE GOSPEL (*See* Psalm 95:8)
℣. Praise to you, Lord Jesus Christ, king of endless glory!
℟. **Praise to you, Lord Jesus Christ, king of endless glory!**
℣. If today you hear his voice,
>> harden not your hearts. ℟.

✠ **A reading from the holy Gospel according to Matthew**

All: **Glory to you, Lord.**

Your Father who sees in secret will repay you.

Jesus said to his disciples:
>> "Take care not to perform righteous deeds
>> in order that people may see them;
>> otherwise, you will have no recompense from your
>>>> heavenly Father.
> When you give alms,
>> do not blow a trumpet before you,
>> as the hypocrites do in the synagogues and in the streets
>> to win the praise of others.
> Amen, I say to you,
>> they have received their reward.
> But when you give alms,
>> do not let your left hand know what your right is doing,
>> so that your almsgiving may be secret.
> And your Father who sees in secret will repay you.
> "When you pray,
>> do not be like the hypocrites,
>> who love to stand and pray in the synagogues and on
>>>> street corners
>> so that others may see them.

Amen, I say to you,
   they have received their reward.
But when you pray, go to your inner room,
   close the door, and pray to your Father in secret.
And your Father who sees in secret will repay you.

"When you fast,
   do not look gloomy like the hypocrites.
They neglect their appearance,
   so that they may appear to others to be fasting.
Amen, I say to you, they have received their reward.
But when you fast,
   anoint your head and wash your face,
   so that you may not appear to be fasting,
   except to your Father who is hidden.
And your Father who sees what is hidden will repay you."

The Gospel of the Lord. All: **Praise to you, Lord Jesus Christ.**

BLESSING AND GIVING OF ASHES
After the homily the priest joins his hands and says:
Dear friends in Christ,
let us ask our Father
to bless these ashes
which we will use
as the mark of our repentance.

Lord,
bless the sinner who asks for your forgiveness
and bless ✠ all those who receive these ashes.
May they keep this lenten season
in preparation for the joy of Easter.
We ask this through Christ our Lord. All: **Amen.**

or:

Lord,
bless these ashes ✠
by which we show that we are dust.
Pardon our sins
and keep us faithful to the discipline of Lent,
for you do not want sinners to die
but to live with the risen Christ,
who reigns with you for ever and ever. All: **Amen.**

The priest sprinkles the ashes with holy water in silence. He then imposes the ashes on those who come forward and stand in front of him. To each he says:

Turn away from sin and be faithful to the gospel. (Mark 1:15)

or:

Remember, man, you are dust, and to dust you will return. (*See* Genesis 3:19)

Responsory (*See* Baruch 3:5)

Priest: Direct our hearts to better things, O Lord;
heal our sin and ignorance.
Lord, do not face us suddenly with death,
but give us time to repent.
People: **Turn to us with mercy, Lord; we have sinned against you.**
Priest: Help us, God our Savior, rescue us for the honor of your name.
People: **Turn to us with mercy, Lord; we have sinned against you.**

After the imposition, the priest washes his hands. The rite concludes with the Prayer of the Faithful. The profession of faith is not said.

The blessing and imposition of ashes may also take place outside Mass. In this case the liturgy of the word may be celebrated, using the entrance song, opening prayer, and the readings with their chants as at Mass. The homily and the blessing and imposition of ashes follow. The rite concludes with the Prayer of the Faithful.

Prayer over the Gifts

Lord,
help us to resist temptation
by our lenten works of charity and penance.
By this sacrifice
may we be prepared to celebrate
the death and resurrection of Christ our Savior
and be cleansed from sin and renewed in spirit.
We ask this through Christ our Lord. All: **Amen.**

Communion Antiphon (Psalm 1:2-3)

The man who meditates day and night on the law of the Lord will yield fruit in due season.

Prayer after Communion

Lord,
through this communion
may our lenten penance give you glory
and bring us your protection.
We ask this in the name of Jesus the Lord. All: **Amen.**

First Sunday of Lent

February 21, 2010

Reflection on the Gospel

Each temptation put to Jesus by the devil involved some misguided personal gain: seeking easy solutions to human hungers, pursuing "power and glory," defying death. By resisting these temptations Jesus shows us that our true gain is found not in satisfying ourselves, but in something better—utter fidelity to God. This same choice between self-satisfaction and fidelity to God frees us, like Jesus, to be who we are meant to be, persons "led by the Spirit."

• *The misguided personal gain I am most tempted to pursue is . . .*

—Living Liturgy™, *First Sunday of Lent 2010*

Entrance Antiphon (Psalm 90:15-16)
When he calls to me, I will answer; I will rescue him and give him honor. Long life and contentment will be his.

Opening Prayer
Father,
through our observance of Lent,
help us to understand the meaning
of your Son's death and resurrection,
and teach us to reflect it in our lives.
Grant this through our Lord Jesus Christ, your Son,
who lives and reigns with you and the Holy Spirit,
one God, for ever and ever. All: **Amen.**

Reading I (L 24-C) (Deuteronomy 26:4-10)
A reading from the Book of Deuteronomy

The confession of faith of the chosen people.

Moses spoke to the people, saying:
   "The priest shall receive the basket from you
      and shall set it in front of the altar of the Lord,
      your God.

Then you shall declare before the Lord, your God,
 'My father was a wandering Aramean
 who went down to Egypt with a small household
 and lived there as an alien.
But there he became a nation
 great, strong, and numerous.
When the Egyptians maltreated and oppressed us,
 imposing hard labor upon us,
 we cried to the Lord, the God of our fathers,
 and he heard our cry
 and saw our affliction, our toil, and our oppression.
He brought us out of Egypt
 with his strong hand and outstretched arm,
 with terrifying power, with signs and wonders;
 and bringing us into this country,
 he gave us this land flowing with milk and honey.
Therefore, I have now brought you the firstfruits
 of the products of the soil
 which you, O Lord, have given me.'
And having set them before the Lord, your God,
 you shall bow down in his presence."

The word of the Lord. **All:** Thanks be to God.

Responsorial Psalm 91

Be with me, Lord, when I am in trouble.

Music: Jay F. Hunstiger, © 1991, administered by Liturgical Press. All rights reserved.

February 21
Psalm 91:1-2, 10-11, 12-13, 14-15

℞. (*See* 15b) **Be with me, Lord, when I am in trouble.**

You who dwell in the shelter of the Most High,
 who abide in the shadow of the Almighty,
say to the Lord, "My refuge and fortress,
 my God in whom I trust." ℞.

No evil shall befall you,
 nor shall affliction come near your tent,
for to his angels he has given command about you,
 that they guard you in all your ways. ℞.

Upon their hands they shall bear you up,
 lest you dash your foot against a stone.
You shall tread upon the asp and the viper;
 you shall trample down the lion and the dragon. ℞.

Because he clings to me, I will deliver him;
 I will set him on high because he acknowledges
  my name.
He shall call upon me, and I will answer him;
 I will be with him in distress;
 I will deliver him and glorify him. ℞.

Reading II (Romans 10:8-13)
A reading from the Letter of Saint Paul to the Romans

The confession of faith of all believers in Christ.

**Brothers and sisters:
What does Scripture say?**
 *The word is near you,
  in your mouth and in your heart*
 **—that is, the word of faith that we preach—,
 for, if you confess with your mouth that Jesus is Lord
 and believe in your heart that God raised him from
  the dead,
 you will be saved.
For one believes with the heart and so is justified,
 and one confesses with the mouth and so is saved.**

For the Scripture says,
> *No one who believes in him will be put to shame.*

For there is no distinction between Jew and Greek;
> the same Lord is Lord of all,
> enriching all who call upon him.

For "everyone who calls on the name of the Lord will
> be saved."

The word of the Lord. ℟. Thanks be to God.

Gospel (Luke 4:1-13)
Verse before the Gospel (Matthew 4:4b)

℣. Praise to you, Lord Jesus Christ, king of endless glory!
℟. **Praise to you, Lord Jesus Christ, king of endless glory!**
℣. One does not live on bread alone,
> but on every word that comes forth from the mouth
> of God. ℟.

✠ **A reading from the holy Gospel according to Luke**

All: **Glory to you, Lord.**

Jesus was led by the Spirit into the desert and was tempted.

Filled with the Holy Spirit, Jesus returned from the Jordan
> and was led by the Spirit into the desert for forty days,
> to be tempted by the devil.

He ate nothing during those days,
> and when they were over he was hungry.

The devil said to him,
> "If you are the Son of God,
> command this stone to become bread."

Jesus answered him,
> "It is written, *One does not live on bread alone.*"

Then he took him up and showed him
> all the kingdoms of the world in a single instant.

The devil said to him,
> "I shall give to you all this power and glory;
> for it has been handed over to me,
> and I may give it to whomever I wish.

All this will be yours, if you worship me."

Jesus said to him in reply,
> "It is written:
> *You shall worship the Lord, your God,*
> > *and him alone shall you serve."*

Then he led him to Jerusalem,
> made him stand on the parapet of the temple, and
> > said to him,

"If you are the Son of God,
> throw yourself down from here, for it is written:
> > *He will command his angels concerning you,*
> > > *to guard you,*

and:
> *With their hands they will support you,*
> *lest you dash your foot against a stone."*

Jesus said to him in reply,
> "It also says,
> *You shall not put the Lord, your God, to the test."*

When the devil had finished every temptation,
> he departed from him for a time.

The Gospel of the Lord. All: **Praise to you, Lord Jesus Christ.**

Prayer over the Gifts
Lord,
make us worthy to bring you these gifts.
May this sacrifice
help to change our lives.
We ask this in the name of Jesus the Lord. All: **Amen.**

Communion Antiphon (Matthew 4:4)
Man does not live on bread alone, but on every word that comes from the mouth of God.

or:

(Psalm 91:4)
The Lord will overshadow you, and you will find refuge under his wings.

Prayer after Communion
Father,
you increase our faith and hope,

you deepen our love in this communion.
Help us to live by your words
and to seek Christ, our bread of life,
who is Lord for ever and ever. All: **Amen.**

Second Sunday of Lent

February 28, 2010

Reflection on the Gospel
Luke's account of the transfiguration event is the only one that includes the necessity of the passion on the journey to glory ("his exodus that he was going to accomplish in Jerusalem"). Peter, James, and John were privileged to see Jesus' transfigured glory. But they clearly missed the most important point: this transfigured glory also foreshadowed his dying, the only way to risen glory. Luke's insight is that glory always presupposes embracing passion.

• *I have experienced a share in Jesus' transfigured glory when . . .*

—*Living Liturgy™, Second Sunday of Lent 2010*

Entrance Antiphon (Psalm 24:6, 3, 22)
Remember your mercies, Lord, your tenderness from ages past. Do not let our enemies triumph over us; O God, deliver Israel from all her distress.

Opening Prayer
God our Father,
help us to hear your Son.
Enlighten us with your word,
that we may find the way to your glory.
We ask this through our Lord Jesus Christ, your Son,
who lives and reigns with you and the Holy Spirit,
one God, for ever and ever. All: **Amen.**

Reading I (L 27-C) (Genesis 15:5-12, 17-18)
A reading from the Book of Genesis

God made a covenant with Abraham, his faithful servant.

The Lord God took Abram outside and said,
  "Look up at the sky and count the stars, if you can.
Just so," he added, "shall your descendants be."
Abram put his faith in the LORD,
  who credited it to him as an act of righteousness.

He then said to him,
  "I am the LORD who brought you from Ur of the
      Chaldeans
  to give you this land as a possession."
"O Lord GOD," he asked,
  "how am I to know that I shall possess it?"
He answered him,
  "Bring me a three-year-old heifer, a three-year-old
      she-goat,
  a three-year-old ram, a turtledove, and a young pigeon."
Abram brought him all these, split them in two,
  and placed each half opposite the other;
  but the birds he did not cut up.
Birds of prey swooped down on the carcasses,
  but Abram stayed with them.
As the sun was about to set, a trance fell upon Abram,
  and a deep, terrifying darkness enveloped him.

When the sun had set and it was dark,
  there appeared a smoking fire pot and a flaming torch,
  which passed between those pieces.
It was on that occasion that the LORD made a covenant
      with Abram,
  saying: "To your descendants I give this land,
  from the Wadi of Egypt to the Great River, the
      Euphrates."
The word of the Lord. All: Thanks be to God.

Responsorial Psalm 27

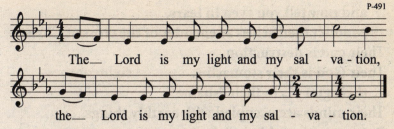

The Lord is my light and my salvation, the Lord is my light and my salvation.

Music: Jay F. Hunstiger, © 1992, administered by Liturgical Press. All rights reserved.

Psalm 27:1, 7-8, 8-9, 13-14

℟. (1a) **The Lord is my light and my salvation.**

The LORD is my light and my salvation;
  whom should I fear?
The LORD is my life's refuge;
  of whom should I be afraid? ℟.

Hear, O LORD, the sound of my call;
  have pity on me, and answer me.
Of you my heart speaks; you my glance seeks. ℟.

Your presence, O LORD, I seek.
  Hide not your face from me;
do not in anger repel your servant.
  You are my helper: cast me not off. ℟.

I believe that I shall see the bounty of the LORD
  in the land of the living.
Wait for the LORD with courage;
  be stouthearted, and wait for the LORD. ℟.

Reading II (Philippians 3:17—4:1) *or* Shorter Form [ ]
(Philippians 3:20—4:1)

A reading from the Letter of Saint Paul to the Philippians

Christ will change our lowly body to conform with his glorified body.

**Join with others in being imitators of me, [brothers and sisters,]
  and observe those who thus conduct themselves
  according to the model you have in us.**

For many, as I have often told you
and now tell you even in tears,
conduct themselves as enemies of the cross of Christ.
Their end is destruction.
Their God is their stomach;
their glory is in their "shame."
Their minds are occupied with earthly things.
But [our citizenship is in heaven,
and from it we also await a savior, the Lord Jesus Christ.
He will change our lowly body
to conform with his glorified body
by the power that enables him also
to bring all things into subjection to himself.

Therefore, my brothers and sisters,
whom I love and long for, my joy and crown,
in this way stand firm in the Lord.]

The word of the Lord. All: **Thanks be to God.**

GOSPEL (Luke 9:28b–36)
VERSE BEFORE THE GOSPEL (See Matthew 17:5)
℣. Praise and honor to you, Lord Jesus Christ!
℟. **Praise and honor to you, Lord Jesus Christ!**
℣. From the shining cloud the Father's voice is heard:
This is my beloved Son, hear him. ℟.

✠ **A reading from the holy Gospel according to Luke**

All: **Glory to you, Lord.**

While he was praying his face changed in appearance and his clothing became dazzling white.

Jesus took Peter, John, and James
and went up the mountain to pray.
While he was praying his face changed in appearance
and his clothing became dazzling white.
And behold, two men were conversing with him, Moses
and Elijah,
who appeared in glory and spoke of his exodus
that he was going to accomplish in Jerusalem.

Peter and his companions had been overcome by sleep,
   but becoming fully awake,
   they saw his glory and the two men standing with him.
As they were about to part from him, Peter said to Jesus,
   "Master, it is good that we are here;
   let us make three tents,
   one for you, one for Moses, and one for Elijah."
But he did not know what he was saying.
While he was still speaking,
   a cloud came and cast a shadow over them,
   and they became frightened when they entered the
      cloud.
Then from the cloud came a voice that said,
   "This is my chosen Son; listen to him."
After the voice had spoken, Jesus was found alone.
They fell silent and did not at that time
   tell anyone what they had seen.

The Gospel of the Lord. All: **Praise to you, Lord Jesus Christ.**

Prayer over the Gifts
Lord,
make us holy.
May this eucharist take away our sins
that we may be prepared
to celebrate the resurrection.
We ask this in the name of Jesus the Lord. All: **Amen.**

Communion Antiphon (Matthew 17:5)
This is my Son, my beloved, in whom is all my delight:
listen to him.

Prayer after Communion
Lord,
we give thanks for these holy mysteries
which bring to us here on earth
a share in the life to come,
through Christ our Lord. All: **Amen.**

Third Sunday of Lent

March 7, 2010

Reflection on the Gospel

The first two events reported in the gospel involve tragic death, and Jesus uses these tragedies to teach us that unless we repent, we too will die. Then in the parable of the fig tree, Jesus reveals the patience of God with us, despite our slowness to repent. This is God's work of mercy: to take what is almost dead and coax it to new life. This is our work of repentance: to turn from sinfulness toward God's transforming mercy.

- *This Lent, how God is cultivating and fertilizing my life is . . . The fruit I hope to bear in the future is . . .*

—Living Liturgy™, *Third Sunday of Lent 2010*

Entrance Antiphon (Ezekiel 36:23-26)

I will prove my holiness through you. I will gather you from the ends of the earth; I will pour clean water on you and wash away all your sins. I will give you a new spirit within you, says the Lord.

Opening Prayer

Father,
you have taught us to overcome our sins
by prayer, fasting and works of mercy.
When we are discouraged by our weakness,
give us confidence in your love.
We ask this through our Lord Jesus Christ, your Son,
who lives and reigns with you and the Holy Spirit,
one God, for ever and ever. All: **Amen.**

The readings given for Year A, n. 28, may be used in place of these.

Reading I (L 30-C) (Exodus 3:1-8a, 13-15)

A reading from the Book of Exodus

"I AM" sent me to you.

Moses was tending the flock of his father-in-law Jethro, the priest of Midian.

Leading the flock across the desert, he came to Horeb,
   the mountain of God.
There an angel of the Lord appeared to Moses in fire
   flaming out of a bush.
As he looked on, he was surprised to see that the bush,
   though on fire, was not consumed.
So Moses decided,
   "I must go over to look at this remarkable sight,
   and see why the bush is not burned."
When the Lord saw him coming over to look at it more
      closely,
   God called out to him from the bush, "Moses! Moses!"
He answered, "Here I am."
God said, "Come no nearer!
Remove the sandals from your feet,
   for the place where you stand is holy ground.
I am the God of your fathers," he continued,
   "the God of Abraham, the God of Isaac, the God of
      Jacob."
Moses hid his face, for he was afraid to look at God.
But the Lord said,
   "I have witnessed the affliction of my people in Egypt
   and have heard their cry of complaint against their
      slave drivers,
   so I know well what they are suffering.
Therefore I have come down to rescue them
   from the hands of the Egyptians
   and lead them out of that land into a good and
      spacious land,
   a land flowing with milk and honey."
Moses said to God, "But when I go to the Israelites
   and say to them, 'The God of your fathers has sent me
      to you,'
   if they ask me, 'What is his name?' what am I to tell
      them?"

God replied, "I am who am."
Then he added, "This is what you shall tell the Israelites:
 I AM sent me to you."

God spoke further to Moses, "Thus shall you say to the
 Israelites:
The LORD, the God of your fathers,
the God of Abraham, the God of Isaac, the God of
 Jacob,
has sent me to you.

"This is my name forever;
 thus am I to be remembered through all
 generations."

The word of the Lord. All: **Thanks be to God.**

RESPONSORIAL PSALM 103

The Lord is kind and mer-ci-ful, is kind and mer-ci-ful.

Music: Jay F. Hunstiger, © 1991, administered by Liturgical Press. All rights reserved.

Psalm 103:1-2, 3-4, 6-7, 8, 11

℟. (8a) **The Lord is kind and merciful.**

Bless the LORD, O my soul;
 and all my being, bless his holy name.
Bless the LORD, O my soul,
 and forget not all his benefits. ℟.

He pardons all your iniquities,
 heals all your ills.
He redeems your life from destruction,
 crowns you with kindness and compassion. ℟.

The LORD secures justice
 and the rights of all the oppressed.
He has made known his ways to Moses,
 and his deeds to the children of Israel. ℟.

> Merciful and gracious is the L ORD,
>> slow to anger and abounding in kindness.
>> For as the heavens are high above the earth,
>> so surpassing is his kindness toward those who fear him. ℟.

R EADING II (1 Corinthians 10:1-6, 10-12)

A reading from the first Letter of Saint Paul to the Corinthians

The life of the people with Moses in the desert was written down as a warning to us.

I do not want you to be unaware, brothers and sisters,
   that our ancestors were all under the cloud
   and all passed through the sea,
   and all of them were baptized into Moses
   in the cloud and in the sea.
All ate the same spiritual food,
   and all drank the same spiritual drink,
   for they drank from a spiritual rock that followed them,
   and the rock was the Christ.
Yet God was not pleased with most of them,
   for they were struck down in the desert.

These things happened as examples for us,
   so that we might not desire evil things, as they did.
Do not grumble as some of them did,
   and suffered death by the destroyer.
These things happened to them as an example,
   and they have been written down as a warning to us,
   upon whom the end of the ages has come.
Therefore, whoever thinks he is standing secure
   should take care not to fall.

The word of the Lord. All: **Thanks be to God.**

March 7

GOSPEL (Luke 13:1-9)
VERSE BEFORE THE GOSPEL (Matthew 4:17)

℣. Praise to you, Lord Jesus Christ, king of endless glory!
℟. **Praise to you, Lord Jesus Christ, king of endless glory!**
℣. Repent, says the Lord;
the kingdom of heaven is at hand. ℟.

✠ **A reading from the holy Gospel according to Luke**

All: **Glory to you, Lord.**

If you do not repent, you will all perish as they did.

**Some people told Jesus about the Galileans
whose blood Pilate had mingled with the blood of
their sacrifices.
Jesus said to them in reply,
"Do you think that because these Galileans suffered
in this way
they were greater sinners than all other Galileans?
By no means!
But I tell you, if you do not repent,
you will all perish as they did!
Or those eighteen people who were killed
when the tower at Siloam fell on them—
do you think they were more guilty
than everyone else who lived in Jerusalem?
By no means!
But I tell you, if you do not repent,
you will all perish as they did!"
And he told them this parable:
"There once was a person who had a fig tree planted
in his orchard,
and when he came in search of fruit on it but found
none,
he said to the gardener,
'For three years now I have come in search of fruit on
this fig tree
but have found none.**

So cut it down.
Why should it exhaust the soil?'
He said to him in reply,
   'Sir, leave it for this year also,
     and I shall cultivate the ground around it and
        fertilize it;
   it may bear fruit in the future.
If not you can cut it down.'"

The Gospel of the Lord. All: **Praise to you, Lord Jesus Christ.**

PRAYER OVER THE GIFTS
Lord,
by the grace of this sacrifice
may we who ask forgiveness
be ready to forgive one another.
We ask this in the name of Jesus the Lord. All: **Amen.**

COMMUNION ANTIPHON (John 4:13-14)
Whoever drinks the water that I shall give him, says the Lord, will have a spring inside him, welling up for eternal life.

PRAYER AFTER COMMUNION
Lord,
in sharing this sacrament
may we receive your forgiveness
and be brought together in unity and peace.
We ask this through Christ our Lord. All: **Amen.**

Fourth Sunday of Lent

March 14, 2010

Reflection on the Gospel

When the prodigal son came "to his senses" and returned home, the most he hoped from his father was to be given a place as a servant and adequate food to eat. But the merciful father was prodigious: he embraced him, clothed him in dignity, and honored him with a feast. Sinners though we are, our merciful Father longs to embrace and celebrate with us. We have only to return to him.

- The people who regularly help me to "come to my senses" and get my life back on track are . . .

—*Living Liturgy*™, *Fourth Sunday of Lent 2010*

Entrance Antiphon (See Isaiah 66:10-11)

Rejoice, Jerusalem! Be glad for her, you who love her; rejoice with her, you who mourned for her, and you will find contentment at her consoling breasts.

Opening Prayer

Father of peace,
we are joyful in your Word,
your Son Jesus Christ,
who reconciles us to you.
Let us hasten toward Easter
with the eagerness of faith and love.
We ask this through our Lord Jesus Christ, your Son,
who lives and reigns with you and the Holy Spirit,
one God, for ever and ever. All: **Amen.**

The readings given for Year A, n. 31, may be used in place of these.

Reading I (L 33-C) (Joshua 5:9a, 10-12)

A reading from the Book of Joshua

The people of God entered the promised land and there kept the Passover.

The Lord said to Joshua,
   "Today I have removed the reproach of Egypt from you."
While the Israelites were encamped at Gilgal on the plains of Jericho,
   they celebrated the Passover
   on the evening of the fourteenth of the month.
On the day after the Passover,
   they ate of the produce of the land
   in the form of unleavened cakes and parched grain.

On that same day after the Passover,
> on which they ate of the produce of the land, the manna ceased.

No longer was there manna for the Israelites,
> who that year ate of the yield of the land of Canaan.

The word of the Lord. All: **Thanks be to God.**

RESPONSORIAL PSALM 34

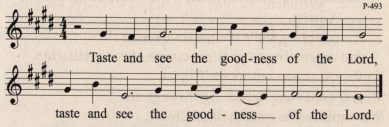

Music: Jay F. Hunstiger, © 1990, administered by Liturgical Press. All rights reserved.

Psalm 34:2-3, 4-5, 6-7

℟. (9a) **Taste and see the goodness of the Lord.**

> I will bless the LORD at all times;
>> his praise shall be ever in my mouth.
>
> Let my soul glory in the LORD;
>> the lowly will hear me and be glad. ℟.

> Glorify the LORD with me,
>> let us together extol his name.
>
> I sought the LORD, and he answered me
>> and delivered me from all my fears. ℟.

> Look to him that you may be radiant with joy,
>> and your faces may not blush with shame.
>
> When the poor one called out, the LORD heard,
>> and from all his distress he saved him. ℟.

READING II (2 Corinthians 5:17-21)

A reading from the second Letter of Saint Paul to the Corinthians

God reconciled us to himself through Christ.

Brothers and sisters:
Whoever is in Christ is a new creation:
> the old things have passed away;
> behold, new things have come.
And all this is from God,
> who has reconciled us to himself through Christ
> and given us the ministry of reconciliation,
> namely, God was reconciling the world to himself in Christ,
> not counting their trespasses against them
> and entrusting to us the message of reconciliation.
So we are ambassadors for Christ,
> as if God were appealing through us.
We implore you on behalf of Christ,
> be reconciled to God.
For our sake he made him to be sin who did not know sin,
> so that we might become the righteousness of God in him.

The word of the Lord. All: **Thanks be to God.**

Gospel (Luke 15:1-3, 11-32)
Verse before the Gospel (Luke 15:18)

℣. Praise to you, Lord Jesus Christ, king of endless glory!
℟. **Praise to you, Lord Jesus Christ, king of endless glory!**
℣. I will get up and go to my Father and shall say to him:
Father, I have sinned against heaven and against you. ℟.

✠ A reading from the holy Gospel according to Luke

All: **Glory to you, Lord.**

Your brother was dead and has come to life again.

Tax collectors and sinners were all drawing near to listen to Jesus,
> but the Pharisees and scribes began to complain, saying,
> "This man welcomes sinners and eats with them."
So to them Jesus addressed this parable:
"A man had two sons, and the younger son said to his father,

'Father give me the share of your estate that should
   come to me.'
So the father divided the property between them.
After a few days, the younger son collected all his
      belongings
   and set off to a distant country
      where he squandered his inheritance on a life of
         dissipation.
When he had freely spent everything,
   a severe famine struck that country,
   and he found himself in dire need.
So he hired himself out to one of the local citizens
   who sent him to his farm to tend the swine.
And he longed to eat his fill of the pods on which the
      swine fed,
   but nobody gave him any.
Coming to his senses he thought,
   'How many of my father's hired workers
   have more than enough food to eat,
   but here am I, dying from hunger.
I shall get up and go to my father and I shall say to him,
   "Father, I have sinned against heaven and against you.
I no longer deserve to be called your son;
   treat me as you would treat one of your hired workers."'
So he got up and went back to his father.
While he was still a long way off,
   his father caught sight of him, and was filled with
      compassion.
He ran to his son, embraced him and kissed him.
His son said to him,
   'Father, I have sinned against heaven and against you;
   I no longer deserve to be called your son.'
But his father ordered his servants,
   'Quickly bring the finest robe and put it on him;
   put a ring on his finger and sandals on his feet.

Take the fattened calf and slaughter it.
Then let us celebrate with a feast,
> because this son of mine was dead, and has come to life again;
> he was lost, and has been found.'
Then the celebration began.
Now the older son had been out in the field
> and, on his way back, as he neared the house,
> he heard the sound of music and dancing.
He called one of the servants and asked what this might mean.
The servant said to him,
> 'Your brother has returned
> and your father has slaughtered the fattened calf
> because he has him back safe and sound.'
He became angry,
> and when he refused to enter the house,
> his father came out and pleaded with him.
He said to his father in reply,
> 'Look, all these years I served you
> and not once did I disobey your orders;
> yet you never gave me even a young goat to feast on with my friends.
But when your son returns
> who swallowed up your property with prostitutes,
> for him you slaughter the fattened calf.'
He said to him,
> 'My son, you are here with me always;
> everything I have is yours.
But now we must celebrate and rejoice,
> because your brother was dead and has come to life again;
> he was lost and has been found.'"

The Gospel of the Lord. All: **Praise to you, Lord Jesus Christ.**

Prayer over the Gifts
Lord,
we offer you these gifts
which bring us peace and joy.
Increase our reverence by this eucharist,
and bring salvation to the world.
We ask this in the name of Jesus the Lord. All: **Amen.**

Communion Antiphon (Luke 15:32)
My son, you should rejoice, because your brother was dead and has come back to life; he was lost and is found.

Prayer after Communion
Father,
you enlighten all who come into the world.
Fill our hearts with the light of your gospel,
that our thoughts may please you,
and our love be sincere.
Grant this through Christ our Lord. All: **Amen.**

Fifth Sunday of Lent

March 21, 2010

Reflection on the Gospel

The crowd brings before Jesus a woman caught in adultery, condemns her, and demands her life. Jesus doesn't condemn the woman. He does condemn her act ("sin no more"), then calls her to repent and choose a new way of living. Lent calls us to the same kind of encounter with Jesus so that we face our own sinfulness, hear his invitation to embrace a new way of living, and make the right choice.

- *When Jesus has said to me "Neither do I condemn you," I have felt . . .*

—*Living Liturgy™, Fifth Sunday of Lent 2010*

Entrance Antiphon (Psalm 42:1-2)
Give me justice, O God, and defend my cause against the wicked; rescue me from deceitful and unjust men. You, O God, are my refuge.

March 21

OPENING PRAYER
Father,
help us to be like Christ your Son,
who loved the world and died for our salvation.
Inspire us by his love,
guide us by his example,
who lives and reigns with you and the Holy Spirit,
one God, for ever and ever. All: **Amen.**

The readings given for Year A, n. 34, may be used in place of these.

READING I (L 36-C) (Isaiah 43:16-21)

A reading from the Book of the Prophet Isaiah

See, I am doing something new and I give my people drink.

Thus says the LORD,
    who opens a way in the sea
    and a path in the mighty waters,
who leads out chariots and horsemen,
    a powerful army,
till they lie prostrate together, never to rise,
    snuffed out and quenched like a wick.
Remember not the events of the past,
    the things of long ago consider not;
see, I am doing something new!
    Now it springs forth, do you not perceive it?
In the desert I make a way,
    in the wasteland, rivers.
Wild beasts honor me,
    jackals and ostriches,
for I put water in the desert
    and rivers in the wasteland
    for my chosen people to drink,
the people whom I formed for myself,
    that they might announce my praise.

The word of the Lord. All: **Thanks be to God.**

Responsorial Psalm 126

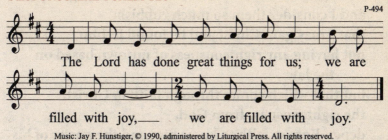

The Lord has done great things for us; we are filled with joy, we are filled with joy.

Music: Jay F. Hunstiger, © 1990, administered by Liturgical Press. All rights reserved.

Psalm 126:1-2, 2-3, 4-5, 6

℟. (3) **The Lord has done great things for us; we are filled with joy.**

> When the Lord brought back the captives of Zion,
>   we were like men dreaming.
> Then our mouth was filled with laughter,
>   and our tongue with rejoicing. ℟.
>
> Then they said among the nations,
>   "The Lord has done great things for them."
> The Lord has done great things for us;
>   we are glad indeed. ℟.
>
> Restore our fortunes, O Lord,
>   like the torrents in the southern desert.
> Those that sow in tears
>   shall reap rejoicing. ℟.
>
> Although they go forth weeping,
>   carrying the seed to be sown,
> they shall come back rejoicing,
>   carrying their sheaves. ℟.

Reading II (Philippians 3:8-14)
A reading from the Letter of Saint Paul to the Philippians

Because of Christ, I consider everything as a loss, being conformed to his death.

**Brothers and sisters:
I consider everything as a loss
   because of the supreme good of knowing Christ Jesus
      my Lord.**

For his sake I have accepted the loss of all things
   and I consider them so much rubbish,
   that I may gain Christ and be found in him,
   not having any righteousness of my own based on
      the law
   but that which comes through faith in Christ,
   the righteousness from God,
   depending on faith to know him and the power of his
      resurrection
   and the sharing of his sufferings by being conformed
      to his death,
   if somehow I may attain the resurrection from the dead.
It is not that I have already taken hold of it
   or have already attained perfect maturity,
   but I continue my pursuit in hope that I may possess it,
   since I have indeed been taken possession of by
      Christ Jesus.
Brothers and sisters, I for my part
   do not consider myself to have taken possession.
Just one thing: forgetting what lies behind
   but straining forward to what lies ahead,
   I continue my pursuit toward the goal,
   the prize of God's upward calling, in Christ Jesus.

The word of the Lord. All: Thanks be to God.

Gospel (John 8:1-11)
Verse before the Gospel (Joel 2:12-13)

℣. Glory to you, Word of God, Lord Jesus Christ!
℟. **Glory to you, Word of God, Lord Jesus Christ!**
℣. Even now, says the Lord,
   return to me with your whole heart;
   for I am gracious and merciful. ℟.

✠ **A reading from the holy Gospel according to John**

All: **Glory to you, Lord.**

Let the one among you who is without sin be the first to throw a stone at her.

Jesus went to the Mount of Olives.
But early in the morning he arrived again in the temple
    area,
    and all the people started coming to him,
    and he sat down and taught them.
Then the scribes and the Pharisees brought a woman
    who had been caught in adultery
    and made her stand in the middle.
They said to him,
    "Teacher, this woman was caught
    in the very act of committing adultery.
Now in the law, Moses commanded us to stone such
    women.
So what do you say?"
They said this to test him,
    so that they could have some charge to bring against
    him.
Jesus bent down and began to write on the ground with
    his finger.
But when they continued asking him,
    he straightened up and said to them,
    "Let the one among you who is without sin
    be the first to throw a stone at her."
Again he bent down and wrote on the ground.
And in response, they went away one by one,
    beginning with the elders.
So he was left alone with the woman before him.
Then Jesus straightened up and said to her,
    "Woman, where are they?
Has no one condemned you?"
She replied, "No one, sir."
Then Jesus said, "Neither do I condemn you.
Go, and from now on do not sin any more."

The Gospel of the Lord. All: **Praise to you, Lord Jesus Christ.**

Prayer over the Gifts
Almighty God,
may the sacrifice we offer
take away the sins of those
whom you enlighten with the Christian faith.
We ask this in the name of Jesus the Lord. All: **Amen.**

Communion Antiphon (John 8:10-11)
Has no one condemned you? The woman answered:
No one, Lord. Neither do I condemn you: go and do not sin again.

Prayer after Communion
Almighty Father,
by this sacrifice
may we always remain one with your Son, Jesus Christ,
whose body and blood we share,
for he is Lord for ever and ever. All: **Amen.**

Palm Sunday of the Lord's Passion

March 28, 2010

Reflection on the Gospel

On five occasions in Luke's passion account Jesus is declared innocent (three times by Pilate, once by the Good Thief, once by the centurion at the foot of the cross). Jesus died, not because of guilt, but because of his infinitely compassionate love for us. We pray that our compassion might increase and abound so that we have the same utter confidence in God's presence and care as did Jesus.

- *Jesus "emptied himself" (second reading) in his passion and death. Occasions calling me to self-emptying are . . .*

—Living Liturgy™, *Palm Sunday 2010*

Commemoration of the Lord's Entrance into Jerusalem

FIRST FORM: THE PROCESSION

The congregation assembles in a secondary church or chapel or in some other suitable place distinct from the church to which the procession will move. The faithful carry palm branches.

Dear friends in Christ, for five weeks of Lent we have been preparing, by works of charity and self-sacrifice, for the celebration of our Lord's paschal mystery. Today we come together to begin this solemn celebration in union with the whole Church throughout the world. Christ entered in triumph into his own city, to complete his work as our Messiah: to suffer, to die, and to rise again. Let us remember with devotion this entry which began his saving work and follow him with a lively faith. United with him in his suffering on the cross, may we share his resurrection and new life.

A Almighty God,
we pray you
bless ✝ these branches
and make them holy.
Today we joyfully acclaim Jesus our Messiah and King.
May we reach one day the happiness of the new and everlasting Jerusalem
by faithfully following him
who lives and reigns for ever and ever. All: **Amen.**

B Lord,
increase the faith of your people
and listen to our prayers.
Today we honor Christ our triumphant King
by carrying these branches.
May we honor you every day
by living always in him,
for he is Lord for ever and ever. All: **Amen.**

The Reading of the Gospel

Gospel (L 37-C) (Luke 19:28-40)

✝ **A reading from the holy Gospel according to Luke**

Blessed is he who comes in the name of the Lord.

**Jesus proceeded on his journey up to Jerusalem.
As he drew near to Bethphage and Bethany
at the place called the Mount of Olives,
he sent two of his disciples.**

He said, "Go into the village opposite you,
    and as you enter it you will find a colt tethered
    on which no one has ever sat.
Untie it and bring it here.
And if anyone should ask you,
    'Why are you untying it?'
    you will answer,
    'The Master has need of it.'"
So those who had been sent went off
    and found everything just as he had told them.
And as they were untying the colt, its owners said to them,
    "Why are you untying this colt?"
They answered,
    "The Master has need of it."
So they brought it to Jesus,
    threw their cloaks over the colt,
    and helped Jesus to mount.
As he rode along,
    the people were spreading their cloaks on the road;
    and now as he was approaching the slope of the
        Mount of Olives,
    the whole multitude of his disciples
    began to praise God aloud with joy
    for all the mighty deeds they had seen.
They proclaimed:
      "Blessed is the king who comes
        in the name of the Lord.
      Peace in heaven
        and glory in the highest."
Some of the Pharisees in the crowd said to him,
    "Teacher, rebuke your disciples."
He said in reply,
    "I tell you, if they keep silent,
    the stones will cry out!"

The Gospel of the Lord. All: **Praise to you, Lord Jesus Christ.**

Procession with the Blessed Branches

SECOND FORM: THE SOLEMN ENTRANCE
The commemoration of the Lord's entrance may be celebrated before the principal Mass with the solemn entrance, which takes place within the church.

THIRD FORM: THE SIMPLE ENTRANCE
The Lord's entrance is commemorated with the following simple entrance.

Entrance Antiphon
Six days before the solemn passover the Lord came to Jerusalem, and children waving palm branches ran out to welcome him. They loudly praised the Lord: Hosanna in the highest. Blessed are you who have come to us so rich in love and mercy.

Opening Prayer
Almighty, ever-living God,
you have given the human race Jesus Christ our Savior
as a model of humility.
He fulfilled your will by becoming man
and giving his life on the cross.
Help us to bear witness to you
by following his example of suffering
and make us worthy to share in his resurrection.
We ask this through our Lord Jesus Christ, your Son,
who lives and reigns with you and the Holy Spirit,
one God, for ever and ever. All: **Amen.**

Reading I (L 38-ABC) (Isaiah 50:4-7)
A reading from the Book of the Prophet Isaiah
My face I did not shield from buffets and spitting, knowing that I shall not be put to shame.

**The Lord God has given me
    a well-trained tongue,
that I might know how to speak to the weary
    a word that will rouse them.
Morning after morning
    he opens my ear that I may hear;
and I have not rebelled,
    have not turned back.**

I gave my back to those who beat me,
>my cheeks to those who plucked my beard;
my face I did not shield
>from buffets and spitting.

The Lord GOD is my help,
>therefore I am not disgraced;
I have set my face like flint,
>knowing that I shall not be put to shame.

The word of the Lord. All: Thanks be to God.

RESPONSORIAL PSALM 22

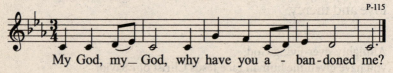

My God, my God, why have you a-ban-doned me?

Music: Jay F. Hunstiger, © 1990, administered by Liturgical Press. All rights reserved.

Psalm 22:8-9, 17-18, 19-20, 23-24

℟. (2a) **My God, my God, why have you abandoned me?**

All who see me scoff at me;
>they mock me with parted lips, they wag their heads:
"He relied on the LORD; let him deliver him,
>let him rescue him, if he loves him." ℟.

Indeed, many dogs surround me,
>a pack of evildoers closes in upon me;
they have pierced my hands and my feet;
>I can count all my bones. ℟.

They divide my garments among them,
>and for my vesture they cast lots.
But you, O LORD, be not far from me;
>O my help, hasten to aid me. ℟.

I will proclaim your name to my brethren;
>in the midst of the assembly I will praise you:
"You who fear the LORD, praise him;
>all you descendants of Jacob, give glory to him;
revere him, all you descendants of Israel!" ℟.

Reading II (Philippians 2:6-11)

A reading from the Letter of Saint Paul to the Philippians

Christ humbled himself. Because of this God greatly exalted him.

**Christ Jesus, though he was in the form of God,
did not regard equality with God
something to be grasped.
Rather, he emptied himself,
taking the form of a slave,
coming in human likeness;
and found human in appearance,
he humbled himself,
becoming obedient to the point of death,
even death on a cross.
Because of this, God greatly exalted him
and bestowed on him the name
which is above every name,
that at the name of Jesus
every knee should bend,
of those in heaven and on earth and under the earth,
and every tongue confess that
Jesus Christ is Lord,
to the glory of God the Father.**

The word of the Lord. All: **Thanks be to God.**

* The message of the liturgy in proclaiming the passion narratives in full is to enable the assembly to see vividly the love of Christ for each person, despite their sins, a love that even death could not vanquish. The crimes during the Passion of Christ cannot be attributed indiscriminately to all Jews of that time, nor to Jews today. The Jewish people should not be referred to as though rejected or cursed, as if this view followed from Scripture. The Church ever keeps in mind that Jesus, his mother Mary, and the Apostles all were Jewish. As the Church has always held, Christ freely suffered his passion and death because of the sins of all, that all might be saved.

GOSPEL (Luke 22:14—23:56) *or* Shorter Form [ ] (Luke 23:1-49)
VERSE BEFORE THE GOSPEL (Philippians 2:8-9)

℣. Praise to you, Lord Jesus Christ, king of endless glory!
℟. **Praise to you, Lord Jesus Christ, king of endless glory!**
℣. Christ became obedient to the point of death,
   even death on a cross.
   Because of this, God greatly exalted him
   and bestowed on him the name which is above every
         name. ℟.

The symbols in the following passion narrative represent:

C.   Narrator;
✠   Christ;
S.   speakers other than Christ;
SS. groups of speakers.

The Passion of our Lord Jesus Christ according to Luke

The Passion of our Lord Jesus Christ.

C. **When the hour came,**
    Jesus took his place at table with the apostles.
    He said to them,
✠   **"I have eagerly desired to eat this Passover with**
            you before I suffer,
    for, I tell you, I shall not eat it again
    until there is fulfillment in the kingdom of God."
C. **Then he took a cup, gave thanks, and said,**
✠   **"Take this and share it among yourselves;**
    for I tell you that from this time on
    I shall not drink of the fruit of the vine
    until the kingdom of God comes."
C. **Then he took the bread, said the blessing,**
    broke it, and gave it to them, saying,
✠   **"This is my body, which will be given for you;**
    do this in memory of me."
C. **And likewise the cup after they had eaten, saying,**
✠   **"This cup is the new covenant in my blood,**
    which will be shed for you.

"And yet behold, the hand of the one who is to
 betray me
 is with me on the table;
 for the Son of Man indeed goes as it has been
 determined;
 but woe to that man by whom he is betrayed."

C. And they began to debate among themselves
 who among them would do such a deed.

Then an argument broke out among them
 about which of them should be regarded as the
 greatest.
He said to them,
✢ "The kings of the Gentiles lord it over them
 and those in authority over them are addressed as
 'Benefactors';
 but among you it shall not be so.
Rather, let the greatest among you be as the youngest,
 and the leader as the servant.
For who is greater:
 the one seated at table or the one who serves?
Is it not the one seated at table?
I am among you as the one who serves.
It is you who have stood by me in my trials;
 and I confer a kingdom on you,
 just as my Father has conferred one on me,
 that you may eat and drink at my table in my
 kingdom;
 and you will sit on thrones
 judging the twelve tribes of Israel.

"Simon, Simon, behold Satan has demanded
 to sift all of you like wheat,
 but I have prayed that your own faith may not fail;
 and once you have turned back,
 you must strengthen your brothers."

C.	He said to him,
S.	"Lord, I am prepared to go to prison and to die with you."
C.	But he replied,
✠	"I tell you, Peter, before the cock crows this day, you will deny three times that you know me."
C.	He said to them,
✠	"When I sent you forth without a money bag or a sack or sandals, were you in need of anything?"
S.	"No, nothing,"
C.	they replied. He said to them,
✠	"But now one who has a money bag should take it, and likewise a sack, and one who does not have a sword should sell his cloak and buy one. For I tell you that this Scripture must be fulfilled in me, namely, *He was counted among the wicked*; and indeed what is written about me is coming to fulfillment."
C.	Then they said,
SS.	"Lord, look, there are two swords here."
C.	But he replied,
✠	"It is enough!"
C.	Then going out, he went, as was his custom, to the Mount of Olives, and the disciples followed him. When he arrived at the place he said to them,
✠	"Pray that you may not undergo the test."
C.	After withdrawing about a stone's throw from them and kneeling, he prayed, saying,
✠	"Father, if you are willing, take this cup away from me; still, not my will but yours be done."

C. And to strengthen him an angel from heaven appeared
       to him.
   He was in such agony and he prayed so fervently
       that his sweat became like drops of blood
       falling on the ground.
   When he rose from prayer and returned to his
       disciples,
       he found them sleeping from grief.
   He said to them,
✠   "Why are you sleeping?
   Get up and pray that you may not undergo the test."
C. While he was still speaking, a crowd approached
       and in front was one of the Twelve, a man named
       Judas.
   He went up to Jesus to kiss him.
   Jesus said to him,
✠   "Judas, are you betraying the Son of Man with a
       kiss?"
C. His disciples realized what was about to happen,
       and they asked,
SS.   "Lord, shall we strike with a sword?"
C. And one of them struck the high priest's servant
       and cut off his right ear.
   But Jesus said in reply,
✠   "Stop, no more of this!"
C. Then he touched the servant's ear and healed him.
   And Jesus said to the chief priests and temple guards
       and elders who had come for him,
✠   "Have you come out as against a robber, with
       swords and clubs?
   Day after day I was with you in the temple area,
       and you did not seize me;
       but this is your hour, the time for the power of
       darkness."

C.	After arresting him they led him away
	and took him into the house of the high priest;
	Peter was following at a distance.
	They lit a fire in the middle of the courtyard and sat around it,
	and Peter sat down with them.
	When a maid saw him seated in the light,
	she looked intently at him and said,
S.	"This man too was with him."
C.	But he denied it saying,
S.	"Woman, I do not know him."
C.	A short while later someone else saw him and said,
S.	"You too are one of them";
C.	but Peter answered,
S.	"My friend, I am not."
C.	About an hour later, still another insisted,
S.	"Assuredly, this man too was with him,
	for he also is a Galilean."
C.	But Peter said,
S.	"My friend, I do not know what you are talking about."
C.	Just as he was saying this, the cock crowed,
	and the Lord turned and looked at Peter;
	and Peter remembered the word of the Lord,
	how he had said to him,
	"Before the cock crows today, you will deny me three times."
	He went out and began to weep bitterly.
	The men who held Jesus in custody were ridiculing and beating him.
	They blindfolded him and questioned him, saying,
SS.	"Prophesy! Who is it that struck you?"
C.	And they reviled him in saying many other things against him.
	When day came the council of elders of the people met,

both chief priests and scribes,
and they brought him before their Sanhedrin.
They said,

SS. "If you are the Christ, tell us,"
C. but he replied to them,
✠ "If I tell you, you will not believe,
and if I question, you will not respond.
But from this time on the Son of Man will be seated
at the right hand of the power of God."
C. They all asked,
SS. "Are you then the Son of God?"
C. He replied to them,
✠ "You say that I am."
C. Then they said,
SS. "What further need have we for testimony?
We have heard it from his own mouth."

C. [Then the whole assembly of them arose and brought
him before Pilate.
They brought charges against him, saying,
SS. "We found this man misleading our people;
he opposes the payment of taxes to Caesar
and maintains that he is the Christ, a king."
C. Pilate asked him,
S. "Are you the king of the Jews?"
C. He said to him in reply,
✠ "You say so."
C. Pilate then addressed the chief priests and the crowds,
S. "I find this man not guilty."
C. But they were adamant and said,
SS. "He is inciting the people with his teaching
throughout all Judea,
from Galilee where he began even to here."

C. On hearing this Pilate asked if the man was a
Galilean;
and upon learning that he was under Herod's
jurisdiction,

      he sent him to Herod who was in Jerusalem at
         that time.
    Herod was very glad to see Jesus;
      he had been wanting to see him for a long time,
      for he had heard about him
      and had been hoping to see him perform some sign.
    He questioned him at length,
      but he gave him no answer.
    The chief priests and scribes, meanwhile,
      stood by accusing him harshly.
    Herod and his soldiers treated him contemptuously
         and mocked him,
      and after clothing him in resplendent garb,
      he sent him back to Pilate.
    Herod and Pilate became friends that very day,
      even though they had been enemies formerly.
    Pilate then summoned the chief priests, the rulers,
         and the people
      and said to them,

S.   "You brought this man to me
      and accused him of inciting the people to revolt.
    I have conducted my investigation in your presence
      and have not found this man guilty
      of the charges you have brought against him,
      nor did Herod, for he sent him back to us.
    So no capital crime has been committed by him.
    Therefore I shall have him flogged and then release
         him."

C.   But all together they shouted out,
SS. "Away with this man!
      Release Barabbas to us."
C.   —Now Barabbas had been imprisoned for a rebellion
      that had taken place in the city and for murder.—
    Again Pilate addressed them, still wishing to release
      Jesus,
      but they continued their shouting,

SS.   "Crucify him! Crucify him!"
C.   Pilate addressed them a third time,
S.   "What evil has this man done?
      I found him guilty of no capital crime.
      Therefore I shall have him flogged and then release him."
C.   With loud shouts, however,
      they persisted in calling for his crucifixion,
      and their voices prevailed.
   The verdict of Pilate was that their demand should be granted.
   So he released the man who had been imprisoned
      for rebellion and murder, for whom they asked,
      and he handed Jesus over to them to deal with as they wished.

   As they led him away
      they took hold of a certain Simon, a Cyrenian,
      who was coming in from the country;
      and after laying the cross on him,
      they made him carry it behind Jesus.
   A large crowd of people followed Jesus,
      including many women who mourned and lamented him.
   Jesus turned to them and said,
✝   "Daughters of Jerusalem, do not weep for me;
      weep instead for yourselves and for your children
      for indeed, the days are coming when people will say,
      'Blessed are the barren,
      the wombs that never bore
      and the breasts that never nursed.'
   At that time people will say to the mountains,
      'Fall upon us!'
      and to the hills, 'Cover us!'
      for if these things are done when the wood is green
      what will happen when it is dry?"

C. Now two others, both criminals,
    were led away with him to be executed.

    When they came to the place called the Skull,
        they crucified him and the criminals there,
        one on his right, the other on his left.
    Then Jesus said,

✝   "Father, forgive them, they know not what they do."

C. They divided his garments by casting lots.
    The people stood by and watched;
        the rulers, meanwhile, sneered at him and said,

SS. "He saved others, let him save himself
        if he is the chosen one, the Christ of God."

C. Even the soldiers jeered at him.
    As they approached to offer him wine they called out,

SS. "If you are King of the Jews, save yourself."

C. Above him there was an inscription that read,
    "This is the King of the Jews."

    Now one of the criminals hanging there reviled Jesus,
        saying,

S. "Are you not the Christ?
    Save yourself and us."

C. The other, however, rebuking him, said in reply,

S. "Have you no fear of God,
        for you are subject to the same condemnation?
    And indeed, we have been condemned justly,
        for the sentence we received corresponds to our crimes,
    but this man has done nothing criminal."

C. Then he said,

S. "Jesus, remember me when you come into your kingdom."

C. He replied to him,

✝   "Amen, I say to you,
    today you will be with me in Paradise."

C. It was now about noon and darkness came over the whole land

until three in the afternoon
because of an eclipse of the sun.
Then the veil of the temple was torn down the middle.
Jesus cried out in a loud voice,

✝ "Father, into your hands I commend my spirit";
C. and when he had said this he breathed his last.

Here all kneel and pause for a short time.

C. The centurion who witnessed what had happened
glorified God and said,
S. "This man was innocent beyond doubt."
C. When all the people who had gathered for this spectacle
saw what had happened,
they returned home beating their breasts;
but all his acquaintances stood at a distance,
including the women who had followed him
from Galilee
and saw these events.]

Now there was a virtuous and righteous man named
Joseph who,
though he was a member of the council,
had not consented to their plan of action.
He came from the Jewish town of Arimathea
and was awaiting the kingdom of God.
He went to Pilate and asked for the body of Jesus.
After he had taken the body down,
he wrapped it in a linen cloth
and laid him in a rock-hewn tomb
in which no one had yet been buried.
It was the day of preparation,
and the sabbath was about to begin.
The women who had come from Galilee with him
followed behind,
and when they had seen the tomb
and the way in which his body was laid in it,

> they returned and prepared spices and
> perfumed oils.
> Then they rested on the sabbath according to the
> commandment.

The Gospel of the Lord. All: **Praise to you, Lord Jesus Christ.**

Prayer over the Gifts
Lord,
may the suffering and death of Jesus, your only Son,
make us pleasing to you.
Alone we can do nothing,
but may this perfect sacrifice
win us your mercy and love.
We ask this in the name of Jesus the Lord. All: **Amen.**

Communion Antiphon (Matthew 26:42)
Father, if this cup may not pass, but I must drink it, then your will be done.

Prayer after Communion
Lord,
you have satisfied our hunger with this eucharistic food.
The death of your Son gives us hope and strengthens our faith.
May his resurrection give us perseverance
and lead us to salvation.
We ask this through Christ our Lord. All: **Amen.**

The Easter Triduum

These next days of entering into Jesus' paschal mystery through the Triduum liturgies and our own everyday living can be a clarion call to us, reminding us that we were created in God's image, and that means we love with an unselfish love, we give without counting the cost, we sacrifice without recoiling. These are days in which we re-learn the deepest meaning of sacrifice. —Living Liturgy™, *Easter Triduum 2010*

Holy Thursday solemnly inaugurates "the triduum during which the Lord died, was buried and rose again" (St. Augustine). To these days Jesus referred when he prophesied: "Destroy this temple and in three days I will raise it up again" (John 2:14).

Holy Thursday

April 1, 2010

Reflection on the Gospel

The simple gesture of Jesus in the gospel reminds us that love knows no bounds, excludes no one, is a remarkable gesture of self-sacrifice. Yes, Jesus loved us to the end. But the end isn't the cross. The end is the ongoing invitation to stand at the messianic table and be nourished by the Body and Blood of Christ. We come to the table worthily when we do as the Master has done: empty ourselves in self-sacrifice for the good of others.

- *The way serving others (footwashing) and being nourished at the eucharistic table are connected for me is . . .*

—Living Liturgy™, *Holy Thursday 2010*

Evening Mass of the Lord's Supper

Entrance Antiphon (*See* Galatians 6:14)
We should glory in the cross of our Lord Jesus Christ, for he is our salvation, our life and our resurrection; through him we are saved and made free.

Opening Prayer
God our Father,
we are gathered here to share in the supper
which your only Son left to his Church to reveal his love.
He gave it to us when he was about to die
and commanded us to celebrate it as the new and eternal sacrifice.
We pray that in this eucharist
we may find the fullness of love and life.
Grant this through our Lord Jesus Christ, your Son,
who lives and reigns with you and the Holy Spirit,
one God, for ever and ever. All: **Amen.**

Reading I (L 39) (Exodus 12:1-8, 11-14)
A reading from the Book of Exodus

The law regarding the Passover meal.

April 1

The LORD said to Moses and Aaron in the land of Egypt,
"This month shall stand at the head of your calendar;
you shall reckon it the first month of the year.
Tell the whole community of Israel:
On the tenth of this month every one of your families
must procure for itself a lamb, one apiece for each
household.
If a family is too small for a whole lamb,
it shall join the nearest household in procuring one
and shall share in the lamb
in proportion to the number of persons who partake
of it.
The lamb must be a year-old male and without blemish.
You may take it from either the sheep or the goats.
You shall keep it until the fourteenth day of this month,
and then, with the whole assembly of Israel present,
it shall be slaughtered during the evening twilight.
They shall take some of its blood
and apply it to the two doorposts and the lintel
of every house in which they partake of the lamb.
That same night they shall eat its roasted flesh
with unleavened bread and bitter herbs.

"This is how you are to eat it:
with your loins girt, sandals on your feet and your
staff in hand,
you shall eat like those who are in flight.
It is the Passover of the LORD.
For on this same night I will go through Egypt,
striking down every firstborn of the land, both man
and beast,
and executing judgment on all the gods of Egypt—
I, the LORD!
But the blood will mark the houses where you are.
Seeing the blood, I will pass over you;
thus, when I strike the land of Egypt,
no destructive blow will come upon you.

"This day shall be a memorial feast for you,
  which all your generations shall celebrate
  with pilgrimage to the Lord, as a perpetual institution."

The word of the Lord. All: **Thanks be to God.**

Responsorial Psalm 116

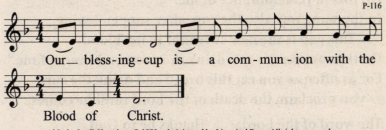

Music: Jay F. Hunstiger, © 1990, administered by Liturgical Press. All rights reserved.

Psalm 116:12-13, 15-16bc, 17-18

℟. (*See* 1 Corinthians 10:16) **Our blessing-cup is a communion with the Blood of Christ.**

> How shall I make a return to the Lord
>   for all the good he has done for me?
> The cup of salvation I will take up,
>   and I will call upon the name of the Lord. ℟.

> Precious in the eyes of the Lord
>   is the death of his faithful ones.
> I am your servant, the son of your handmaid;
>   you have loosed my bonds. ℟.

> To you will I offer sacrifice of thanksgiving,
>   and I will call upon the name of the Lord.
> My vows to the Lord I will pay
>   in the presence of all his people. ℟.

Reading II (1 Corinthians 11:23-26)

A reading from the first Letter of Saint Paul to the Corinthians

For as often as you eat this bread and drink the cup, you proclaim the death of the Lord.

Brothers and sisters:
I received from the Lord what I also handed on to you,
> that the Lord Jesus, on the night he was handed over,
> took bread, and, after he had given thanks,
> broke it and said, "This is my body that is for you.
Do this in remembrance of me."
In the same way also the cup, after supper, saying,
> "This cup is the new covenant in my blood.
Do this, as often as you drink it, in remembrance of me."
For as often as you eat this bread and drink the cup,
> you proclaim the death of the Lord until he comes.

The word of the Lord. All: Thanks be to God.

GOSPEL (John 13:1-15)
VERSE BEFORE THE GOSPEL (John 13:34)

℣. Praise to you, Lord Jesus Christ, king of endless glory!
℟. **Praise to you, Lord Jesus Christ, king of endless glory!**
℣. I give you a new commandment, says the Lord:
love one another as I have loved you. ℟.

✠ **A reading from the holy Gospel according to John**

All: **Glory to you, Lord.**

Jesus loved them to the end.

Before the feast of Passover, Jesus knew that his hour had come
> to pass from this world to the Father.
He loved his own in the world and he loved them to
> the end.
The devil had already induced Judas, son of Simon the
> Iscariot, to hand him over.
So, during supper,
> fully aware that the Father had put everything into
> > his power
> and that he had come from God and was returning
> > to God,
> he rose from supper and took off his outer garments.
He took a towel and tied it around his waist.

Then he poured water into a basin
    and began to wash the disciples' feet
    and dry them with the towel around his waist.
He came to Simon Peter, who said to him,
    "Master, are you going to wash my feet?"
Jesus answered and said to him,
    "What I am doing, you do not understand now,
    but you will understand later."
Peter said to him, "You will never wash my feet."
Jesus answered him,
    "Unless I wash you, you will have no inheritance
        with me."
Simon Peter said to him,
    "Master, then not only my feet, but my hands and
        head as well."
Jesus said to him,
    "Whoever has bathed has no need except to have his
        feet washed,
        for he is clean all over;
    so you are clean, but not all."
For he knew who would betray him;
    for this reason, he said, "Not all of you are clean."

So when he had washed their feet
    and put his garments back on and reclined at table
        again,
    he said to them, "Do you realize what I have done
        for you?
You call me 'teacher' and 'master,' and rightly so,
    for indeed I am.
If I, therefore, the master and teacher, have washed
    your feet,
    you ought to wash one another's feet.
I have given you a model to follow,
    so that as I have done for you, you should also do."

The Gospel of the Lord. All: **Praise to you, Lord Jesus Christ.**

WASHING OF FEET
Antiphons or other appropriate songs are sung.

Prayer over the Gifts
Lord,
make us worthy to celebrate these mysteries.
Each time we offer this memorial sacrifice
the work of our redemption is accomplished.
We ask this in the name of Jesus the Lord. All: **Amen.**

Communion Antiphon (1 Corinthians 11:24-25)
This body will be given for you. This is the cup of the new covenant in my blood; whenever you receive them, do so in remembrance of me.

Prayer after Communion
Almighty God,
we receive new life
from the supper your Son gave us in this world.
May we find full contentment
in the meal we hope to share
in your eternal kingdom.
We ask this through Christ our Lord. All: **Amen.**

TRANSFER OF THE HOLY EUCHARIST

Good Friday

April 2, 2010 (First Friday)

Reflection on the Gospel

Good Friday is more than a step to resurrection; it is a day on which we celebrate Jesus' obedience, his kingship, the everlasting establishment of his reign, his side being opened and himself being poured out so that we can be washed in his very blood and water. The real scandal of the cross isn't suffering and death; the real scandal of the cross is that death is vindicated by Jesus' self-sacrificing love.

- *The cross of self-sacrifice I must yet take up and carry is . . .*

—Living Liturgy™, *Good Friday 2010*

Celebration of the Lord's Passion

Prayer (Let us pray is not said)
Lord,
by shedding his blood for us,
your Son, Jesus Christ,
established the paschal mystery.
In your goodness, make us holy
and watch over us always.
We ask this through Christ our Lord. All: **Amen.**

or:

Lord,
by the suffering of Christ your Son
you have saved us all from the death
we inherited from sinful Adam.
By the law of nature
we have borne the likeness of his manhood.
May the sanctifying power of grace
help us to put on the likeness of our Lord in heaven,
who lives and reigns for ever and ever. All: **Amen.**

Reading I (L 40) (Isaiah 52:13—53:12)

A reading from the Book of the Prophet Isaiah

He himself was wounded for our sins.

(Fourth oracle of the Servant of the Lord.)

**See, my servant shall prosper,
    he shall be raised high and greatly exalted.
Even as many were amazed at him—
    so marred was his look beyond human semblance
    and his appearance beyond that of the sons of man—
so shall he startle many nations,
    because of him kings shall stand speechless;
for those who have not been told shall see,
    those who have not heard shall ponder it.**

**Who would believe what we have heard?
    To whom has the arm of the LORD been revealed?
He grew up like a sapling before him,
    like a shoot from the parched earth;**

> there was in him no stately bearing to make us look
>   at him,
>   nor appearance that would attract us to him.
> He was spurned and avoided by people,
>   a man of suffering, accustomed to infirmity,
> one of those from whom people hide their faces,
>   spurned, and we held him in no esteem.
>
> Yet it was our infirmities that he bore,
>   our sufferings that he endured,
> while we thought of him as stricken,
>   as one smitten by God and afflicted.
> But he was pierced for our offenses,
>   crushed for our sins;
> upon him was the chastisement that makes us whole,
>   by his stripes we were healed.
> We had all gone astray like sheep,
>   each following his own way;
> but the LORD laid upon him
>   the guilt of us all.
>
> Though he was harshly treated, he submitted
>   and opened not his mouth;
> like a lamb led to the slaughter
>   or a sheep before the shearers,
>   he was silent and opened not his mouth.
> Oppressed and condemned, he was taken away,
>   and who would have thought any more of his destiny?
> When he was cut off from the land of the living,
>   and smitten for the sin of his people,
> a grave was assigned him among the wicked
>   and a burial place with evildoers,
> though he had done no wrong
>   nor spoken any falsehood.
> But the LORD was pleased
>   to crush him in infirmity.
>
> If he gives his life as an offering for sin,
>   he shall see his descendants in a long life,

April 2   181

    and the will of the Lord shall be accomplished
       through him.

Because of his affliction
  he shall see the light
    in fullness of days;
through his suffering, my servant shall justify many,
  and their guilt he shall bear.
Therefore I will give him his portion among the great,
  and he shall divide the spoils with the mighty,
because he surrendered himself to death
  and was counted among the wicked;
and he shall take away the sins of many,
  and win pardon for their offenses.

The word of the Lord. All: **Thanks be to God.**

Responsorial Psalm 31

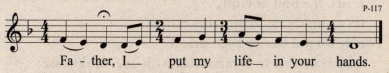

Music: Jay F. Hunstiger, © 1990, administered by Liturgical Press. All rights reserved.

Psalm 31:2, 6, 12-13, 15-16, 17, 25

℟. (Luke 23:46) **Father, into your hands I commend my spirit.**

In you, O Lord, I take refuge;
  let me never be put to shame.
In your justice rescue me.
Into your hands I commend my spirit;
  you will redeem me, O Lord, O faithful God. ℟.

For all my foes I am an object of reproach,
  a laughingstock to my neighbors, and a dread to my friends;
  they who see me abroad flee from me.
I am forgotten like the unremembered dead;
  I am like a dish that is broken. ℟.

(continued)

But my trust is in you, O Lord;
  I say, "You are my God.
In your hands is my destiny; rescue me
  from the clutches of my enemies and my persecutors." ℟.

Let your face shine upon your servant;
  save me in your kindness.
Take courage and be stouthearted,
  all you who hope in the Lord. ℟.

Reading II (Hebrews 4:14-16; 5:7-9)
A reading from the Letter to the Hebrews

Jesus learned obedience and became the source of salvation for all who obey him.

Brothers and sisters:
Since we have a great high priest who has passed through
  the heavens,
  Jesus, the Son of God,
  let us hold fast to our confession.
For we do not have a high priest
  who is unable to sympathize with our weaknesses,
  but one who has similarly been tested in every way,
  yet without sin.
So let us confidently approach the throne of grace
  to receive mercy and to find grace for timely help.

In the days when Christ was in the flesh,
  he offered prayers and supplications with loud cries
    and tears
  to the one who was able to save him from death,
  and he was heard because of his reverence.
Son though he was, he learned obedience from what he
    suffered;
  and when he was made perfect,
  he became the source of eternal salvation for all who
    obey him.

The word of the Lord. All: **Thanks be to God.**

GOSPEL (John 18:1—19:42)
VERSE BEFORE THE GOSPEL (Philippians 2:8-9)

℣. Praise to you, Lord Jesus Christ, king of endless glory!
℟. **Praise to you, Lord Jesus Christ, king of endless glory!**
℣. Christ became obedient to the point of death,
  even death on a cross.
  Because of this, God greatly exalted him
  and bestowed on him the name which is above every
    other name. ℟.

The symbols in the following passion narrative represent:

  C. Narrator;
  ✟ Christ;
  S. speakers other than Christ;
  SS. groups of speakers.

The Passion of our Lord Jesus Christ according to John

The Passion of our Lord Jesus Christ.

C. **Jesus went out with his disciples across the Kidron
    valley
    to where there was a garden,
    into which he and his disciples entered.
  Judas his betrayer also knew the place,
    because Jesus had often met there with his disciples.
  So Judas got a band of soldiers and guards
    from the chief priests and the Pharisees
    and went there with lanterns, torches, and weapons.
  Jesus, knowing everything that was going to happen
    to him,
    went out and said to them,**
✟ **"Whom are you looking for?"**
C. **They answered him,**
SS. **"Jesus the Nazorean."**
C. **He said to them,**
✟ **"I AM."**
C. **Judas his betrayer was also with them.
  When he said to them, "I AM,"
    they turned away and fell to the ground.**

So he again asked them,
✝   "Whom are you looking for?"
C. They said,
SS.   "Jesus the Nazorean."
C. Jesus answered,
✝   "I told you that I AM.
So if you are looking for me, let these men go."
C. This was to fulfill what he had said,
   "I have not lost any of those you gave me."

Then Simon Peter, who had a sword, drew it,
   struck the high priest's slave, and cut off his right ear.
The slave's name was Malchus.
Jesus said to Peter,
✝   "Put your sword into its scabbard.
Shall I not drink the cup that the Father gave me?"
C. So the band of soldiers, the tribune, and the Jewish guards seized Jesus,
   bound him, and brought him to Annas first.
He was the father-in-law of Caiaphas,
   who was high priest that year.
It was Caiaphas who had counseled the Jews
   that it was better that one man should die rather than the people.

Simon Peter and another disciple followed Jesus.
Now the other disciple was known to the high priest,
   and he entered the courtyard of the high priest with Jesus.
But Peter stood at the gate outside.
So the other disciple, the acquaintance of the high priest,
   went out and spoke to the gatekeeper and brought Peter in.
Then the maid who was the gatekeeper said to Peter,
S.   "You are not one of this man's disciples, are you?"

C.	He said,
S.	"I am not."
C.	Now the slaves and the guards were standing around a charcoal fire
that they had made, because it was cold, and were warming themselves.
Peter was also standing there keeping warm.

The high priest questioned Jesus about his disciples and about his doctrine.
Jesus answered him, |
| ✢ | "I have spoken publicly to the world.
I have always taught in a synagogue or in the temple area where all the Jews gather, and in secret I have said nothing. Why ask me?
Ask those who heard me what I said to them.
They know what I said." |
| C. | When he had said this,
one of the temple guards standing there struck Jesus and said, |
S.	"Is this the way you answer the high priest?"
C.	Jesus answered him,
✢	"If I have spoken wrongly, testify to the wrong; but if I have spoken rightly, why do you strike me?"
C.	Then Annas sent him bound to Caiaphas the high priest.

Now Simon Peter was standing there keeping warm.
And they said to him, |
S.	"You are not one of his disciples, are you?"
C.	He denied it and said,
S.	"I am not."
C.	One of the slaves of the high priest,
a relative of the one whose ear Peter had cut off, said,
S.	"Didn't I see you in the garden with him?"
C.	Again Peter denied it.
And immediately the cock crowed.

Then they brought Jesus from Caiaphas to the
>   praetorium.
It was morning.
And they themselves did not enter the praetorium,
>   in order not to be defiled so that they could eat
>   the Passover.
So Pilate came out to them and said,

S. "What charge do you bring against this man?"
C. They answered and said to him,
SS. "If he were not a criminal,
>   we would not have handed him over to you."
C. At this, Pilate said to them,
S. "Take him yourselves, and judge him according
>   to your law."
C. The Jews answered him,
SS. "We do not have the right to execute anyone,"
C. in order that the word of Jesus might be fulfilled
>   that he said indicating the kind of death he would
>   die.
So Pilate went back into the praetorium
and summoned Jesus and said to him,
S. "Are you the King of the Jews?"
C. Jesus answered,
✝ "Do you say this on your own
>   or have others told you about me?"
C. Pilate answered,
S. "I am not a Jew, am I?
Your own nation and the chief priests handed you
>   over to me.
What have you done?"
C. Jesus answered,
✝ "My kingdom does not belong to this world.
If my kingdom did belong to this world,
>   my attendants would be fighting
>   to keep me from being handed over to the Jews.
But as it is, my kingdom is not here."

C.	So Pilate said to him,
S.	"Then you are a king?"
C.	Jesus answered,
✝	"You say I am a king. For this I was born and for this I came into the world, to testify to the truth. Everyone who belongs to the truth listens to my voice."
C.	Pilate said to him,
S.	"What is truth?"
C.	When he had said this, he again went out to the Jews and said to them,
S.	"I find no guilt in him. But you have a custom that I release one prisoner to you at Passover. Do you want me to release to you the King of the Jews?"
C.	They cried out again,
SS.	"Not this one but Barabbas!"
C.	Now Barabbas was a revolutionary. Then Pilate took Jesus and had him scourged. And the soldiers wove a crown out of thorns and placed it on his head, and clothed him in a purple cloak, and they came to him and said,
SS.	"Hail, King of the Jews!"
C.	And they struck him repeatedly. Once more Pilate went out and said to them,
S.	"Look, I am bringing him out to you, so that you may know that I find no guilt in him."
C.	So Jesus came out, wearing the crown of thorns and the purple cloak. And Pilate said to them,
S.	"Behold, the man!"
C.	When the chief priests and the guards saw him they cried out,
SS.	"Crucify him, crucify him!"

C. Pilate said to them,
S. "Take him yourselves and crucify him.
I find no guilt in him."
C. The Jews answered,
SS. "We have a law, and according to that law he ought
to die,
because he made himself the Son of God."
C. Now when Pilate heard this statement,
he became even more afraid,
and went back into the praetorium and said to Jesus,
S. "Where are you from?"
C. Jesus did not answer him.
So Pilate said to him,
S. "Do you not speak to me?
Do you not know that I have power to release you
and I have power to crucify you?"
C. Jesus answered him,
✠ "You would have no power over me
if it had not been given to you from above.
For this reason the one who handed me over to you
has the greater sin."
C. Consequently, Pilate tried to release him; but the
Jews cried out,
SS. "If you release him, you are not a Friend of Caesar.
Everyone who makes himself a king opposes Caesar."
C. When Pilate heard these words he brought Jesus out
and seated him on the judge's bench
in the place called Stone Pavement, in Hebrew,
Gabbatha.
It was preparation day for Passover, and it was
about noon.
And he said to the Jews,
S. "Behold, your king!"
C. They cried out,
SS. "Take him away, take him away! Crucify him!"

C.	Pilate said to them,
S.	"Shall I crucify your king?"
C.	The chief priests answered,
SS.	"We have no king but Caesar."
C.	Then he handed him over to them to be crucified.

> So they took Jesus, and, carrying the cross himself,
>> he went out to what is called the Place of the Skull,
>> in Hebrew, Golgotha.
> There they crucified him, and with him two others,
>> one on either side, with Jesus in the middle.
> Pilate also had an inscription written and put on
>> the cross.
> It read,
>> "Jesus the Nazorean, the King of the Jews."
> Now many of the Jews read this inscription,
>> because the place where Jesus was crucified was
>>> near the city;
>> and it was written in Hebrew, Latin, and Greek.
> So the chief priests of the Jews said to Pilate,

SS.	"Do not write 'The King of the Jews,' but that he said, 'I am the King of the Jews.'"
C.	Pilate answered,
S.	"What I have written, I have written."
C.	When the soldiers had crucified Jesus,

> they took his clothes and divided them into four
>> shares,
>> a share for each soldier.
> They also took his tunic, but the tunic was seamless,
>> woven in one piece from the top down.
> So they said to one another,

SS.	"Let's not tear it, but cast lots for it to see whose it will be,"
C.	in order that the passage of Scripture might be fulfilled that says:

> They divided my garments among them,
> and for my vesture they cast lots.

This is what the soldiers did.
Standing by the cross of Jesus were his mother
   and his mother's sister, Mary the wife of Clopas,
   and Mary of Magdala.
When Jesus saw his mother and the disciple there
   whom he loved he said to his mother,

✠   "Woman, behold, your son."
C. Then he said to the disciple,
✠   "Behold, your mother."
C. And from that hour the disciple took her into his home.

After this, aware that everything was now finished,
   in order that the Scripture might be fulfilled,
   Jesus said,

✠   "I thirst."
C. There was a vessel filled with common wine.
So they put a sponge soaked in wine on a sprig of
   hyssop
   and put it up to his mouth.
When Jesus had taken the wine, he said,
✠   "It is finished."
C. And bowing his head, he handed over the spirit.

Here all kneel and pause for a short time.

Now since it was preparation day,
   in order that the bodies might not remain
     on the cross on the sabbath,
   for the sabbath day of that week was a solemn one,
   the Jews asked Pilate that their legs be broken
   and that they be taken down.
So the soldiers came and broke the legs of the first
   and then of the other one who was crucified
     with Jesus.
But when they came to Jesus and saw that he was
   already dead,

they did not break his legs,
   but one soldier thrust his lance into his side,
   and immediately blood and water flowed out.
An eyewitness has testified, and his testimony is true;
   he knows that he is speaking the truth,
   so that you also may come to believe.
For this happened so that the Scripture passage
      might be fulfilled:
   Not a bone of it will be broken.
And again another passage says:
   They will look upon him whom they have pierced.

After this, Joseph of Arimathea,
   secretly a disciple of Jesus for fear of the Jews,
   asked Pilate if he could remove the body of Jesus.
And Pilate permitted it.
So he came and took his body.
Nicodemus, the one who had first come to him at
      night,
   also came bringing a mixture of myrrh and aloes
   weighing about one hundred pounds.
They took the body of Jesus
   and bound it with burial cloths along with the
      spices,
   according to the Jewish burial custom.
Now in the place where he had been crucified there
      was a garden,
   and in the garden a new tomb, in which no one
      had yet been buried.
So they laid Jesus there because of the Jewish
      preparation day;
   for the tomb was close by.

The Gospel of the Lord. All: **Praise to you, Lord Jesus Christ.**

General Intercessions

I. For the Church

Let us pray, dear friends,
for the holy Church of God throughout the world,
that God the almighty Father
guide it and gather it together
so that we may worship him
in peace and tranquility.

Silent prayer. Then the priest sings or says:

Almighty and eternal God,
you have shown your glory to all nations
in Christ, your Son.
Guide the work of your Church.
Help it to persevere in faith,
proclaim your name,
and bring your salvation to people everywhere.
We ask this through Christ our Lord. All: **Amen.**

II. For the Pope

Let us pray
for our Holy Father, Pope N.,
that God who chose him to be bishop
may give him health and strength
to guide and govern God's holy people.

Silent prayer. Then the priest sings or says:

Almighty and eternal God,
you guide all things by your word,
you govern all Christian people.
In your love protect the Pope you have chosen for us.
Under his leadership deepen our faith
and make us better Christians.
We ask this through Christ our Lord. All: **Amen.**

III. For the Clergy and Laity of the Church

Let us pray
for N., our bishop,
for all bishops, priests, and deacons;
for all who have a special ministry in the Church
and for all God's people.

Silent prayer. Then the priest sings or says:

Almighty and eternal God,
your Spirit guides the Church
and makes it holy.

Listen to our prayers
and help each of us
in his own vocation
to do your work more faithfully.
We ask this through Christ our Lord. All: **Amen.**

IV. For those Preparing for Baptism

Let us pray
for those [among us] preparing for baptism,
that God in his mercy
make them responsive to his love,
forgive their sins through the waters of new birth,
and give them life in Jesus Christ our Lord.

Silent prayer. Then the priest sings or says:

Almighty and eternal God,
you continually bless your Church with new members.
Increase the faith and understanding
of those [among us] preparing for baptism.
Give them a new birth in these living waters
and make them members of your chosen family.
We ask this through Christ our Lord. All: **Amen.**

V. For the Unity of Christians

Let us pray
for all our brothers and sisters
who share our faith in Jesus Christ,
that God may gather and keep together in one Church
all those who seek the truth with sincerity.

Silent prayer. Then the priest sings or says:

Almighty and eternal God,
you keep together those you have united.
Look kindly on all who follow Jesus your Son.
We are all consecrated to you by our common baptism.
Make us one in the fullness of faith,
and keep us one in the fellowship of love.
We ask this through Christ our Lord. All: **Amen.**

VI. For the Jewish People

Let us pray
for the Jewish people,
the first to hear the word of God,
that they may continue to grow in the love of his name
and in faithfulness to his covenant.

Silent prayer. Then the priest sings or says:

Almighty and eternal God,
long ago you gave your promise to Abraham and his posterity.
Listen to your Church as we pray
that the people you first made your own
may arrive at the fullness of redemption.
We ask this through Christ our Lord. All: **Amen.**

VII. FOR THOSE WHO DO NOT BELIEVE IN CHRIST

Let us pray
for those who do not believe in Christ,
that the light of the Holy Spirit
may show them the way to salvation.

Silent prayer. Then the priest sings or says:

Almighty and eternal God,
enable those who do not acknowledge Christ
to find the truth
as they walk before you in sincerity of heart.
Help us to grow in love for one another,
to grasp more fully the mystery of your godhead,
and to become more perfect witnesses of your love
in the sight of men.
We ask this through Christ our Lord. All: **Amen.**

VIII. FOR THOSE WHO DO NOT BELIEVE IN GOD

Let us pray
for those who do not believe in God,
that they may find him
by sincerely following all that is right.

Silent prayer. Then the priest sings or says:

Almighty and eternal God,
you created mankind
so that all might long to find you
and have peace when you are found.
Grant that, in spite of the hurtful things
that stand in their way,
they may all recognize in the lives of Christians
the tokens of your love and mercy,
and gladly acknowledge you
as the one true God and Father of us all.
We ask this through Christ our Lord. All: **Amen.**

IX. FOR ALL IN PUBLIC OFFICE

Let us pray
for those who serve us in public office,

that God may guide their minds and hearts,
so that all men may live in true peace and freedom.

Silent prayer. Then the priest sings or says:

Almighty and eternal God,
you know the longings of men's hearts
and you protect their rights.
In your goodness
watch over those in authority,
so that people everywhere may enjoy
religious freedom, security, and peace.
We ask this through Christ our Lord. All: **Amen.**

X. For Those in Special Need
Let us pray, dear friends,
that God the almighty Father
may heal the sick,
comfort the dying,
give safety to travelers,
free those unjustly deprived of liberty,
and rid the world of falsehood,
hunger, and disease.

Silent prayer. Then the priest sings or says:

Almighty, ever-living God,
you give strength to the weary
and new courage to those who have lost heart.
Hear the prayers of all who call on you in any trouble
that they may have the joy of receiving your help in their need.
We ask this through Christ our Lord. All: **Amen.**

VENERATION OF THE CROSS

First Form of Showing the Cross
℣. This is the wood of the cross, on which hung the Savior of the world.
All respond: **Come, let us worship.**

Second Form of Showing the Cross
℣. This is the wood of the cross, on which hung the Savior of the world.
All respond: **Come, let us worship.**

Veneration of the Cross
The priest, clergy, and faithful approach to venerate the cross in a kind of procession.

HOLY COMMUNION

Let us pray with confidence to the Father
in the words our Savior gave us:

He extends his hands and continues, with all present:
Our Father, who art in heaven,
hallowed be thy name;
thy kingdom come;
thy will be done on earth as it is in heaven.
Give us this day our daily bread;
and forgive us our trespasses
as we forgive those who trespass against us;
and lead us not into temptation,
but deliver us from evil.

With hands extended, the priest continues alone:
Deliver us, Lord, from every evil,
and grant us peace in our day.
In your mercy keep us free from sin
and protect us from all anxiety
as we wait in joyful hope
for the coming of our Savior, Jesus Christ.

He joins his hands. The people end the prayer with the acclamation:
For the kingdom, the power, and the glory are yours, now and for ever.

23. *Then the priest joins his hands and says inaudibly:*
Lord Jesus Christ,
with faith in your love and mercy
I eat your body and drink your blood.
Let it not bring me condemnation,
but health in mind and body.

24. *The priest genuflects. Taking the host, he raises it slightly over the ciborium and, facing the people, says aloud:*
This is the Lamb of God
who takes away the sins of the world.
Happy are those who are called to his supper.

He adds, once only, with the people:
Lord, I am not worthy to receive you,
but only say the word and I shall be healed.

Prayer after Communion
Almighty and eternal God,
you have restored us to life
by the triumphant death and resurrection of Christ.
Continue this healing work within us.
May we who participate in this mystery

never cease to serve you.
We ask this through Christ our Lord. All: **Amen.**

All depart in silence. The altar is stripped; the cross remains, however, with four candles.

HOLY SATURDAY

The Easter Vigil

April 3, 2010 (First Saturday)

Reflection on the Gospel

This is the night when the stones of our Lenten penance are rolled away and we are invited to peer into the empty space of this dark night and see ourselves in "dazzling garments." This is the night we announce all these things to anyone who will hear—even though sometimes we are still puzzled at the seeming nonsense. This is the night God surprises humanity yet another time: he who is dead has risen!

- *The way I understand resurrection is . . . One way I experience resurrection in my daily living is . . .*

—Living Liturgy™, *Easter Vigil 2010*

PART ONE: SOLEMN BEGINNING OF THE VIGIL:
THE SERVICE OF LIGHT

Dear friends in Christ,
on this most holy night,
when our Lord Jesus Christ passed from death to life,
the Church invites her children throughout the world
to come together in vigil and prayer.
This is the passover of the Lord:
if we honor the memory of his death and resurrection
by hearing his word and celebrating his mysteries,
then we may be confident
that we shall share his victory over death
and live with him for ever in God.

Let us pray.
Father,
we share in the light of your glory
through your Son, the light of the world.
Make this new fire ✣ holy, and inflame us with new hope.
Purify our minds by this Easter celebration,
and bring us one day to the feast of eternal light.
We ask this through Christ our Lord. All: **Amen.**

Preparation of the Candle

(1) **Christ yesterday and today** (as he traces the vertical arm of the cross),
(2) **the beginning and the end** (the horizontal arm),
(3) **alpha** (alpha, above the cross),
(4) **and omega** (omega, below the cross);
(5) **all time belongs to him** (the first numeral, in the upper left corner of the cross),
(6) **and all the ages** (the second numeral in the upper right corner),
(7) **to him be glory and power** (the third numeral in the lower left corner),
(8) **through every age for ever. Amen.** (the last numeral in the lower right corner).

```
        A
     2     0
     0     N
        Ω
```

(1) **By his holy**   1
(2) **and glorious wounds**
(3) **may Christ our Lord**   4 2 5
(4) **guard us**
(5) **and keep us. Amen.**   3

May the light of Christ, rising in glory,
dispel the darkness of our hearts and minds.

Procession

℣. Christ our Light. ℟. **Thanks be to God.**
℣. Christ our Light. ℟. **Thanks be to God.**
℣. Christ our Light. ℟. **Thanks be to God.**

Easter Proclamation
Long Form of the Easter Proclamation (Exsultet)

Rejoice, heavenly powers! Sing, choirs of angels!
  Exult, all creation around God's throne!
  Jesus Christ, our King, is risen!
  Sound the trumpet of salvation!

Rejoice, O earth, in shining splendor,
    radiant in the brightness of your King!
    Christ has conquered! Glory fills you!
    Darkness vanishes for ever!
Rejoice, O Mother Church! Exult in glory!
    The risen Savior shines upon you!
    Let this place resound with joy,
    echoing the mighty song of all God's people!
[My dearest friends, standing with me in this holy light,
    join me in asking God for mercy,
    that he may give his unworthy minister
    grace to sing his Easter praises.]
[℣. The Lord be with you.
℟. **And also with you.**]
℣. Lift up your hearts.
℟. **We lift them up to the Lord.**
℣. Let us give thanks to the Lord our God.
℟. **It is right to give him thanks and praise.**
It is truly right
    that with full hearts and minds and voices
    we should praise the unseen God, the all-powerful Father,
    and his only Son, our Lord Jesus Christ.
For Christ has ransomed us with his blood,
    and paid for us the price of Adam's sin
    to our eternal Father!
This is our passover feast,
    when Christ, the true Lamb, is slain,
    whose blood consecrates the homes of all believers.
This is the night when first you saved our fathers:
    you freed the people of Israel from their slavery
    and led them dry-shod through the sea.
This is the night when the pillar of fire
    destroyed the darkness of sin!
This is the night when Christians everywhere,
    washed clean of sin
    and freed from all defilement,
    are restored to grace and grow together in holiness.

This is the night when Jesus Christ
    broke the chains of death
    and rose triumphant from the grave.
What good would life have been to us,
    had Christ not come as our Redeemer?
Father, how wonderful your care for us!
    How boundless your merciful love!
    To ransom a slave
    you gave away your Son.
O happy fault, O necessary sin of Adam,
    which gained for us so great a Redeemer!
Most blessed of all nights, chosen by God
    to see Christ rising from the dead!
Of this night scripture says:
    "The night will be as clear as day:
    it will become my light, my joy."
The power of this holy night
    dispels all evil, washes guilt away,
    restores lost innocence, brings mourners joy;
    it casts out hatred, brings us peace, and humbles
        earthly pride.
Night truly blessed when heaven is wedded to earth
    and man is reconciled with God!
Therefore heavenly Father, in the joy of this night,
    receive our evening sacrifice of praise,
    your Church's solemn offering.
Accept this Easter candle,
    a flame divided but undimmed,
    a pillar of fire that glows to the honor of God.
Let it mingle with the lights of heaven
    and continue bravely burning
    to dispel the darkness of this night!
May the Morning Star which never sets find this flame still
      burning:
    Christ, that Morning Star, who came back from the dead,
    and shed his peaceful light on all mankind,
    your Son who lives and reigns for ever and ever. All: **Amen.**

PART TWO: LITURGY OF THE WORD

Dear friends in Christ,
we have begun our solemn vigil.
Let us now listen attentively to the word of God,
recalling how he saved his people throughout history
and, in the fullness of time,
sent his own Son to be our Redeemer.

Through this Easter celebration,
may God bring to perfection
the saving work he has begun in us.

READING I (L 41) (Genesis 1:1—2:2) *or* Shorter Form [ ]
(Genesis 1:1, 26-31a)

A reading from the Book of Genesis

God looked at everything he had made, and he found it very good.

[In the beginning, when God created the heavens and
  the earth,]
  the earth was a formless wasteland, and darkness
    covered the abyss,
  while a mighty wind swept over the waters.
Then God said,
  "Let there be light," and there was light.
God saw how good the light was.
God then separated the light from the darkness.
God called the light "day," and the darkness he called
  "night."
Thus evening came, and morning followed—the first day.
Then God said,
  "Let there be a dome in the middle of the waters,
  to separate one body of water from the other."
And so it happened:
  God made the dome,
  and it separated the water above the dome from the
    water below it.
God called the dome "the sky."
Evening came, and morning followed—the second day.

Then God said,
> "Let the water under the sky be gathered into a single basin,
> so that the dry land may appear."

And so it happened:
> the water under the sky was gathered into its basin,
> and the dry land appeared.

God called the dry land "the earth,"
> and the basin of the water he called "the sea."

God saw how good it was.

Then God said,
> "Let the earth bring forth vegetation:
> every kind of plant that bears seed
> and every kind of fruit tree on earth
> that bears fruit with its seed in it."

And so it happened:
> the earth brought forth every kind of plant that bears seed
> and every kind of fruit tree on earth
> that bears fruit with its seed in it.

God saw how good it was.

Evening came, and morning followed—the third day.

Then God said:
> "Let there be lights in the dome of the sky,
> to separate day from night.

Let them mark the fixed times, the days and the years,
> and serve as luminaries in the dome of the sky,
> to shed light upon the earth."

And so it happened:
> God made the two great lights,
> the greater one to govern the day,
> and the lesser one to govern the night;
> and he made the stars.

God set them in the dome of the sky,
> to shed light upon the earth,

>   to govern the day and the night,
>   and to separate the light from the darkness.
> God saw how good it was.
> Evening came, and morning followed—the fourth day.
>
> Then God said,
>   "Let the water teem with an abundance of living creatures,
>   and on the earth let birds fly beneath the dome of the sky."
> And so it happened:
>   God created the great sea monsters
>   and all kinds of swimming creatures with which the water teems,
>   and all kinds of winged birds.
> God saw how good it was, and God blessed them, saying,
>   "Be fertile, multiply, and fill the water of the seas;
>   and let the birds multiply on the earth."
> Evening came, and morning followed—the fifth day.
>
> Then God said,
>   "Let the earth bring forth all kinds of living creatures:
>   cattle, creeping things, and wild animals of all kinds."
> And so it happened:
>   God made all kinds of wild animals, all kinds of cattle,
>   and all kinds of creeping things of the earth.
> God saw how good it was.
> Then [God said:
>   "Let us make man in our image, after our likeness.
> Let them have dominion over the fish of the sea,
>   the birds of the air, and the cattle,
>   and over all the wild animals
>   and all the creatures that crawl on the ground."
> God created man in his image;
>   in the image of God he created him;
>   male and female he created them.

God blessed them, saying:
"Be fertile and multiply;
fill the earth and subdue it.
Have dominion over the fish of the sea, the birds of the air,
and all the living things that move on the earth."
God also said:
"See, I give you every seed-bearing plant all over the earth
and every tree that has seed-bearing fruit on it to be your food;
and to all the animals of the land, all the birds of the air,
and all the living creatures that crawl on the ground,
I give all the green plants for food."
And so it happened.
God looked at everything he had made, and he found it very good.]
Evening came, and morning followed—the sixth day.

Thus the heavens and the earth and all their array were completed.
Since on the seventh day God was finished
with the work he had been doing,
he rested on the seventh day from all the work he had undertaken.

The word of the Lord.

The response Thanks be to God is not said after the readings.

Responsorial Psalm 104 or 33

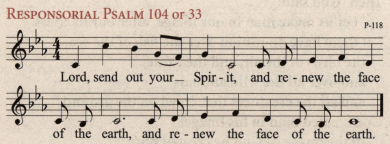

Lord, send out your Spirit, and renew the face of the earth, and renew the face of the earth.

Music: Jay F. Hunstiger, © 1990, administered by Liturgical Press. All rights reserved.

April 3   205

A   Psalm 104:1-2, 5-6, 10, 12, 13-14, 24, 35

℟. (30) **Lord, send out your Spirit, and renew the face of the earth.**

> Bless the Lord, O my soul!
> > O Lord, my God, you are great indeed!
>
> You are clothed with majesty and glory,
> > robed in light as with a cloak. ℟.
>
> You fixed the earth upon its foundation,
> > not to be moved forever;
>
> with the ocean, as with a garment, you covered it;
> > above the mountains the waters stood. ℟.
>
> You send forth springs into the watercourses
> > that wind among the mountains.
>
> Beside them the birds of heaven dwell;
> > from among the branches they send forth their song. ℟.
>
> You water the mountains from your palace;
> > the earth is replete with the fruit of your works.
>
> You raise grass for the cattle,
> > and vegetation for man's use,
>
> producing bread from the earth. ℟.
>
> How manifold are your works, O Lord!
> > In wisdom you have wrought them all—
>
> the earth is full of your creatures.
> > Bless the Lord, O my soul! ℟.

or:

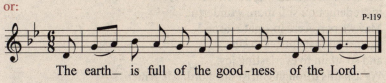

The earth is full of the goodness of the Lord.

Music: Jay F. Hunstiger, © 1990, administered by Liturgical Press. All rights reserved.

B   Psalm 33:4-5, 6-7, 12-13, 20 and 22

℟. (5b) **The earth is full of the goodness of the Lord.**

> Upright is the word of the Lord,
> > and all his works are trustworthy.
>
> He loves justice and right;
> > of the kindness of the Lord the earth is full. ℟.

(continued)

By the word of the LORD the heavens were made;
  by the breath of his mouth all their host.
He gathers the waters of the sea as in a flask;
  in cellars he confines the deep. ℟.

Blessed the nation whose God is the LORD,
  the people he has chosen for his own inheritance.
From heaven the LORD looks down;
  he sees all mankind. ℟.

Our soul waits for the LORD,
  who is our help and our shield.
May your kindness, O LORD, be upon us
  who have put our hope in you. ℟.

PRAYER
Let us pray.
Almighty and eternal God,
you created all things in wonderful beauty and order.
Help us now to perceive
how still more wonderful is the new creation
by which in the fullness of time
you redeemed your people
through the sacrifice of our passover, Jesus Christ,
who lives and reigns for ever and ever. All: **Amen.**

or:

Let us pray.
Lord God,
the creation of man was a wonderful work,
his redemption still more wonderful.
May we persevere in right reason
against all that entices to sin
and so attain to everlasting joy.
We ask this through Christ our Lord. All: **Amen.**

READING II (Genesis 22:1-18) *or* Shorter Form [ ] (Genesis 22:1-2, 9a, 10-13, 15-18)

A reading from the Book of Genesis

The sacrifice of Abraham, our father in faith.

[God put Abraham to the test.
He called to him, "Abraham!"
"Here I am," he replied.

Then God said:
>"Take your son Isaac, your only one, whom you love,
>and go to the land of Moriah.
>There you shall offer him up as a holocaust
>on a height that I will point out to you."]

Early the next morning Abraham saddled his donkey,
>took with him his son Isaac and two of his servants as well,
>and with the wood that he had cut for the holocaust,
>set out for the place of which God had told him.

On the third day Abraham got sight of the place from afar.
Then he said to his servants:
>"Both of you stay here with the donkey,
>while the boy and I go on over yonder.
>We will worship and then come back to you."

Thereupon Abraham took the wood for the holocaust
>and laid it on his son Isaac's shoulders,
>while he himself carried the fire and the knife.

As the two walked on together, Isaac spoke to his father Abraham:
>"Father!" Isaac said.
"Yes, son," he replied.
Isaac continued, "Here are the fire and the wood,
>but where is the sheep for the holocaust?"
"Son," Abraham answered,
>"God himself will provide the sheep for the holocaust."
Then the two continued going forward.

[When they came to the place of which God had told him,
>Abraham built an altar there and arranged the wood on it.]
Next he tied up his son Isaac,
>and put him on top of the wood on the altar.
[Then he reached out and took the knife to slaughter his son.
But the LORD's messenger called to him from heaven,
>"Abraham, Abraham!"

"Here I am!" he answered.
"Do not lay your hand on the boy," said the messenger.
"Do not do the least thing to him.
I know now how devoted you are to God,
　　since you did not withhold from me your own
　　　　beloved son."
As Abraham looked about,
　　he spied a ram caught by its horns in the thicket.
So he went and took the ram
　　and offered it up as a holocaust in place of his son.]
Abraham named the site Yahweh-yireh;
　　hence people now say, "On the mountain the Lord
　　　　will see."

[Again the Lord's messenger called to Abraham from
　　　　heaven and said:
"I swear by myself, declares the Lord,
that because you acted as you did
in not withholding from me your beloved son,
I will bless you abundantly
and make your descendants as countless
as the stars of the sky and the sands of the seashore;
your descendants shall take possession
of the gates of their enemies,
and in your descendants all the nations of the earth
　　shall find blessing—
all this because you obeyed my command."]

The word of the Lord.

Responsorial Psalm 16

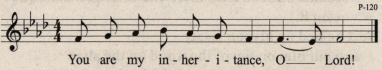

You are my in-her-i-tance, O＿ Lord!

Music: Jay F. Hunstiger, © 1990, administered by Liturgical Press. All rights reserved.

Psalm 16:5, 8, 9-10, 11

℟. (1) **You are my inheritance, O Lord.**

> O Lord, my allotted portion and my cup,
>   you it is who hold fast my lot.
> I set the Lord ever before me;
>   with him at my right hand I shall not be disturbed. ℟.
>
> Therefore my heart is glad and my soul rejoices,
>   my body, too, abides in confidence;
> because you will not abandon my soul to the netherworld,
>   nor will you suffer your faithful one to undergo
>   corruption. ℟.
>
> You will show me the path to life,
>   fullness of joys in your presence,
>   the delights at your right hand forever. ℟.

Prayer

Let us pray.
God and Father of all who believe in you,
you promised Abraham that he would become the father of all nations,
and through the death and resurrection of Christ
you fulfill that promise:
everywhere throughout the world you increase your chosen people.
May we respond to your call
by joyfully accepting your invitation to the new life of grace.
We ask this through Christ our Lord. All: **Amen.**

Reading III (Exodus 14:15—15:1)

A reading from the Book of Exodus

The Israelites marched on dry land through the midst of the sea.

**The Lord said to Moses, "Why are you crying out to me?
Tell the Israelites to go forward.
And you, lift up your staff and, with hand outstretched
    over the sea,
  split the sea in two,
  that the Israelites may pass through it on dry land.
But I will make the Egyptians so obstinate
  that they will go in after them.
Then I will receive glory through Pharaoh and all his army,
  his chariots and charioteers.**

The Egyptians shall know that I am the LORD,
  when I receive glory through Pharaoh
  and his chariots and charioteers."

The angel of God, who had been leading Israel's camp,
  now moved and went around behind them.
The column of cloud also, leaving the front,
  took up its place behind them,
  so that it came between the camp of the Egyptians
  and that of Israel.
But the cloud now became dark, and thus the night passed
  without the rival camps coming any closer together
    all night long.
Then Moses stretched out his hand over the sea,
  and the LORD swept the sea
  with a strong east wind throughout the night
  and so turned it into dry land.
When the water was thus divided,
  the Israelites marched into the midst of the sea on
    dry land,
  with the water like a wall to their right and to their left.

The Egyptians followed in pursuit;
  all Pharaoh's horses and chariots and charioteers went
    after them
  right into the midst of the sea.
In the night watch just before dawn
  the LORD cast through the column of the fiery cloud
  upon the Egyptian force a glance that threw it into a
    panic;
  and he so clogged their chariot wheels
  that they could hardly drive.
With that the Egyptians sounded the retreat before Israel,
  because the LORD was fighting for them against the
    Egyptians.

Then the LORD told Moses, "Stretch out your hand over
  the sea,

that the water may flow back upon the Egyptians,
   upon their chariots and their charioteers."
So Moses stretched out his hand over the sea,
   and at dawn the sea flowed back to its normal depth.
The Egyptians were fleeing head on toward the sea,
   when the L̲o̲r̲d̲ hurled them into its midst.
As the water flowed back,
   it covered the chariots and the charioteers of Pharaoh's
      whole army
   which had followed the Israelites into the sea.
Not a single one of them escaped.
But the Israelites had marched on dry land
   through the midst of the sea,
   with the water like a wall to their right and to their left.
Thus the L̲o̲r̲d̲ saved Israel on that day
   from the power of the Egyptians.
When Israel saw the Egyptians lying dead on the seashore
   and beheld the great power that the L̲o̲r̲d̲
      had shown against the Egyptians,
   they feared the L̲o̲r̲d̲ and believed in him and in his
      servant Moses.

Then Moses and the Israelites sang this song to the L̲o̲r̲d̲:
   I will sing to the L̲o̲r̲d̲, for he is gloriously triumphant;
   horse and chariot he has cast into the sea.

The word of the Lord.

Responsorial Psalm (Exodus 15)

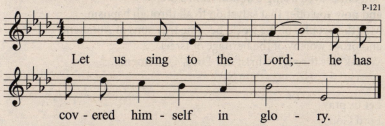

Let us sing to the Lord; he has covered himself in glory.

Music: Jay F. Hunstiger, © 1990, administered by Liturgical Press. All rights reserved.

April 3
Exodus 15:1-2, 3-4, 5-6, 17-18

℟. (1b) **Let us sing to the Lord; he has covered himself in glory.**

> I will sing to the LORD, for he is gloriously triumphant;
>> horse and chariot he has cast into the sea.
>
> My strength and my courage is the LORD,
>> and he has been my savior.
>
> He is my God, I praise him;
>> the God of my father, I extol him. ℟.
>
> The LORD is a warrior,
>> LORD is his name!
>
> Pharaoh's chariots and army he hurled into the sea;
>> the elite of his officers were submerged in the Red Sea. ℟.
>
> The flood waters covered them,
>> they sank into the depths like a stone.
>
> Your right hand, O LORD, magnificent in power,
>> your right hand, O LORD, has shattered the enemy. ℟.
>
> You brought in the people you redeemed
>> and planted them on the mountain of your inheritance—
>
> the place where you made your seat, O LORD,
>> the sanctuary, LORD, which your hands established.
>
> The LORD shall reign forever and ever. ℟.

PRAYER
Let us pray.
Father,
even today we see the wonders
of the miracles you worked long ago.
You once saved a single nation from slavery,
and now you offer that salvation to all through baptism.
May the peoples of the world become true sons of Abraham
and prove worthy of the heritage of Israel.
We ask this through Christ our Lord. All: **Amen.**

or:

Let us pray.
Lord God,
in the new covenant
you shed light on the miracles you worked in ancient times:
the Red Sea is a symbol of our baptism,

and the nation you freed from slavery
is a sign of your Christian people.
May every nation
share the faith and privilege of Israel,
and come to new birth in the Holy Spirit.
We ask this through Christ our Lord. All: **Amen.**

Reading IV (Isaiah 54:5-14)
A reading from the Book of the Prophet Isaiah

With enduring love, the Lord your redeemer takes pity on you.

> The One who has become your husband is your Maker;
>> his name is the Lord of hosts;
>
> your redeemer is the Holy One of Israel,
>> called God of all the earth.
>
> The Lord calls you back,
>> like a wife forsaken and grieved in spirit,
>> a wife married in youth and then cast off,
>> says your God.
>
> For a brief moment I abandoned you,
>> but with great tenderness I will take you back.
>
> In an outburst of wrath, for a moment
>> I hid my face from you;
>
> but with enduring love I take pity on you,
>> says the Lord, your redeemer.
>
> This is for me like the days of Noah,
>> when I swore that the waters of Noah
>> should never again deluge the earth;
>
> so I have sworn not to be angry with you,
>> or to rebuke you.
>
> Though the mountains leave their place
>> and the hills be shaken,
>
> my love shall never leave you
>> nor my covenant of peace be shaken,
>> says the Lord, who has mercy on you.
>
> O afflicted one, storm-battered and unconsoled,
>> I lay your pavements in carnelians,
>> and your foundations in sapphires;

I will make your battlements of rubies,
>   your gates of carbuncles,
>   and all your walls of precious stones.
> All your children shall be taught by the LORD,
>   and great shall be the peace of your children.
> In justice shall you be established,
>   far from the fear of oppression,
>   where destruction cannot come near you.

The word of the Lord.

Responsorial Psalm 30

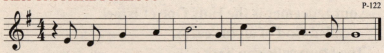

I will praise you, Lord, for you have rescued me.

Music: Jay F. Hunstiger, © 1990, administered by Liturgical Press. All rights reserved.

Psalm 30:2, 4, 5-6, 11-12, 13

℟. (2a) **I will praise you, Lord, for you have rescued me.**

> I will extol you, O LORD, for you drew me clear
>   and did not let my enemies rejoice over me.
> O LORD, you brought me up from the netherworld;
>   you preserved me from among those going down into
>   the pit. ℟.

> Sing praise to the LORD, you his faithful ones,
>   and give thanks to his holy name.
> For his anger lasts but a moment;
>   a lifetime, his good will.
> At nightfall, weeping enters in,
>   but with the dawn, rejoicing. ℟.

> Hear, O LORD, and have pity on me;
>   O LORD, be my helper.
> You changed my mourning into dancing;
>   O LORD, my God, forever will I give you thanks. ℟.

Prayer

Let us pray.
Almighty and eternal God,
glorify your name by increasing your chosen people

as you promised long ago.
In reward for their trust,
may we see in the Church the fulfillment of your promise.
We ask this through Christ our Lord. All: **Amen.**

Reading V (Isaiah 55:1-11)
A reading from the Book of the Prophet Isaiah

Come to me that you may have life. I will renew with you an everlasting covenant.

> Thus says the Lord:
> All you who are thirsty,
>   come to the water!
> You who have no money,
>   come, receive grain and eat;
> come, without paying and without cost,
>   drink wine and milk!
> Why spend your money for what is not bread,
>   your wages for what fails to satisfy?
> Heed me, and you shall eat well,
>   you shall delight in rich fare.
> Come to me heedfully,
>   listen, that you may have life.
> I will renew with you the everlasting covenant,
>   the benefits assured to David.
> As I made him a witness to the peoples,
>   a leader and commander of nations,
> so shall you summon a nation you knew not,
>   and nations that knew you not shall run to you,
> because of the Lord, your God,
>   the Holy One of Israel, who has glorified you.
>
> Seek the Lord while he may be found,
>   call him while he is near.
> Let the scoundrel forsake his way,
>   and the wicked man his thoughts;
> let him turn to the Lord for mercy;
>   to our God, who is generous in forgiving.

216 April 3

> For my thoughts are not your thoughts,
>> nor are your ways my ways, says the Lord.
> As high as the heavens are above the earth,
>> so high are my ways above your ways
>> and my thoughts above your thoughts.
>
> For just as from the heavens
>> the rain and snow come down
> and do not return there
>> till they have watered the earth,
>> making it fertile and fruitful,
> giving seed to the one who sows
>> and bread to the one who eats,
> so shall my word be
>> that goes forth from my mouth;
> my word shall not return to me void,
>> but shall do my will,
>> achieving the end for which I sent it.

The word of the Lord.

Responsorial Psalm (Isaiah 12)

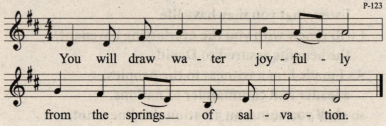

Music: Jay F. Hunstiger, © 1990, administered by Liturgical Press. All rights reserved.

Isaiah 12:2-3, 4, 5-6

℟. (3) **You will draw water joyfully from the springs of salvation.**

> God indeed is my savior;
>> I am confident and unafraid.
> My strength and my courage is the Lord,
>> and he has been my savior.
> With joy you will draw water
>> at the fountain of salvation. ℟.

Give thanks to the Lord, acclaim his name;
> among the nations make known his deeds,
> proclaim how exalted is his name. ℟.

Sing praise to the Lord for his glorious achievement;
> let this be known throughout all the earth.

Shout with exultation, O city of Zion,
> for great in your midst
> is the Holy One of Israel! ℟.

Prayer
Let us pray.
Almighty, ever-living God,
only hope of the world,
by the preaching of the prophets
you proclaimed the mysteries we are celebrating tonight.
Help us to be your faithful people,
for it is by your inspiration alone
that we can grow in goodness.
We ask this through Christ our Lord. All: **Amen.**

Reading VI (Baruch 3:9-15, 32—4:4)
A reading from the Book of the Prophet Baruch

Walk toward the splendor of the Lord.

Hear, O Israel, the commandments of life:
> **listen, and know prudence!**

How is it, Israel,
> **that you are in the land of your foes,**
> **grown old in a foreign land,**

defiled with the dead,
> **accounted with those destined for the netherworld?**

You have forsaken the fountain of wisdom!
> **Had you walked in the way of God,**
> **you would have dwelt in enduring peace.**

Learn where prudence is,
> **where strength, where understanding;**

that you may know also
> **where are length of days, and life,**
> **where light of the eyes, and peace.**

Who has found the place of wisdom,
  who has entered into her treasuries?

The One who knows all things knows her;
  he has probed her by his knowledge—
the One who established the earth for all time,
  and filled it with four-footed beasts;
  he who dismisses the light, and it departs,
  calls it, and it obeys him trembling;
before whom the stars at their posts
  shine and rejoice;
when he calls them, they answer, "Here we are!"
  shining with joy for their Maker.
Such is our God;
  no other is to be compared to him:
he has traced out the whole way of understanding,
  and has given her to Jacob, his servant,
  to Israel, his beloved son.

Since then she has appeared on earth,
  and moved among people.
She is the book of the precepts of God,
  the law that endures forever;
all who cling to her will live,
  but those will die who forsake her.
Turn, O Jacob, and receive her:
  walk by her light toward splendor.
Give not your glory to another,
  your privileges to an alien race.
Blessed are we, O Israel;
  for what pleases God is known to us!

The word of the Lord.

Responsorial Psalm 19

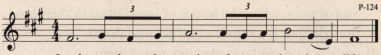

Lord, you have the words of ev-er-last-ing life.

Music: Jay F. Hunstiger, © 1990, administered by Liturgical Press. All rights reserved.

Psalm 19:8, 9, 10, 11

℟. (John 6:68c) **Lord, you have the words of everlasting life.**

The law of the Lord is perfect,
    refreshing the soul;
the decree of the Lord is trustworthy,
    giving wisdom to the simple. ℟.

The precepts of the Lord are right,
    rejoicing the heart;
the command of the Lord is clear,
    enlightening the eye. ℟.

The fear of the Lord is pure,
    enduring forever;
the ordinances of the Lord are true,
    all of them just. ℟.

They are more precious than gold,
    than a heap of purest gold;
sweeter also than syrup
    or honey from the comb. ℟.

Prayer
Let us pray.
Father,
you increase your Church
by continuing to call all people to salvation.
Listen to our prayers
and always watch over those you cleanse in baptism.
We ask this through Christ our Lord. All: **Amen.**

Reading VII (Ezekiel 36:16-17a, 18-28)
A reading from the Book of the Prophet Ezekiel

I shall sprinkle clean water upon you and I shall give you a new heart.

The word of the Lord came to me, saying:
> Son of man, when the house of Israel lived in their land,
> they defiled it by their conduct and deeds.

Therefore I poured out my fury upon them
> because of the blood that they poured out on the ground,
> and because they defiled it with idols.

I scattered them among the nations,
> dispersing them over foreign lands;
> according to their conduct and deeds I judged them.

But when they came among the nations wherever they came,
> they served to profane my holy name,
> because it was said of them: "These are the people of the Lord,
> yet they had to leave their land."

So I have relented because of my holy name
> which the house of Israel profaned
> among the nations where they came.

Therefore say to the house of Israel: Thus says the Lord God:
> Not for your sakes do I act, house of Israel,
> but for the sake of my holy name,
> which you profaned among the nations to which you came.

I will prove the holiness of my great name, profaned among the nations,
> in whose midst you have profaned it.

Thus the nations shall know that I am the Lord, says the Lord God,
> when in their sight I prove my holiness through you.

For I will take you away from among the nations,
> gather you from all the foreign lands,
> and bring you back to your own land.

I will sprinkle clean water upon you
> to cleanse you from all your impurities,
> and from all your idols I will cleanse you.

I will give you a new heart and place a new spirit within you,
  taking from your bodies your stony hearts
  and giving you natural hearts.
I will put my spirit within you and make you live by my statutes,
  careful to observe my decrees.
You shall live in the land I gave your fathers;
  you shall be my people, and I will be your God.
The word of the Lord.

Responsorial Psalm

A *When baptism is celebrated*

Music: Jay F. Hunstiger, © 1984, administered by Liturgical Press. All rights reserved.

Psalm 42:3, 5; 43:3, 4

℟. (42:2) **Like a deer that longs for running streams,**
  my soul longs for you, my God.

Athirst is my soul for God, the living God.
  When shall I go and behold the face of God? ℟.

I went with the throng
  and led them in procession to the house of God,
amid loud cries of joy and thanksgiving,
  with the multitude keeping festival. ℟.

Send forth your light and your fidelity;
  they shall lead me on
and bring me to your holy mountain,
  to your dwelling-place. ℟.

Then will I go in to the altar of God,
  the God of my gladness and joy;

(continued)

April 3

> then will I give you thanks upon the harp,
> > O God, my God! ℟.

B *When baptism is not celebrated*

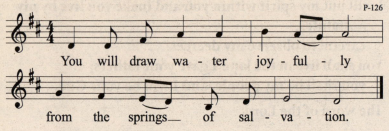

You will draw water joyfully from the springs of salvation.

Music: Jay F. Hunstiger, © 1990, administered by Liturgical Press. All rights reserved.

Isaiah 12:2-3, 4bcd, 5-6

℟. (3) **You will draw water joyfully from the springs of salvation.**

God indeed is my savior;
> I am confident and unafraid.
My strength and my courage is the Lord,
> and he has been my savior.
With joy you will draw water
> at the fountain of salvation. ℟.

Give thanks to the Lord, acclaim his name;
> among the nations make known his deeds,
> proclaim how exalted is his name. ℟.

Sing praise to the Lord for his glorious achievement;
> let this be known throughout all the earth.
Shout with exultation, O city of Zion,
> for great in your midst
> is the Holy One of Israel! ℟.

C *When baptism is not celebrated*

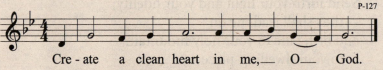

Create a clean heart in me, O God.

Music: Jay F. Hunstiger, © 1990, administered by Liturgical Press. All rights reserved.

Psalm 51:12-13, 14-15, 18-19

℟. (12a) **Create a clean heart in me, O God.**

A clean heart create for me, O God,
 and a steadfast spirit renew within me.
Cast me not out from your presence,
 and your Holy Spirit take not from me. ℟.

Give me back the joy of your salvation,
 and a willing spirit sustain in me.
I will teach transgressors your ways,
 and sinners shall return to you. ℟.

For you are not pleased with sacrifices;
 should I offer a holocaust, you would not accept it.
My sacrifice, O God, is a contrite spirit;
 a heart contrite and humbled, O God, you will not
  spurn. ℟.

Prayer
Let us pray.
God of unchanging power and light,
look with mercy and favor on your entire Church.
Bring lasting salvation to mankind,
so that the world may see
the fallen lifted up,
the old made new,
and all things brought to perfection,
through him who is their origin,
our Lord Jesus Christ,
who lives and reigns for ever and ever. All: **Amen.**

or:

Father,
you teach us in both the Old and the New Testament
to celebrate this passover mystery.
Help us to understand your great love for us.
May the goodness you now show us
confirm our hope in your future mercy.
We ask this through Christ our Lord. All: **Amen.**

Opening Prayer
Lord God,
you have brightened this night
with the radiance of the risen Christ.

Quicken the spirit of sonship in your Church;
renew us in mind and body
to give you whole-hearted service.
Grant this through our Lord Jesus Christ, your Son,
who lives and reigns with you and the Holy Spirit,
one God, for ever and ever. All: **Amen.**

Epistle (Romans 6:3-11)

A reading from the Letter of Saint Paul to the Romans

Christ, raised from the dead, dies no more.

Brothers and sisters:
Are you unaware that we who were baptized into Christ Jesus
   were baptized into his death?
We were indeed buried with him through baptism into death,
   so that, just as Christ was raised from the dead
   by the glory of the Father,
   we too might live in newness of life.

For if we have grown into union with him through a death like his,
   we shall also be united with him in the resurrection.
We know that our old self was crucified with him,
   so that our sinful body might be done away with,
   that we might no longer be in slavery to sin.
For a dead person has been absolved from sin.
If, then, we have died with Christ,
   we believe that we shall also live with him.
We know that Christ, raised from the dead, dies no more;
   death no longer has power over him.
As to his death, he died to sin once and for all;
   as to his life, he lives for God.
Consequently, you too must think of yourselves as being dead to sin
   and living for God in Christ Jesus.

The word of the Lord.

Responsorial Psalm 118

Music: Jay F. Hunstiger, © 1990, administered by Liturgical Press. All rights reserved.

Psalm 118:1-2, 16-17, 22-23

℟. **Alleluia, alleluia, alleluia.**

> Give thanks to the Lord, for he is good,
>> for his mercy endures forever.
>
> Let the house of Israel say,
>> "His mercy endures forever." ℟.
>
> "The right hand of the Lord has struck with power;
>> the right hand of the Lord is exalted.
>
> I shall not die, but live,
>> and declare the works of the Lord." ℟.
>
> The stone which the builders rejected
>> has become the cornerstone.
>
> By the Lord has this been done;
>> it is wonderful in our eyes. ℟.

Gospel C (Luke 24:1-12)

✠ A reading from the holy Gospel according to Luke

All: **Glory to you, Lord.**

Why do you seek the Living One among the dead?

**At daybreak on the first day of the week
the women who had come from Galilee with Jesus
took the spices they had prepared
and went to the tomb.**

They found the stone rolled away from the tomb;
>   but when they entered,
>   they did not find the body of the Lord Jesus.
> While they were puzzling over this, behold,
>   two men in dazzling garments appeared to them.
> They were terrified and bowed their faces to the ground.
> They said to them,
>   "Why do you seek the living one among the dead?
> He is not here, but he has been raised.
> Remember what he said to you while he was still in Galilee,
>   that the Son of Man must be handed over to sinners
>   and be crucified, and rise on the third day."
> And they remembered his words.
> Then they returned from the tomb
>   and announced all these things to the eleven
>   and to all the others.
> The women were Mary Magdalene, Joanna, and Mary the
>   mother of James;
>   the others who accompanied them also told this to
>   the apostles,
>   but their story seemed like nonsense
>   and they did not believe them.
> But Peter got up and ran to the tomb,
>   bent down, and saw the burial cloths alone;
>   then he went home amazed at what had happened.

The Gospel of the Lord. **All: Praise to you, Lord Jesus Christ.**

PART THREE: LITURGY OF BAPTISM

If there are candidates to be baptized:

Dear friends in Christ,
as our brothers and sisters approach the waters of rebirth,
let us help them by our prayers
and ask God, our almighty Father,
to support them with his mercy and love.

If the font is to be blessed, but there is no one to be baptized:

Dear friends in Christ,
let us ask God, the almighty Father,

to bless this font,
that those reborn in it
may be made one with his adopted children in Christ.

39. The litany is sung by two cantors. All present stand (as is customary during the Easter season) and answer.

The Litany of the Saints

If there are candidates to be baptized, the priest, says the following prayer:

Almighty and eternal God,
be present in this sacrament of your love.
Send your Spirit of adoption
on those to be born again in baptism.
And may the work of our humble ministry
be brought to perfection by your mighty power.
We ask this through Christ our Lord. All: **Amen.**

Blessing of Water

Father, you give us grace through sacramental signs,
    which tell us of the wonders of your unseen power.
In baptism we use your gift of water,
    which you have made a rich symbol
    of the grace you give us in this sacrament.
At the very dawn of creation
    your Spirit breathed on the waters,
    making them the wellspring of all holiness.
The waters of the great flood
    you made a sign of the waters of baptism,
    that make an end of sin and a new beginning of goodness.
Through the waters of the Red Sea
    you led Israel out of slavery,
    to be an image of God's holy people,
    set free from sin by baptism.
In the waters of the Jordan
    your Son was baptized by John
    and anointed with the Spirit.
Your Son willed that water and blood
    should flow from his side
    as he hung upon the cross.
After his resurrection he told his disciples:
    "Go out and teach all nations,
    baptizing them in the name of the Father
    and of the Son and of the Holy Spirit."
Father, look now with love upon your Church,
    and unseal for her the fountain of baptism.

By the power of the Holy Spirit
   give to the water of this font
   the grace of your Son.
You created man in your own likeness:
   cleanse him from sin in a new birth of innocence
   by water and the Spirit.
We ask you, Father, with your Son
   to send the Holy Spirit upon the waters of this font.
May all who are buried with Christ
   in the death of baptism
   rise also with him to newness of life.
We ask this through Christ our Lord. All: **Amen.**

Celebration of Baptism

Renunciation of Sin and Profession of Faith

Dear parents and godparents: You have come here to present these children for baptism. By water and the Holy Spirit they are to receive the gift of new life from God, who is love.

On your part, you must make it your constant care to bring them up in the practice of the faith. See that the divine life which God gives them is kept safe from the poison of sin, to grow always stronger in their hearts.

If your faith makes you ready to accept this responsibility, renew now the vows of your own baptism. Reject sin; profess your faith in Christ Jesus. This is the faith of the Church. This is the faith in which these children are about to be baptized.

The celebrant questions the candidates and the parents and godparents:

A Celebrant: Do you reject Satan?
Candidates, parents, and godparents: **I do.**

Celebrant: And all his works?
Candidates, parents, and godparents: **I do.**

Celebrant: And all his empty promises?
Candidates, parents, and godparents: **I do.**

B Celebrant: Do you reject sin, so as to live in the freedom of God's children?
Candidates, parents, and godparents: **I do.**

Celebrant: Do you reject the glamor of evil, and refuse to be mastered by sin?
Candidates, parents, and godparents: **I do.**

Celebrant: Do you reject Satan, father of sin and prince of darkness?
Candidates, parents, and godparents: **I do.**

Next the celebrant asks for the threefold profession of faith from the candidates, parents, and godparents:

Celebrant: Do you believe in God, the Father almighty, creator of heaven and earth?

Candidates, parents, and godparents: **I do.**

Celebrant: Do you believe in Jesus Christ, his only Son, our Lord, who was born of the Virgin Mary, was crucified, died, and was buried, rose from the dead, and is now seated at the right hand of the Father?

Candidates, parents, and godparents: **I do.**

Celebrant: Do you believe in the Holy Spirit, the holy catholic Church, the communion of saints, the forgiveness of sins, the resurrection of the body, and life everlasting?

Candidates, parents, and godparents: **I do.**

Baptism of Adults

Celebrant: Is it your will to be baptized in the faith of the Church, which we have all professed with you?

Candidate: **It is.**

He baptizes the candidate, saying:

N., I baptize you in the name of the Father,

He immerses the candidate or pours water upon him.

and of the Son,

He immerses the candidate or pours water upon him a second time.

and of the Holy Spirit.

He immerses the candidate or pours water upon him a third time. He asks the same question and performs the same action for each candidate.

After each baptism it is appropriate for the people to sing a short acclamation:

**This is the fountain of life,
water made holy by the suffering of Christ, washing all the world.
You who are washed in this water have hope of heaven's kingdom.**

Baptism of Children

Celebrant: Is it your will that N. should be baptized in the faith of the Church, which we have all professed with you?

Parents and godparents: **It is.**

He baptizes the child, saying:

N., I baptize you in the name of the Father,

He immerses the child or pours water upon it.

and of the Son,

He immerses the child or pours water upon it a second time.

and of the Holy Spirit.

He immerses the child or pours water upon it a third time. He asks the same question and performs the same action for each child.

After each baptism it is appropriate for the people to sing a short acclamation:

**This is the fountain of life,
water made holy by the suffering of Christ, washing all the world.
You who are washed in this water have hope of heaven's kingdom.**

Anointing with Chrism
God the Father of our Lord Jesus Christ has freed you from sin, given you a new birth by water and the Holy Spirit, and welcomed you into his holy people. He now anoints you with the chrism of salvation. As Christ was anointed Priest, Prophet, and King, so may you live always as members of his body, sharing everlasting life. All: **Amen.**

Clothing with the White Garment
(N., N.,) you have become a new creation, and have clothed yourselves in Christ. See in this white garment the outward sign of your Christian dignity. With your family and friends to help you by word and example, bring that dignity unstained into the everlasting life of heaven.
All: **Amen.**

Celebration of Confirmation *
If the bishop has conferred baptism, he should now also confer confirmation. If the bishop is not present, the priest who conferred baptism and received the candidates into full communion is authorized to confirm. The infants who were baptized during this celebration are not confirmed. However, the newly baptized children who have gone through the RCIA process are confirmed.

Invitation
My dear friends, let us pray to God our Father, that he will pour out the Holy Spirit on these candidates for confirmation to strengthen them with his gifts and anoint them to be more like Christ, the Son of God.

Laying on of Hands
**All-powerful God, Father of our Lord Jesus Christ,
by water and the Holy Spirit
you freed your sons
and daughters from sin and gave them new life.
Send your Holy Spirit upon them to be their helper and guide.
Give them the spirit of wisdom and understanding,
the spirit of right judgment and courage,
the spirit of knowledge and reverence.**

*From the RCIA, nos. 588–591.

Fill them with the spirit of wonder and awe in your presence.
We ask this through Christ our Lord. All: **Amen.**

ANOINTING WITH CHRISM
N., be sealed with the Gift of the Holy Spirit.
Newly confirmed: **Amen.**

The minister of the sacrament adds: Peace be with you.
Newly confirmed: **And also with you.**

45. If no one is to be baptized and the font is not to be blessed, the priest blesses the water with the following prayer:

My brothers and sisters, let us ask the Lord our God
to bless this water he has created,
which we shall use to recall our baptism.
May he renew us and keep us faithful to the Spirit
we have all received.

All pray silently for a short while. With hands joined, the priest continues:

Lord our God,
this night your people keep prayerful vigil.
Be with us as we recall the wonder of our creation
and the greater wonder of our redemption.
Bless this water: it makes the seed to grow,
it refreshes us and makes us clean.
You have made of it a servant of your loving kindness:
through water you set your people free,
and quenched their thirst in the desert.
With water the prophets announced a new covenant
that you would make with man.
By water, made holy by Christ in the Jordan,
you made our sinful nature new in the bath that gives rebirth.
Let this water remind us of our baptism;
let us share the joys of our brothers who are baptized this Easter.
We ask this through Christ our Lord. All: **Amen.**

RENEWAL OF BAPTISMAL PROMISES
Dear friends,
through the paschal mystery,
we have been buried with Christ in baptism,
so that we may rise with him to a new life.
Now that we have completed our lenten observance,
let us renew the promises we made in baptism
when we rejected Satan and his works,
and promised to serve God faithfully
in his holy catholic Church.
And so:

A Priest: Do you reject Satan? All: **I do.**
Priest: And all his works? All: **I do.**
Priest: And all his empty promises? All: **I do.**

or:

B Priest: Do you reject sin, so as to live in the freedom of God's children?
All: **I do.**

Priest: Do you reject the glamor of evil, and refuse to be mastered by sin?
All: **I do.**

Priest: Do you reject Satan, father of sin and prince of darkness?
All: **I do.**

Then the priest continues:
Priest: Do you believe in God, the Father almighty, creator of heaven and earth?
All: **I do.**

Priest: Do you believe in Jesus Christ, his only Son, our Lord, who was born of the Virgin Mary, was crucified, died, and was buried, rose from the dead, and is now seated at the right hand of the Father?
All: **I do.**

Priest: Do you believe in the Holy Spirit, the holy catholic Church, the communion of saints, the forgiveness of sins, the resurrection of the body, and life everlasting?
All: **I do.**

God, the all-powerful Father of our Lord Jesus Christ,
has given us a new birth by water and the Holy Spirit,
and forgiven all our sins.
May he also keep us faithful to our Lord Jesus Christ
for ever and ever. All: **Amen.**

PRAYER OF THE FAITHFUL

PART FOUR: LITURGY OF THE EUCHARIST

PRAYER OVER THE GIFTS
Lord,
accept the prayers and offerings of your people.
With your help
may this Easter mystery of our redemption
bring to perfection the saving work you have begun in us.
We ask this through Christ our Lord. All: **Amen.**

Communion Antiphon (1 Corinthians 5:7-8)
Christ has become our paschal sacrifice; let us feast with the unleavened bread of sincerity and truth, alleluia.

Prayer after Communion
Lord,
you have nourished us with your Easter sacraments.
Fill us with your Spirit,
and make us one in peace and love.
We ask this through Christ our Lord. All: **Amen.**

Easter Sunday

THE RESURRECTION OF THE LORD

April 4, 2010

Reflection on the Gospel

Even on this Easter day when we rejoice in the risen life of Jesus, we are reminded that resurrection has its cost: self-emptying for the sake of others. The paradox of Christianity is that dying to self isn't something to avoid, but it is the way we remove the stone that blocks our own hearts from receiving new life. We need to see beyond the obvious—an empty tomb and the demands of self-emptying—to the glory that God has bestowed through Christ Jesus.

- *"Seeing" and "believing" in Jesus' resurrection means to me . . . The way I try to live this mystery is . . .*

—Living Liturgy™, *Easter Sunday 2010*

Entrance Antiphon (Psalm 139:18, 5-6)
I have risen: I am with you once more; you placed your hand on me to keep me safe. How great is the depth of your wisdom, alleluia.

or:

(Luke 24:34; *see* Revelation 1:6)
The Lord has indeed risen, alleluia. Glory and kingship be his for ever and ever.

Opening Prayer

God our Father,
by raising Christ your Son
you conquered the power of death
and opened for us the way to eternal life.
Let our celebration today
raise us up and renew our lives
by the Spirit that is within us.
Grant this through our Lord Jesus Christ, your Son,
who lives and reigns with you and the Holy Spirit,
one God, for ever and ever. All: **Amen.**

Reading I (L 42) (Acts of the Apostles 10:34a, 37-43)

A reading from the Acts of the Apostles

We ate and drank with him after he rose from the dead.

Peter proceeded to speak and said:
  "You know what has happened all over Judea,
  beginning in Galilee after the baptism
  that John preached,
  how God anointed Jesus of Nazareth
  with the Holy Spirit and power.
He went about doing good
  and healing all those oppressed by the devil,
  for God was with him.
We are witnesses of all that he did
  both in the country of the Jews and in Jerusalem.
They put him to death by hanging him on a tree.
This man God raised on the third day and granted that
     he be visible,
  not to all the people, but to us,
  the witnesses chosen by God in advance,
  who ate and drank with him after he rose from the dead.
He commissioned us to preach to the people
  and testify that he is the one appointed by God
  as judge of the living and the dead.
To him all the prophets bear witness,
  that everyone who believes in him
  will receive forgiveness of sins through his name."

The word of the Lord. All: **Thanks be to God.**

Responsorial Psalm 118

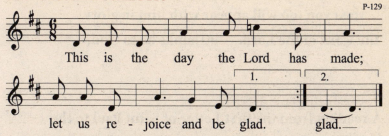

Music: Jay F. Hunstiger, © 1990, administered by Liturgical Press. All rights reserved.

Psalm 118:1-2, 16-17, 22-23

℟. (24) **This is the day the Lord has made; let us rejoice and be glad.** *or:* ℟. **Alleluia.**

Give thanks to the LORD, for he is good,
    for his mercy endures forever.
Let the house of Israel say,
    "His mercy endures forever." ℟.

"The right hand of the LORD has struck with power;
    the right hand of the LORD is exalted.
I shall not die, but live,
    and declare the works of the LORD." ℟.

The stone which the builders rejected
    has become the cornerstone.
By the LORD has this been done;
    it is wonderful in our eyes. ℟.

Reading II

A (Colossians 3:1-4)

A reading from the Letter of Saint Paul to the Colossians

Seek what is above, where Christ is.

Brothers and sisters:
If then you were raised with Christ, seek what is above,
    where Christ is seated at the right hand of God.
Think of what is above, not of what is on earth.
For you have died, and your life is hidden with Christ
    in God.

When Christ your life appears,
　　then you too will appear with him in glory.

The word of the Lord. All: Thanks be to God.

or:

B (1 Corinthians 5:6b-8)

A reading from the first Letter of Saint Paul to the Corinthians

Clear out the old yeast, so that you may become a fresh batch of dough.

Brothers and sisters:
Do you not know that a little yeast leavens all the dough?
Clear out the old yeast,
　　so that you may become a fresh batch of dough,
　　inasmuch as you are unleavened.
For our paschal lamb, Christ, has been sacrificed.
Therefore, let us celebrate the feast,
　　not with the old yeast, the yeast of malice and
　　　　wickedness,
　　but with the unleavened bread of sincerity and truth.

The word of the Lord. All: Thanks be to God.

SEQUENCE
Victimae paschali laudes

Christians, to the Paschal Victim
　　Offer your thankful praises!
A Lamb the sheep redeems;
　　Christ, who only is sinless,
　　Reconciles sinners to the Father.
Death and life have contended in that combat stupendous:
　　The Prince of life, who died, reigns immortal.
Speak, Mary, declaring
　　What you saw, wayfaring.
"The tomb of Christ, who is living,
　　The glory of Jesus' resurrection;

Bright angels attesting,
  The shroud and napkin resting.
Yes, Christ my hope is arisen;
  To Galilee he goes before you."
Christ indeed from death is risen, our new life obtaining.
  Have mercy, victor King, ever reigning!
  Amen. Alleluia.

Gospel (John 20:1-9)
Alternative readings can be found in the Lectionary for Mass.
Alleluia (*See* 1 Corinthians 5:7b-8a)
℣. Alleluia, alleluia. ℟. **Alleluia, alleluia.**
℣. Christ, our paschal lamb, has been sacrificed;
   let us then feast with joy in the Lord. ℟.

✠ **A reading from the holy Gospel according to John**

All: **Glory to you, Lord.**

He had to rise from the dead.

**On the first day of the week,
  Mary of Magdala came to the tomb early in the morning,
  while it was still dark,
  and saw the stone removed from the tomb.
So she ran and went to Simon Peter
  and to the other disciple whom Jesus loved, and
      told them,
  "They have taken the Lord from the tomb,
  and we don't know where they put him."
So Peter and the other disciple went out and came to
      the tomb.
They both ran, but the other disciple ran faster than Peter
  and arrived at the tomb first;
  he bent down and saw the burial cloths there, but did
      not go in.
When Simon Peter arrived after him,
  he went into the tomb and saw the burial cloths there,
  and the cloth that had covered his head,
  not with the burial cloths but rolled up in a separate
      place.**

Then the other disciple also went in,
> the one who had arrived at the tomb first,
> and he saw and believed.
For they did not yet understand the Scripture
> that he had to rise from the dead.

The Gospel of the Lord. All: **Praise to you, Lord Jesus Christ.**

Renewal of Baptismal Promises
The renewal of baptismal promises takes place at all Masses today. The form followed is the same as at the Easter Vigil, *see* nos. 46–47, page •••.

Prayer over the Gifts
Lord,
with Easter joy we offer you the sacrifice
by which your Church is reborn and nourished,
through Christ our Lord. All: **Amen.**

Communion Antiphon (1 Corinthians 5:7-8)
Christ has become our paschal sacrifice; let us feast with the unleavened bread of sincerity and truth, alleluia.

Prayer after Communion
Father of love
watch over your Church
and bring us to the glory of the resurrection
promised by this Easter sacrament.
We ask this in the name of Jesus the Lord. All: **Amen.**

Second Sunday of Easter
(or DIVINE MERCY SUNDAY)

April 11, 2010

Reflection on the Gospel

Three times the risen Lord addresses the gathered disciples, "Peace be with you." What is this peace he brings? It is a peace that allays fears, empowers forgiveness, and prompts us to accept the reality of suffering and death as doorways to new life. This peace is new life: the Spirit breathed into us by the risen Lord. It is not a peace we can make for ourselves. It is a peace that is the gift of the risen Lord.

- *Where God is calling me to receive the peace of the risen Lord is . . . to extend this peace is . . .*

—Living Liturgy™, *Second Sunday of Easter 2010*

Entrance Antiphon (1 Peter 2:2)
Like newborn children you should thirst for milk, on which your spirit can grow to strength, alleluia.

or:

(4 Esdras 2:36-37)
Rejoice to the full in the glory that is yours, and give thanks to God who called you to his kingdom, alleluia.

Opening Prayer
God of mercy,
you wash away our sins in water,
you give us new birth in the Spirit,
and redeem us in the blood of Christ.
As we celebrate Christ's resurrection
increase our awareness of these blessings,
and renew your gift of life within us.
We ask this through our Lord Jesus Christ, your Son,
who lives and reigns with you and the Holy Spirit,
one God, for ever and ever. All: **Amen.**

Reading I (L 45-C) (Acts of the Apostles 5:12-16)
A reading from the Acts of the Apostles

More than ever, believers in the Lord, great numbers of men and women, were added to them.

**Many signs and wonders were done among the people
   at the hands of the apostles.
They were all together in Solomon's portico.
None of the others dared to join them, but the people
   esteemed them.
Yet more than ever, believers in the Lord,
   great numbers of men and women, were added to them.**

Thus they even carried the sick out into the streets
   and laid them on cots and mats
   so that when Peter came by,
   at least his shadow might fall on one or another of them.
A large number of people from the towns
   in the vicinity of Jerusalem also gathered,
   bringing the sick and those disturbed by unclean spirits,
   and they were all cured.

The word of the Lord. All: Thanks be to God.

Responsorial Psalm 118

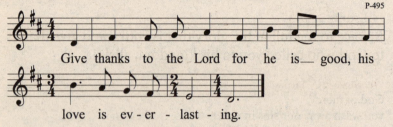

Music: Jay F. Hunstiger, © 1990, administered by Liturgical Press. All rights reserved.

Psalm 118:2-4, 13-15, 22-24

℟. (1) **Give thanks to the Lord for he is good, his love is everlasting.** *or:* ℟. **Alleluia.**

Let the house of Israel say,
   "His mercy endures forever."
Let the house of Aaron say,
   "His mercy endures forever."
Let those who fear the Lord say,
   "His mercy endures forever." ℟.

I was hard pressed and was falling,
   but the Lord helped me.
My strength and my courage is the Lord,
   and he has been my savior.
The joyful shout of victory
   in the tents of the just. ℟.

The stone which the builders rejected
   has become the cornerstone.

By the L ORD has this been done;
   it is wonderful in our eyes.
This is the day the L ORD has made;
   let us be glad and rejoice in it. R⁄.

R EADING II (Revelation 1:9-11a, 12-13, 17-19)
A reading from the Book of Revelation

I was dead, but now I am alive forever and ever.

I, John, your brother, who share with you
   the distress, the kingdom, and the endurance we have
      in Jesus,
   found myself on the island called Patmos
   because I proclaimed God's word and gave testimony
      to Jesus.
I was caught up in spirit on the Lord's day
   and heard behind me a voice as loud as a trumpet,
      which said,
"Write on a scroll what you see."
Then I turned to see whose voice it was that spoke to me,
   and when I turned, I saw seven gold lampstands
   and in the midst of the lampstands one like a son of man,
   wearing an ankle-length robe, with a gold sash
      around his chest.

When I caught sight of him, I fell down at his feet as
      though dead.
He touched me with his right hand and said, "Do not be
      afraid.
I am the first and the last, the one who lives.
Once I was dead, but now I am alive forever and ever.
I hold the keys to death and the netherworld.
Write down, therefore, what you have seen,
   and what is happening, and what will happen
      afterwards."

The word of the Lord. All: Thanks be to God.

GOSPEL (John 20:19-31)
ALLELUIA (John 20:29)

℣. Alleluia, alleluia. ℟. **Alleluia, alleluia.**
℣. You believe in me, Thomas, because you have seen me,
   says the Lord;
   blessed are they who have not seen me, but still believe! ℟.

✠ **A reading from the holy Gospel according to John**

All: **Glory to you, Lord.**

Eight days later Jesus came and stood in their midst.

On the evening of that first day of the week,
   when the doors were locked, where the disciples were,
   for fear of the Jews,
   Jesus came and stood in their midst
   and said to them, "Peace be with you."
When he had said this, he showed them his hands and
   his side.
The disciples rejoiced when they saw the Lord.
Jesus said to them again, "Peace be with you.
As the Father has sent me, so I send you."
And when he had said this, he breathed on them and
   said to them,
   "Receive the Holy Spirit.
Whose sins you forgive are forgiven them,
   and whose sins you retain are retained."

Thomas, called Didymus, one of the Twelve,
   was not with them when Jesus came.
So the other disciples said to him, "We have seen the Lord."
But he said to them,
   "Unless I see the mark of the nails in his hands
   and put my finger into the nailmarks
   and put my hand into his side, I will not believe."

Now a week later his disciples were again inside
   and Thomas was with them.
Jesus came, although the doors were locked,
   and stood in their midst and said, "Peace be with you."

Then he said to Thomas, "Put your finger here and see
 my hands,
 and bring your hand and put it into my side,
 and do not be unbelieving, but believe."
Thomas answered and said to him, "My Lord and my God!"
Jesus said to him, "Have you come to believe because
 you have seen me?
Blessed are those who have not seen and have believed."
Now Jesus did many other signs in the presence of his
 disciples
 that are not written in this book.
But these are written that you may come to believe
 that Jesus is the Christ, the Son of God,
 and that through this belief you may have life in his
 name.

The Gospel of the Lord. All: Praise to you, Lord Jesus Christ.

Prayer over the Gifts
Lord,
through faith and baptism
we have become a new creation.
Accept the offerings of your people
(and of those born again in baptism)
and bring us to eternal happiness.
Grant this through Christ our Lord. All: **Amen.**

Communion Antiphon (See John 20:27)
Jesus spoke to Thomas: Put your hand here, and see the place of the nails. Doubt no longer, but believe, alleluia.

Prayer after Communion
Almighty God,
may the Easter sacraments we have received
live for ever in our minds and hearts.
We ask this through Christ our Lord. All: **Amen.**

Third Sunday of Easter

April 18, 2010

Reflection on the Gospel

The two scenes in the gospel capture two different but interrelated aspects of the Easter mystery. The first scene (miraculous catch of fish) dramatizes what God gives us—abundance of new life. The second scene (encounter between Jesus and Peter) dramatizes our response—love that overflows in faithfully following the risen Christ even to the point of death. We can give our lives because we have first been given life by God.

- *How I have responded to God's abundance to me is . . .*

—Living Liturgy™, *Third Sunday of Easter 2010*

Entrance Antiphon (Psalm 65:1-2)
Let all the earth cry out to God with joy; praise the glory of his name; proclaim his glorious praise, alleluia.

Opening Prayer
God our Father,
may we look forward with hope to our resurrection,
for you have made us your sons and daughters,
and restored the joy of our youth.
We ask this through our Lord Jesus Christ, your Son,
who lives and reigns with you and the Holy Spirit,
one God, for ever and ever. All: **Amen.**

Reading I (L 48-C) (Acts of the Apostles 5:27-32, 40b-41)
A reading from the Acts of the Apostles

We are witnesses of these words as is the Holy Spirit.

**When the captain and the court officers had brought the apostles in
and made them stand before the Sanhedrin,
the high priest questioned them,
"We gave you strict orders, did we not,
to stop teaching in that name?**

Yet you have filled Jerusalem with your teaching
   and want to bring this man's blood upon us."
But Peter and the apostles said in reply,
   "We must obey God rather than men.
The God of our ancestors raised Jesus,
   though you had him killed by hanging him on a tree.
God exalted him at his right hand as leader and savior
   to grant Israel repentance and forgiveness of sins.
We are witnesses of these things,
   as is the Holy Spirit whom God has given to those
      who obey him."
The Sanhedrin ordered the apostles
   to stop speaking in the name of Jesus, and dismissed
      them.
So they left the presence of the Sanhedrin,
   rejoicing that they had been found worthy
   to suffer dishonor for the sake of the name.

The word of the Lord. All: Thanks be to God.

RESPONSORIAL PSALM 30

P-496

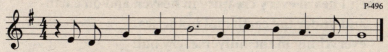

I will praise you, Lord, for you have res-cued me.

Music: Jay F. Hunstiger, © 1990, administered by Liturgical Press. All rights reserved.

Psalm 30:2, 4, 5-6, 11-12, 13

℟. (2a) **I will praise you, Lord, for you have rescued me.**
   or: ℟. **Alleluia.**

I will extol you, O LORD, for you drew me clear
   and did not let my enemies rejoice over me.
O LORD, you brought me up from the netherworld;
   you preserved me from among those going down into
      the pit. ℟.

Sing praise to the LORD, you his faithful ones,
   and give thanks to his holy name.

> For his anger lasts but a moment;
>> a lifetime, his good will.
> At nightfall, weeping enters in,
>> but with the dawn, rejoicing. ℟.
>
> Hear, O Lord, and have pity on me;
>> O Lord, be my helper.
> You changed my mourning into dancing;
>> O Lord, my God, forever will I give you thanks. ℟.

Reading II (Revelation 5:11-14)
A reading from the Book of Revelation

Worthy is the Lamb that was slain to receive power and riches.

**I, John, looked and heard the voices of many angels
who surrounded the throne
and the living creatures and the elders.
They were countless in number, and they cried out in a loud voice:
"Worthy is the Lamb that was slain
to receive power and riches, wisdom and strength,
honor and glory and blessing."
Then I heard every creature in heaven and on earth
and under the earth and in the sea,
everything in the universe, cry out:
"To the one who sits on the throne and to the Lamb
be blessing and honor, glory and might,
forever and ever."
The four living creatures answered, "Amen,"
and the elders fell down and worshiped.**

The word of the Lord. All: **Thanks be to God.**

Gospel (John 21:1-19) *or* Shorter Form [ ] (John 21:1-14)
Alleluia
℣. Alleluia, alleluia. ℟. **Alleluia, alleluia.**
℣. Christ is risen, creator of all;
   he has shown pity on all people. ℟.

✠ **A reading from the holy Gospel according to John**

All: **Glory to you, Lord.**

Jesus came and took the bread and gave it to them and in like manner the fish.

[At that time, Jesus revealed himself again to his disciples
 at the Sea of Tiberias.
He revealed himself in this way.
Together were Simon Peter, Thomas called Didymus,
 Nathanael from Cana in Galilee,
 Zebedee's sons, and two others of his disciples.
Simon Peter said to them, "I am going fishing."
They said to him, "We also will come with you."
So they went out and got into the boat,
 but that night they caught nothing.
When it was already dawn, Jesus was standing on the shore;
 but the disciples did not realize that it was Jesus.
Jesus said to them, "Children, have you caught anything
 to eat?"
They answered him, "No."
So he said to them, "Cast the net over the right side of
 the boat
 and you will find something."
So they cast it, and were not able to pull it in
 because of the number of fish.
So the disciple whom Jesus loved said to Peter, "It is the
 Lord."
When Simon Peter heard that it was the Lord,
 he tucked in his garment, for he was lightly clad,
 and jumped into the sea.
The other disciples came in the boat,
 for they were not far from shore, only about a hundred
 yards,
 dragging the net with the fish.
When they climbed out on shore,
 they saw a charcoal fire with fish on it and bread.

Jesus said to them, "Bring some of the fish you just caught."
So Simon Peter went over and dragged the net ashore
 full of one hundred fifty-three large fish.
Even though there were so many, the net was not torn.
Jesus said to them, "Come, have breakfast."
And none of the disciples dared to ask him, "Who are you?"
 because they realized it was the Lord.
Jesus came over and took the bread and gave it to them,
 and in like manner the fish.
This was now the third time Jesus was revealed to his
 disciples
 after being raised from the dead.]

When they had finished breakfast, Jesus said to Simon
 Peter,
 "Simon, son of John, do you love me more than these?"
Simon Peter answered him, "Yes, Lord, you know that
 I love you."
Jesus said to him, "Feed my lambs."
He then said to Simon Peter a second time,
 "Simon, son of John, do you love me?"
Simon Peter answered him, "Yes, Lord, you know that
 I love you."
Jesus said to him, "Tend my sheep."
Jesus said to him the third time,
 "Simon, son of John, do you love me?"
Peter was distressed that Jesus had said to him a third time,
 "Do you love me?" and he said to him,
 "Lord, you know everything; you know that I love you."
Jesus said to him, "Feed my sheep.
Amen, amen, I say to you, when you were younger,
 you used to dress yourself and go where you wanted;
 but when you grow old, you will stretch out your hands,
 and someone else will dress you
 and lead you where you do not want to go."

He said this signifying by what kind of death he would
   glorify God.
And when he had said this, he said to him, "Follow me."

The Gospel of the Lord. All: **Praise to you, Lord Jesus Christ.**

Prayer over the Gifts
Lord,
receive these gifts from your Church.
May the great joy you give us
come to perfection in heaven.
Grant this through Christ our Lord. All: **Amen.**

Communion Antiphon Year C (*See* John 21:12-13)
Jesus said to his disciples: Come and eat. And he took the bread, and gave it to them, alleluia.

Prayer after Communion
Lord,
look on your people with kindness
and by these Easter mysteries
bring us to the glory of the resurrection.
We ask this in the name of Jesus the Lord. All: **Amen.**

Fourth Sunday of Easter

April 25, 2010

Reflection on the Gospel

The gospel conveys Jesus' great, tender care and concern for his "sheep." This care does not keep his followers from "violent abuse" (first reading) or "great distress" (second reading). It does assure them of protection in the midst of persecution ("no one can take them out of my hand") and of eternal life ("they shall never perish"). But this assurance only comes when we followers of Jesus "hear [his] voice" and live out of the personal relationship God offers us.

- *Where Jesus my Good Shepherd is asking me to follow him is . . .*

—*Living Liturgy™, Fourth Sunday of Easter 2010*

Entrance Antiphon (Psalm 32:5-6)
The earth is full of the goodness of the Lord; by the word of the Lord the heavens were made, alleluia.

Opening Prayer
Almighty and ever-living God,
give us new strength
from the courage of Christ our shepherd,
and lead us to join the saints in heaven,
where he lives and reigns with you and the Holy Spirit,
one God, for ever and ever. All: **Amen.**

Reading I (L 51-C) (Acts of the Apostles 13:14, 43-52)
A reading from the Acts of the Apostles

We now turn to the Gentiles.

**Paul and Barnabas continued on from Perga
and reached Antioch in Pisidia.
On the sabbath they entered the synagogue and took
their seats.
Many Jews and worshipers who were converts to Judaism
followed Paul and Barnabas, who spoke to them
and urged them to remain faithful to the grace of God.**

**On the following sabbath almost the whole city gathered
to hear the word of the Lord.
When the Jews saw the crowds, they were filled with
jealousy
and with violent abuse contradicted what Paul said.
Both Paul and Barnabas spoke out boldly and said,
"It was necessary that the word of God be spoken to
you first,
but since you reject it
and condemn yourselves as unworthy of eternal life,
we now turn to the Gentiles.**

For so the Lord has commanded us,
>   *I have made you a light to the Gentiles,*
>   *that you may be an instrument of salvation*
>   *to the ends of the earth."*

The Gentiles were delighted when they heard this
    and glorified the word of the Lord.
All who were destined for eternal life came to believe,
    and the word of the Lord continued to spread
    through the whole region.
The Jews, however, incited the women of prominence
        who were worshipers
    and the leading men of the city,
    stirred up a persecution against Paul and Barnabas,
    and expelled them from their territory.
So they shook the dust from their feet in protest against them,
    and went to Iconium.
The disciples were filled with joy and the Holy Spirit.

The word of the Lord. All: Thanks be to God.

Responsorial Psalm 100

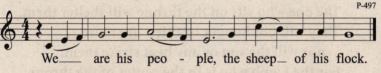

We are his peo-ple, the sheep of his flock.

Music: Jay F. Hunstiger, © 1991, administered by Liturgical Press. All rights reserved.

Psalm 100:1-2, 3, 5

℟. (3c) **We are his people, the sheep of his flock.** *or:*
    ℟. **Alleluia.**

Sing joyfully to the Lord, all you lands;
    serve the Lord with gladness;
    come before him with joyful song. ℟.

Know that the Lord is God;
    he made us, his we are;
    his people, the flock he tends. ℟.

The Lord is good:
　　his kindness endures forever,
　　and his faithfulness, to all generations. ℟.

Reading II (Revelation 7:9, 14b-17)
A reading from the Book of Revelation

The Lamb will shepherd them and lead them to springs of life-giving water.

**I, John, had a vision of a great multitude,
　　which no one could count,
　　from every nation, race, people, and tongue.
They stood before the throne and before the Lamb,
　　wearing white robes and holding palm branches in their hands.
Then one of the elders said to me,
　　"These are the ones who have survived the time of great distress;
they have washed their robes
and made them white in the blood of the Lamb.**

　　**"For this reason they stand before God's throne
　　　　and worship him day and night in his temple.
　　The one who sits on the throne will shelter them.
　　They will not hunger or thirst anymore,
　　　　nor will the sun or any heat strike them.
　　For the Lamb who is in the center of the throne
　　　　will shepherd them
　　　　and lead them to springs of life-giving water,
　　　　and God will wipe away every tear from their eyes."**

The word of the Lord. All: **Thanks be to God.**

Gospel (John 10:27-30)
Alleluia (John 10:14)
℣. Alleluia, alleluia. ℟. **Alleluia, alleluia.**
℣. I am the good shepherd, says the Lord;
　　I know my sheep, and mine know me. ℟.

✢ **A reading from the holy Gospel according to John**
All: **Glory to you, Lord.**
I give my sheep eternal life.

**Jesus said:
"My sheep hear my voice;
  I know them, and they follow me.
I give them eternal life, and they shall never perish.
No one can take them out of my hand.
My Father, who has given them to me, is greater than all,
  and no one can take them out of the Father's hand.
The Father and I are one."

The Gospel of the Lord.** All: **Praise to you, Lord Jesus Christ.**

Prayer over the Gifts
Lord,
restore us by these Easter mysteries.
May the continuing work of our Redeemer
bring us eternal joy.
We ask this through Christ our Lord. All: **Amen.**

Communion Antiphon
The Good Shepherd is risen! He who laid down his life for his sheep, who died for his flock, he is risen, alleluia.

Prayer after Communion
Father, eternal shepherd,
watch over the flock redeemed by the blood of Christ
and lead us to the promised land.
Grant this through Christ our Lord. All: **Amen.**

Fifth Sunday of Easter

May 2, 2010

Reflection on the Gospel

The "new commandment" Jesus gives is not simply to "love" but to love as he has loved us. With respect to loving, "how far?" is the question. Jesus' commandment to love requires a new way of living: regard for the other without counting the cost to ourselves. Jesus' death simultaneously reveals the full measure of his love and his glory. Our death—dying to self—reveals the full measure of our love for others and leads to a share in Jesus' glory. Love is the doorway to glory.

- *As I understand it, the newness of Jesus' commandment to love is . . .*

—Living Liturgy™, *Fifth Sunday of Easter 2010*

Entrance Antiphon (Psalm 97:1-2)

Sing to the Lord a new song, for he has done marvelous deeds; he has revealed to the nations his saving power, alleluia.

Opening Prayer

God our Father,
look upon us with love.
You redeem us and make us your children in Christ.
Give us true freedom
and bring us to the inheritance you promised.
We ask this through our Lord Jesus Christ, your Son,
who lives and reigns with you and the Holy Spirit,
one God, for ever and ever. All: **Amen.**

Reading I (L 54-C) (Acts of the Apostles 14:21-27)

A reading from the Acts of the Apostles

They called the Church together and reported what God had done with them.

After Paul and Barnabas had proclaimed the good news
  to that city
  and made a considerable number of disciples,
    they returned to Lystra and to Iconium and to Antioch.
They strengthened the spirits of the disciples
  and exhorted them to persevere in the faith, saying,
    "It is necessary for us to undergo many hardships
    to enter the kingdom of God."
They appointed elders for them in each church and,
  with prayer and fasting, commended them to the Lord
  in whom they had put their faith.
Then they traveled through Pisidia and reached Pamphylia.
After proclaiming the word at Perga they went down to
    Attalia.
From there they sailed to Antioch,
  where they had been commended to the grace of God
  for the work they had now accomplished.
And when they arrived, they called the church together
  and reported what God had done with them
  and how he had opened the door of faith to the Gentiles.

The word of the Lord. All: Thanks be to God.

Responsorial Psalm 145

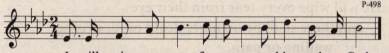

I will praise your name for-ev-er, my king and my God.

Music: Jay F. Hunstiger, © 1991, administered by Liturgical Press. All rights reserved.

Psalm 145:8-9, 10-11, 12-13

℟. (See 1) **I will praise your name forever, my king and
  my God.** or: ℟. **Alleluia.**

The Lord is gracious and merciful,
  slow to anger and of great kindness.
The Lord is good to all
  and compassionate toward all his works. ℟.

Let all your works give you thanks, O Lord,
    and let your faithful ones bless you.
Let them discourse of the glory of your kingdom
    and speak of your might. ℟.

Let them make known your might to the children of Adam,
    and the glorious splendor of your kingdom.
Your kingdom is a kingdom for all ages,
    and your dominion endures through all generations. ℟.

Reading II (Revelation 21:1-5a)
A reading from the Book of Revelation

God will wipe every tear from their eyes.

**Then I, John, saw a new heaven and a new earth.
The former heaven and the former earth had passed away,
    and the sea was no more.
I also saw the holy city, a new Jerusalem,
    coming down out of heaven from God,
    prepared as a bride adorned for her husband.
I heard a loud voice from the throne saying,
    "Behold, God's dwelling is with the human race.
He will dwell with them and they will be his people
    and God himself will always be with them as their God.
He will wipe every tear from their eyes,
    and there shall be no more death or mourning,
        wailing or pain,
    for the old order has passed away."

The One who sat on the throne said,
    "Behold, I make all things new."**

The word of the Lord. All: **Thanks be to God.**

Gospel (John 13:31-33a, 34-35)
Alleluia (John 13:34)
  ℣. Alleluia, alleluia. ℟. **Alleluia, alleluia.**
  ℣. I give you a new commandment, says the Lord:
     love one another as I have loved you. ℟.

✠ **A reading from the holy Gospel according to John**
All: **Glory to you, Lord.**

I give you a new commandment: love one another.

When Judas had left them, Jesus said,
  "Now is the Son of Man glorified, and God is glorified in him.
If God is glorified in him,
  God will also glorify him in himself,
  and God will glorify him at once.
My children, I will be with you only a little while longer.
I give you a new commandment: love one another.
As I have loved you, so you also should love one another.
This is how all will know that you are my disciples,
  if you have love for one another."

The Gospel of the Lord. All: **Praise to you, Lord Jesus Christ.**

Prayer over the Gifts
Lord God,
by this holy exchange of gifts
you share with us your divine life.
Grant that everything we do
may be directed by the knowledge of your truth.
We ask this in the name of Jesus the Lord. All: **Amen.**

Communion Antiphon (John 15:5)
I am the vine and you are the branches, says the Lord;
he who lives in me, and I in him, will bear much fruit,
alleluia.

Prayer after Communion
Merciful Father,
may these mysteries give us new purpose
and bring us to a new life in you.
Grant this through Christ our Lord. All: **Amen.**

Sixth Sunday of Easter

May 9, 2010

Reflection on the Gospel

If we have difficulty keeping our own word (and, realistically, sometimes we do), how in the world can we be successful in keeping Jesus' word? Besides, Jesus' word is much more than simply what Jesus said and taught. It is the way he lived. Jesus' words and deeds coalesce into the same reality, that is, a life of self-giving that brings salvation. It is the same life we are called to in this gospel.

- *This Easter the word of Jesus that I am being called to keep is . . .*

—Living Liturgy™, *Sixth Sunday of Easter 2010*

Entrance Antiphon (*See* Isaiah 48:20)
Speak out with a voice of joy; let it be heard to the ends of the earth: The Lord has set his people free, alleluia.

Opening Prayer
Ever-living God,
help us to celebrate our joy
in the resurrection of the Lord
and to express in our lives
the love we celebrate.
Grant this through our Lord Jesus Christ, your Son,
who lives and reigns with you and the Holy Spirit,
one God, for ever and ever. All: **Amen.**

When the Ascension of the Lord is celebrated the following Sunday, the second reading and Gospel from the Seventh Sunday of Easter (*see* nos. 59–61) may be read on the Sixth Sunday of Easter.

Reading I (L 57-C) (Acts of the Apostles 15:1-2, 22-29)
A reading from the Acts of the Apostles

It is the decision of the Holy Spirit and of us not to place on you any burden beyond these necessities.

Some who had come down from Judea were instructing
>the brothers,
>>"Unless you are circumcised according to the Mosaic
>>>practice,
>>you cannot be saved."
Because there arose no little dissension and debate
>by Paul and Barnabas with them,
>>it was decided that Paul, Barnabas, and some of the
>>>others
>>>should go up to Jerusalem to the apostles and elders
>>>about this question.

The apostles and elders, in agreement with the whole
>church,
>>decided to choose representatives
>>and to send them to Antioch with Paul and Barnabas.
The ones chosen were Judas, who was called Barsabbas,
>and Silas, leaders among the brothers.
This is the letter delivered by them:

"The apostles and the elders, your brothers,
>to the brothers in Antioch, Syria, and Cilicia
>of Gentile origin: greetings.
Since we have heard that some of our number
>who went out without any mandate from us
>have upset you with their teachings
>and disturbed your peace of mind,
>we have with one accord decided to choose
>>representatives
>and to send them to you along with our beloved
>>Barnabas and Paul,
>who have dedicated their lives to the name of our
>>Lord Jesus Christ.
So we are sending Judas and Silas
>who will also convey this same message by word of
>>mouth:
>'It is the decision of the Holy Spirit and of us
>not to place on you any burden beyond these necessities,

namely, to abstain from meat sacrificed to idols,
from blood, from meats of strangled animals,
and from unlawful marriage.
If you keep free of these,
you will be doing what is right. Farewell.'"

The word of the Lord. All: Thanks be to God.

Responsorial Psalm 67

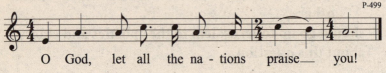

O God, let all the nations praise you!

Music: Jay F. Hunstiger, © 1991, administered by Liturgical Press. All rights reserved.

Psalm 67:2-3, 5, 6, 8

℟. (4) **O God, let all the nations praise you!** *or:* ℟. **Alleluia.**

May God have pity on us and bless us;
   may he let his face shine upon us.
So may your way be known upon earth;
   among all nations, your salvation. ℟.

May the nations be glad and exult
   because you rule the peoples in equity;
   the nations on the earth you guide. ℟.

May the peoples praise you, O God;
   may all the peoples praise you!
May God bless us,
   and may all the ends of the earth fear him! ℟.

Reading II (Revelation 21:10-14, 22-23)

A reading from the Book of Revelation

The angel showed me the holy city coming down out of heaven.

**The angel took me in spirit to a great, high mountain
   and showed me the holy city Jerusalem
   coming down out of heaven from God.
It gleamed with the splendor of God.
Its radiance was like that of a precious stone,
   like jasper, clear as crystal.**

It had a massive, high wall,
>	with twelve gates where twelve angels were stationed
>	and on which names were inscribed,
>	the names of the twelve tribes of the Israelites.

There were three gates facing east,
>	three north, three south, and three west.

The wall of the city had twelve courses of stones as its foundation,
>	on which were inscribed the twelve names
>	of the twelve apostles of the Lamb.

I saw no temple in the city
>	for its temple is the Lord God almighty and the Lamb.

The city had no need of sun or moon to shine on it,
>	for the glory of God gave it light,
>	and its lamp was the Lamb.

The word of the Lord. All: **Thanks be to God.**

GOSPEL (John 14:23-29)
ALLELUIA (John 14:23)

℣. Alleluia, alleluia.   ℟. **Alleluia, alleluia.**
℣. Whoever loves me will keep my word, says the Lord,
and my Father will love him and we will come to him. ℟.

✠ **A reading from the holy Gospel according to John**

All: **Glory to you, Lord.**

The Holy Spirit will teach you everything and remind you of all that I told you.

Jesus said to his disciples:
>	**"Whoever loves me will keep my word,**
>	**and my Father will love him,**
>	**and we will come to him and make our dwelling with him.**

Whoever does not love me does not keep my words;
>	**yet the word you hear is not mine**
>	**but that of the Father who sent me.**

"I have told you this while I am with you.
The Advocate, the Holy Spirit,
   whom the Father will send in my name,
   will teach you everything
   and remind you of all that I told you.
Peace I leave with you; my peace I give to you.
Not as the world gives do I give it to you.
Do not let your hearts be troubled or afraid.
You heard me tell you,
   'I am going away and I will come back to you.'
If you loved me,
   you would rejoice that I am going to the Father;
   for the Father is greater than I.
And now I have told you this before it happens,
   so that when it happens you may believe."

The Gospel of the Lord. All: **Praise to you, Lord Jesus Christ.**

Prayer over the Gifts
Lord,
accept our prayers and offerings.
Make us worthy of your sacraments of love
by granting us your forgiveness.
We ask this in the name of Jesus the Lord. All: **Amen.**

Communion Antiphon (John 14:15-16)
If you love me, keep my commandments, says the Lord.
The Father will send you the Holy Spirit, to be with you for ever, alleluia.

Prayer after Communion
Almighty and ever-living Lord,
you restored us to life
by raising Christ from death.
Strengthen us by this Easter sacrament;
may we feel its saving power in our daily life.
We ask this through Christ our Lord. All: **Amen.**

The Ascension of the Lord

May 13, 2010

Reflection on the Gospel

Jesus' disappearance from sight does not mark an absence, but a new kind of presence. In the "absence" left by his ascension, we his followers are commissioned to "preach[ ] in his name to all nations." What is it we preach? That suffering and even death lead to new life and that forgiveness will be granted to all who repent. His very ascension into heaven is our commissioning on earth because, "clothed with power from on high," we are now the visible presence of Jesus.

- *I "preach" Jesus' dying and rising pattern in my life when . . .*

—Living Liturgy™, *Ascension 2010*

Entrance Antiphon (Acts of the Apostles 1:11)

Men of Galilee, why do you stand looking in the sky? The Lord will return, just as you have seen him ascend, alleluia.

Opening Prayer

God our Father,
make us joyful in the ascension of your Son Jesus Christ.
May we follow him into the new creation,
for his ascension is our glory and our hope.
We ask this through our Lord Jesus Christ, your Son,
who lives and reigns with you and the Holy Spirit,
one God, for ever and ever. All: **Amen.**

Reading I (L 58-C) (Acts of the Apostles 1:1-11)

A reading from the beginning of the Acts of the Apostles

As the Apostles were looking on, Jesus was lifted up.

In the first book, Theophilus,
 I dealt with all that Jesus did and taught
 until the day he was taken up,

after giving instructions through the Holy Spirit
to the apostles whom he had chosen.
He presented himself alive to them
by many proofs after he had suffered,
appearing to them during forty days
and speaking about the kingdom of God.
While meeting with them,
he enjoined them not to depart from Jerusalem,
but to wait for "the promise of the Father
about which you have heard me speak;
for John baptized with water,
but in a few days you will be baptized with the
Holy Spirit."
When they had gathered together they asked him,
"Lord, are you at this time going to restore
the kingdom to Israel?"
He answered them, "It is not for you to know the times
or seasons
that the Father has established by his own authority.
But you will receive power when the Holy Spirit comes
upon you,
and you will be my witnesses in Jerusalem,
throughout Judea and Samaria,
and to the ends of the earth."
When he had said this, as they were looking on,
he was lifted up, and a cloud took him from their sight.
While they were looking intently at the sky as he was going,
suddenly two men dressed in white garments stood
beside them.
They said, "Men of Galilee,
why are you standing there looking at the sky?
This Jesus who has been taken up from you into heaven
will return in the same way as you have seen him
going into heaven."

The word of the Lord. All: Thanks be to God.

Responsorial Psalm 47

God mounts his throne to shouts of joy, to shouts of joy.

Music: Jay F. Hunstiger, © 1990, administered by Liturgical Press. All rights reserved.

Psalm 47:2-3, 6-7, 8-9

℟. (6) **God mounts his throne to shouts of joy: a blare of trumpets for the Lord.** *or:* ℟. **Alleluia.**

All you peoples, clap your hands,
    shout to God with cries of gladness,
for the Lord, the Most High, the awesome,
    is the great king over all the earth. ℟.

God mounts his throne amid shouts of joy;
    the Lord, amid trumpet blasts.
Sing praise to God, sing praise;
    sing praise to our king, sing praise. ℟.

For king of all the earth is God;
    sing hymns of praise.
God reigns over the nations,
    God sits upon his holy throne. ℟.

Reading II

A (Ephesians 1:17-23)

A reading from the Letter of Saint Paul to the Ephesians

God seated Jesus at his right hand in the heavens.

**Brothers and sisters:
May the God of our Lord Jesus Christ, the Father of glory,
    give you a Spirit of wisdom and revelation
    resulting in knowledge of him.
May the eyes of your hearts be enlightened,
    that you may know what is the hope that belongs to
        his call,
    what are the riches of glory
    in his inheritance among the holy ones,**

and what is the surpassing greatness of his power
>   for us who believe,
>   in accord with the exercise of his great might,
>   which he worked in Christ,
>   raising him from the dead
>   and seating him at his right hand in the heavens,
>   far above every principality, authority, power, and dominion,
>   and every name that is named
>   not only in this age but also in the one to come.
> And he put all things beneath his feet
>   and gave him as head over all things to the church,
>   which is his body,
>   the fullness of the one who fills all things in every way.

The word of the Lord. All: Thanks be to God.

or:

B (Hebrews 9:24-28; 10:19-23)

A reading from the Letter to the Hebrews

Christ has entered into heaven itself.

**Christ did not enter into a sanctuary made by hands,
>   a copy of the true one, but heaven itself,
>   that he might now appear before God on our behalf.
> Not that he might offer himself repeatedly,
>   as the high priest enters each year into the sanctuary
>   with blood that is not his own;
>   if that were so, he would have had to suffer repeatedly
>   from the foundation of the world.
> But now once for all he has appeared at the end of the ages
>   to take away sin by his sacrifice.
> Just as it is appointed that men and women die once,
>   and after this the judgment, so also Christ,
>   offered once to take away the sins of many,
>   will appear a second time, not to take away sin
>   but to bring salvation to those who eagerly await him.**

Therefore, brothers and sisters, since through the blood
> of Jesus
>> we have confidence of entrance into the sanctuary
>> by the new and living way he opened for us through
>>> the veil,
>> that is, his flesh,
>> and since we have "a great priest over the house of God,"
>> let us approach with a sincere heart and in absolute
>>> trust,
>> with our hearts sprinkled clean from an evil conscience
>> and our bodies washed in pure water.
> Let us hold unwaveringly to our confession that gives us
>> hope,
>> for he who made the promise is trustworthy.

The word of the Lord. All: **Thanks be to God.**

GOSPEL (Luke 24:46-53)
ALLELUIA (Matthew 28:19a, 20b)

℣. Alleluia, alleluia. ℟. **Alleluia, alleluia.**
℣. Go and teach all nations, says the Lord;
I am with you always, until the end of the world. ℟.

✠ A reading from the conclusion of the holy Gospel according to Luke

All: **Glory to you, Lord.**

As he blessed them, he was taken up to heaven.

**Jesus said to his disciples:
> "Thus it is written that the Christ would suffer
> and rise from the dead on the third day
> and that repentance, for the forgiveness of sins,
> would be preached in his name
> to all the nations, beginning from Jerusalem.
You are witnesses of these things.
And behold I am sending the promise of my Father
> upon you;
>> but stay in the city
>> until you are clothed with power from on high."**

Then he led them out as far as Bethany,
   raised his hands, and blessed them.
As he blessed them he parted from them
   and was taken up to heaven.
They did him homage
   and then returned to Jerusalem with great joy,
   and they were continually in the temple praising God.

The Gospel of the Lord. All: **Praise to you, Lord Jesus Christ.**

Prayer over the Gifts
Lord,
receive our offering
as we celebrate the ascension of Christ your Son.
May his gifts help us rise with him
to the joys of heaven,
where he lives and reigns for ever and ever. All: **Amen.**

Communion Antiphon (Matthew 28:20)
I, the Lord, am with you always, until the end of the world, alleluia.

Prayer after Communion
Father,
in this eucharist
we touch the divine life you give to the world.
Help us to follow Christ with love
to eternal life where he is Lord for ever and ever. All: **Amen.**

Seventh Sunday of Easter

May 16, 2010

If the feast of the Ascension is celebrated on the Seventh Sunday of Easter in your diocese, please turn to page 263 for the texts for the feast of the ASCENSION.

Reflection on the Gospel

In this intimate prayer of Jesus before his suffering and death, we see clearly how much Jesus sustains us in our discipleship. Our peek into what is deepest in Jesus' heart encourages us. The gift of the Spirit that we receive helps us see who we are to be as the one Body of Christ: those whose lives are spent in self-sacrificing surrender for the sake of others. Our glory lies in imitating Jesus, knowing that dying to self leads to risen life.

- *As I listen to Jesus' prayer for me, what is most comforting is . . .*

—Living Liturgy™, *Seventh Sunday of Easter 2010*

Entrance Antiphon (Psalm 26:7-9)

Lord, hear my voice when I call to you. My heart has prompted me to seek your face; I seek it, Lord; do not hide from me, alleluia.

Opening Prayer

Father,
help us keep in mind that Christ our Savior
lives with you in glory
and promised to remain with us until the end of time.
We ask this through our Lord Jesus Christ, your Son,
who lives and reigns with you and the Holy Spirit,
one God, for ever and ever. All: **Amen.**

In those places where the solemnity of the Ascension of the Lord has been transferred to the Seventh Sunday of Easter, the Mass and readings of the Ascension are used. *See* page 263.

Reading I (L 61-C) (Acts of the Apostles 7:55-60)
A reading from the Acts of the Apostles

I see the Son of Man standing at the right hand of God.

**Stephen, filled with the Holy Spirit,
    looked up intently to heaven and saw the glory of God
    and Jesus standing at the right hand of God,
    and Stephen said, "Behold, I see the heavens opened
    and the Son of Man standing at the right hand of God."
But they cried out in a loud voice,
    covered their ears, and rushed upon him together.
They threw him out of the city, and began to stone him.
The witnesses laid down their cloaks
    at the feet of a young man named Saul.
As they were stoning Stephen, he called out,
    "Lord Jesus, receive my spirit."
Then he fell to his knees and cried out in a loud voice,
    "Lord, do not hold this sin against them";
    and when he said this, he fell asleep.**

The word of the Lord. All: **Thanks be to God.**

Responsorial Psalm 97

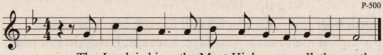

The Lord is king, the Most High o-ver all the earth.

Music: Jay F. Hunstiger, © 1991, administered by Liturgical Press. All rights reserved.

Psalm 97:1-2, 6-7, 9

℟. (1a and 9a) **The Lord is king, the most high over all the earth.** *or:* ℟. **Alleluia.**

The Lord is king; let the earth rejoice;
    let the many islands be glad.
Justice and judgment are the foundation of his throne. ℟.

The heavens proclaim his justice,
    and all peoples see his glory.
All gods are prostrate before him. ℟.

You, O LORD, are the Most High over all the earth,
  exalted far above all gods. ℟.

READING II (Revelation 22:12-14, 16-17, 20)
A reading from the Book of Revelation

Come, Lord Jesus!

I, John, heard a voice saying to me:
  "Behold, I am coming soon.
I bring with me the recompense I will give to each
  according to his deeds.
I am the Alpha and the Omega, the first and the last,
  the beginning and the end."
Blessed are they who wash their robes
  so as to have the right to the tree of life
  and enter the city through its gates.

"I, Jesus, sent my angel to give you this testimony for the churches.
I am the root and offspring of David,
  the bright morning star."

The Spirit and the bride say, "Come."
Let the hearer say, "Come."
Let the one who thirsts come forward,
  and the one who wants it receive the gift of life-giving water.

The one who gives this testimony says, "Yes, I am coming soon."
Amen! Come, Lord Jesus!

The word of the Lord. All: **Thanks be to God.**

GOSPEL (John 17:20-26)
ALLELUIA (*See* John 14:18)
  ℣. Alleluia, alleluia. ℟. **Alleluia, alleluia.**
  ℣. I will not leave you orphans, says the Lord.
  I will come back to you, and your hearts will rejoice. ℟.

✞ **A reading from the holy Gospel according to John**
All: **Glory to you, Lord.**

That they may be brought to perfection as one!

Lifting up his eyes to heaven, Jesus prayed, saying:
   "**Holy Father, I pray not only for them,**
      but also for those who will believe in me through
         their word,
      so that they may all be one,
      as you, Father, are in me and I in you,
      that they also may be in us,
      that the world may believe that you sent me.
And I have given them the glory you gave me,
      so that they may be one, as we are one,
      I in them and you in me,
      that they may be brought to perfection as one,
      that the world may know that you sent me,
      and that you loved them even as you loved me.
Father, they are your gift to me.
I wish that where I am they also may be with me,
      that they may see my glory that you gave me,
      because you loved me before the foundation of the
         world.
Righteous Father, the world also does not know you,
      but I know you, and they know that you sent me.
I made known to them your name and I will make it
      known,
      that the love with which you loved me
      may be in them and I in them."

The Gospel of the Lord. All: **Praise to you, Lord Jesus Christ.**

Prayer over the Gifts
Lord,
accept the prayers and gifts
we offer in faith and love.
May this eucharist
bring us to your glory.
Grant this through Christ our Lord. All: **Amen.**

Communion Antiphon (John 17:22)
This is the prayer of Jesus: that his believers may become one as he is one with the Father, alleluia.

Prayer after Communion
God our Savior,
hear us,
and through this holy mystery give us hope
that the glory you have given Christ
will be given to the Church, his body,
for he is Lord for ever and ever. All: **Amen.**

Pentecost

VIGIL MASS

May 22, 2010

The Mass of the Vigil of Pentecost is used on Saturday evening in those places where the Sunday obligation may be fulfilled on Saturday evening.

Entrance Antiphon (*See* Romans 5:5; 8:11)
The love of God has been poured into our hearts by his Spirit living in us, alleluia.

Opening Prayer
Almighty and ever-living God,
you fulfilled the Easter promise
by sending us your Holy Spirit.
May that Spirit unite the races and nations on earth
to proclaim your glory.
Grant this through our Lord Jesus Christ, your Son,
who lives and reigns with you and the Holy Spirit,
one God, for ever and ever. All: **Amen.**

or:

God our Father,
you have given us new birth.
Strengthen us with your Holy Spirit
and fill us with your light.

Grant this through our Lord Jesus Christ, your Son,
who lives and reigns with you and the Holy Spirit,
one God, for ever and ever. All: **Amen.**

These readings are used at Saturday Evening Mass celebrated either before or after Evening Prayer I of Pentecost Sunday. The first of four options for the First Reading for this Mass is given here. Please see the others in the lectionary: Exodus 19:3-8a, 16-20b; Ezekiel 37:1-14; or Joel 3:1-5.

Reading I (L 62) *A* (Genesis 11:1-9)
A reading from the Book of Genesis

It was called Babel because there the Lord confused the speech of all the world.

**The whole world spoke the same language, using the same words.
While the people were migrating in the east,
   they came upon a valley in the land of Shinar and settled there.
They said to one another,
   "Come, let us mold bricks and harden them with fire."
They used bricks for stone, and bitumen for mortar.
Then they said, "Come, let us build ourselves a city
   and a tower with its top in the sky,
   and so make a name for ourselves;
   otherwise we shall be scattered all over the earth."**

**The Lord came down to see the city and the tower
   that the people had built.
Then the Lord said: "If now, while they are one people,
   all speaking the same language,
   they have started to do this,
   nothing will later stop them from doing whatever they presume to do.
Let us then go down there and confuse their language,
   so that one will not understand what another says."
Thus the Lord scattered them from there all over the earth,
   and they stopped building the city.**

That is why it was called Babel,
> because there the LORD confused the speech of all the
>> world.

It was from that place that he scattered them all over the
> earth.

The word of the Lord. All: Thanks be to God.

RESPONSORIAL PSALM 104

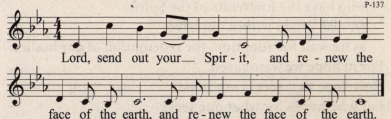

Psalm 104:1-2, 24, 35, 27-28, 29, 30

℟. (*See* 30) **Lord, send out your Spirit, and renew the face of the earth.** *or:* ℟. **Alleluia.**

Bless the LORD, O my soul!
> O LORD, my God, you are great indeed!
You are clothed with majesty and glory,
> robed in light as with a cloak. ℟.

How manifold are your works, O LORD!
> In wisdom you have wrought them all—
> the earth is full of your creatures;
> bless the LORD, O my soul! Alleluia. ℟.

Creatures all look to you
> to give them food in due time.
When you give it to them, they gather it;
> when you open your hand, they are filled with good
>> things. ℟.

If you take away their breath, they perish
> and return to their dust.
When you send forth your spirit, they are created,
> and you renew the face of the earth. ℟.

May 22

Reading II (Romans 8:22-27)
A reading from the Letter of Saint Paul to the Romans

The Spirit intercedes with inexpressible groanings.

Brothers and sisters:
We know that all creation is groaning in labor pains
> **even until now;**
>> **and not only that, but we ourselves,**
>> **who have the firstfruits of the Spirit,**
>> **we also groan within ourselves**
>> **as we wait for adoption, the redemption of our bodies.**

For in hope we were saved.
Now hope that sees is not hope.
For who hopes for what one sees?
But if we hope for what we do not see, we wait with endurance.

In the same way, the Spirit too comes to the aid of our weakness;
> **for we do not know how to pray as we ought,**
> **but the Spirit himself intercedes with inexpressible groanings.**

And the one who searches hearts
> **knows what is the intention of the Spirit,**
> **because he intercedes for the holy ones**
> **according to God's will.**

The word of the Lord. All: **Thanks be to God.**

Gospel (John 7:37-39)
Alleluia

℣. Alleluia, alleluia. ℟. **Alleluia, alleluia.**
℣. Come, Holy Spirit, fill the hearts of the faithful and kindle in them the fire of your love. ℟.

✠ **A reading from the holy Gospel according to John**

All: **Glory to you, Lord.**

Rivers of living water will flow.

On the last and greatest day of the feast,
>	Jesus stood up and exclaimed,
>		"Let anyone who thirsts come to me and drink.
As Scripture says:
>	*Rivers of living water will flow from within him who believes in me."*

He said this in reference to the Spirit
>	that those who came to believe in him were to receive.
There was, of course, no Spirit yet,
>	because Jesus had not yet been glorified.

The Gospel of the Lord. All: **Praise to you, Lord Jesus Christ.**

Prayer over the Gifts
Lord,
send your Spirit on these gifts
and through them help the Church you love
to show your salvation to all the world.
We ask this in the name of Jesus the Lord. All: **Amen.**

Communion Antiphon (John 7:37)
On the last day of the festival, Jesus stood and cried aloud:
If anyone is thirsty, let him come to me and drink, alleluia.

Prayer after Communion
Lord,
through this eucharist,
send the Holy Spirit of Pentecost into our hearts
to keep us always in your love.
We ask this through Christ our Lord. All: **Amen.**

Sunday, May 23

MASS DURING THE DAY

Reflection on the Gospel
With the sending of the Holy Spirit who is "another Advocate," we followers of Jesus are never bereft of divine presence. This new Advocate teaches us just as Jesus taught the first disciples. This new Advocate "calls" (L. advocare = to call) us to faithful discipleship and "supports" (paráklētos = helper) us in our efforts to love Jesus. This new Advocate

enables us to love and live as Jesus did, continuing his saving mission and making him present through us.

- The way I experience the Spirit's indwelling is . . .

—*Living Liturgy*™, *Pentecost 2010*

Entrance Antiphon (Wisdom 1:7)

The Spirit of the Lord fills the whole world. It holds all things together and knows every word spoken by man, alleluia.

or:

(*See* Romans 5:5; 8:11)

The love of God has been poured into our hearts by his Spirit living in us, alleluia.

Opening Prayer

God our Father,
let the Spirit you sent on your Church
to begin the teaching of the gospel
continue to work in the world
through the hearts of all who believe.
We ask this through our Lord Jesus Christ, your Son,
who lives and reigns with you and the Holy Spirit,
one God, for ever and ever. All: **Amen.**

Reading I (L 63) (Acts of the Apostles 2:1-11)

A reading from the Acts of the Apostles

They were all filled with the Holy Spirit and began to speak.

**When the time for Pentecost was fulfilled,
   they were all in one place together.
And suddenly there came from the sky
   a noise like a strong driving wind,
   and it filled the entire house in which they were.
Then there appeared to them tongues as of fire,
   which parted and came to rest on each one of them.
And they were all filled with the Holy Spirit
   and began to speak in different tongues,
   as the Spirit enabled them to proclaim.
Now there were devout Jews from every nation under
   heaven staying in Jerusalem.**

At this sound, they gathered in a large crowd,
> but they were confused
>> because each one heard them speaking in his own language.

They were astounded, and in amazement they asked,
> "Are not all these people who are speaking Galileans?

Then how does each of us hear them in his native language?

We are Parthians, Medes, and Elamites,
> inhabitants of Mesopotamia, Judea and Cappadocia,
> Pontus and Asia, Phrygia and Pamphylia,
> Egypt and the districts of Libya near Cyrene,
> as well as travelers from Rome,
> both Jews and converts to Judaism, Cretans and Arabs,
> yet we hear them speaking in our own tongues
> of the mighty acts of God."

The word of the Lord. **All: Thanks be to God.**

Responsorial Psalm 104

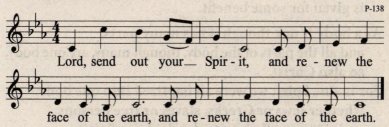

Music: Jay F. Hunstiger, © 1990, administered by Liturgical Press. All rights reserved.

Psalm 104:1, 24, 29-30, 31, 34

℟. (See 30) **Lord, send out your Spirit, and renew the face of the earth.** *or:* ℟. **Alleluia.**

Bless the Lord, O my soul!
> O Lord, my God, you are great indeed!
How manifold are your works, O Lord!
> The earth is full of your creatures. ℟.

If you take away their breath, they perish
> and return to their dust.
When you send forth your spirit, they are created,
> and you renew the face of the earth. ℟.   *(continued)*

May the glory of the Lord endure forever;
  may the Lord be glad in his works!
Pleasing to him be my theme;
  I will be glad in the Lord. ℟.

Reading II

A (1 Corinthians 12:3b-7, 12-13)

A reading from the first Letter of Saint Paul to the Corinthians

In one Spirit we were all baptized into one body.

Brothers and sisters:
No one can say, "Jesus is Lord," except by the Holy Spirit.
There are different kinds of spiritual gifts but the same Spirit;
  there are different forms of service but the same Lord;
  there are different workings but the same God
  who produces all of them in everyone.
To each individual the manifestation of the Spirit
  is given for some benefit.

As a body is one though it has many parts,
  and all the parts of the body, though many, are one body,
  so also Christ.
For in one Spirit we were all baptized into one body,
  whether Jews or Greeks, slaves or free persons,
  and we were all given to drink of one Spirit.

The word of the Lord. All: **Thanks be to God.**

or:

B (Romans 8:8-17)

A reading from the Letter of Saint Paul to the Romans

Those who are led by the Spirit of God are children of God.

Brothers and sisters:
Those who are in the flesh cannot please God.
But you are not in the flesh;
  on the contrary, you are in the spirit,
  if only the Spirit of God dwells in you.

Whoever does not have the Spirit of Christ does not
> belong to him.
But if Christ is in you,
> although the body is dead because of sin,
> the spirit is alive because of righteousness.
If the Spirit of the one who raised Jesus from the dead
> dwells in you,
> the one who raised Christ from the dead
> will give life to your mortal bodies also,
> through his Spirit that dwells in you.
Consequently, brothers and sisters,
> we are not debtors to the flesh,
> to live according to the flesh.
For if you live according to the flesh, you will die,
> but if by the Spirit you put to death the deeds of the
>> body,
> you will live.

For those who are led by the Spirit of God are sons of God.
For you did not receive a spirit of slavery to fall back
> into fear,
> but you received a Spirit of adoption,
> through whom we cry, "Abba, Father!"
The Spirit himself bears witness with our spirit
> that we are children of God,
> and if children, then heirs,
> heirs of God and joint heirs with Christ,
> if only we suffer with him
> so that we may also be glorified with him.

The word of the Lord. All: Thanks be to God.

Sequence
Veni, Sancte Spiritus

Come, Holy Spirit, come!
And from your celestial home
> Shed a ray of light divine!
Come, Father of the poor!

Come, source of all our store!
    Come, within our bosoms shine.
You, of comforters the best;
You, the soul's most welcome guest;
    Sweet refreshment here below;
In our labor, rest most sweet;
Grateful coolness in the heat;
    Solace in the midst of woe.
O most blessed Light divine,
Shine within these hearts of yours,
    And our inmost being fill!
Where you are not, we have naught,
Nothing good in deed or thought,
    Nothing free from taint of ill.
Heal our wounds, our strength renew;
On our dryness pour your dew;
    Wash the stains of guilt away:
Bend the stubborn heart and will;
Melt the frozen, warm the chill;
    Guide the steps that go astray.
On the faithful, who adore
And confess you, evermore
    In your sevenfold gift descend;
Give them virtue's sure reward;
Give them your salvation, Lord;
    Give them joys that never end. Amen.
    Alleluia.

Gospel
Alleluia

℣. Alleluia, alleluia. ℟. **Alleluia, alleluia.**
℣. Come, Holy Spirit, fill the hearts of your faithful
and kindle in them the fire of your love. ℟.

A (John 20:19-23)

✚ **A reading from the holy Gospel according to John**

All: Glory to you, Lord.

As the Father sent me, so I send you. Receive the Holy Spirit.

On the evening of that first day of the week,
   when the doors were locked, where the disciples were,
   for fear of the Jews,
   Jesus came and stood in their midst
   and said to them, "Peace be with you."
When he had said this, he showed them his hands and
   his side.
The disciples rejoiced when they saw the Lord.
Jesus said to them again, "Peace be with you.
As the Father has sent me, so I send you."
And when he had said this, he breathed on them and
   said to them,
   "Receive the Holy Spirit.
Whose sins you forgive are forgiven them,
   and whose sins you retain are retained."

The Gospel of the Lord. All: Praise to you, Lord Jesus Christ.

or:

B (John 14:15-16, 23b-26)

✚ **A reading from the holy Gospel according to John**

All: Glory to you, Lord.

The Holy Spirit will teach you everything.

Jesus said to his disciples:
   "If you love me, you will keep my commandments.
And I will ask the Father,
   and he will give you another Advocate to be with you
      always.

"Whoever loves me will keep my word,
   and my Father will love him,

> and we will come to him and make our dwelling with him.
> Those who do not love me do not keep my words;
> > yet the word you hear is not mine
> > but that of the Father who sent me.
>
> "I have told you this while I am with you.
> The Advocate, the Holy Spirit whom the Father will send in my name,
> > will teach you everything
> > and remind you of all that I told you."

The Gospel of the Lord. All: **Praise to you, Lord Jesus Christ.**

If it is customary or obligatory for the faithful to attend Mass on the Monday or even the Tuesday after Pentecost, the readings from the Mass of Pentecost Sunday may be repeated or the readings of the Ritual Mass for Confirmation, nos. 764–768, may be used in its place.

Prayer over the Gifts
Lord,
may the Spirit you promised
lead us into all truth
and reveal to us the full meaning of this sacrifice.
Grant this through Christ our Lord. All: **Amen.**

Communion Antiphon (Acts of the Apostles 2:4, 11)
They were all filled with the Holy Spirit, and they spoke of the great things God had done, alleluia.

Prayer after Communion
Father,
may the food we receive in the eucharist
help our eternal redemption.
Keep within us the vigor of your Spirit
and protect the gifts you have given to your Church.
We ask this in the name of Jesus the Lord. All: **Amen.**

Trinity Sunday

May 30, 2010

Reflection on the Gospel

The readings for this solemnity describe the majesty of God in the many ways we encounter the divine among us: in creation that is tangible and all around us, in Jesus of Nazareth who lived among us and is then the risen Lord who commands us to continue his saving mission, and in the Holy Spirit who is poured forth in our hearts. The glory of God's presence is encountered through creation, salvation, and each other!

- The revelation of God has come to me through . . . I am the revelation of God for others when . . .

—Living Liturgy™, *Trinity Sunday 2010*

Entrance Antiphon

Blessed be God the Father and his only-begotten Son and the Holy Spirit; for he has shown that he loves us.

Opening Prayer

Father,
you sent your Word to bring us truth
and your Spirit to make us holy.
Through them we come to know the mystery of your life.
Help us to worship you, one God in three Persons,
by proclaiming and living our faith in you.
Grant this through our Lord Jesus Christ, your Son,
who lives and reigns with you and the Holy Spirit,
one God, for ever and ever. All: **Amen.**

Reading I (L 166-C) (Proverbs 8:22-31)

A reading from the Book of Proverbs

Before the earth was made, Wisdom was conceived.

**Thus says the wisdom of God:
"The Lord possessed me, the beginning of his ways,
    the forerunner of his prodigies of long ago;
from of old I was poured forth,
    at the first, before the earth.**

When there were no depths I was brought forth,
   when there were no fountains or springs of water;
before the mountains were settled into place,
   before the hills, I was brought forth;
while as yet the earth and fields were not made,
   nor the first clods of the world.

"When the Lord established the heavens I was there,
   when he marked out the vault over the face of the deep;
when he made firm the skies above,
   when he fixed fast the foundations of the earth;
when he set for the sea its limit,
   so that the waters should not transgress his command;
then was I beside him as his craftsman,
   and I was his delight day by day,
playing before him all the while,
   playing on the surface of his earth;
   and I found delight in the human race."

The word of the Lord. All: **Thanks be to God.**

Responsorial Psalm 8

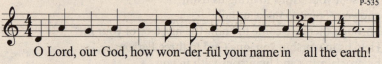

O Lord, our God, how won-der-ful your name in all the earth!

Music: Jay F. Hunstiger, © 1991, administered by Liturgical Press. All rights reserved.

Psalm 8:4-5, 6-7, 8-9

℟. (2a) **O Lord, our God, how wonderful your name in all the earth!**

When I behold your heavens, the work of your fingers,
   the moon and the stars which you set in place—
what is man that you should be mindful of him,
   or the son of man that you should care for him? ℟.

You have made him little less than the angels,
   and crowned him with glory and honor.
You have given him rule over the works of your hands,
   putting all things under his feet. ℟.

All sheep and oxen,
>   yes, and the beasts of the field,
>   the birds of the air, the fishes of the sea,
>   and whatever swims the paths of the seas. ℟.

Reading II (Romans 5:1-5)
A reading from the Letter of Saint Paul to the Romans

To God, through Christ, in love poured out through the Holy Spirit.

Brothers and sisters:
Therefore, since we have been justified by faith,
>   **we have peace with God through our Lord Jesus Christ,**
>   **through whom we have gained access by faith**
>   **to this grace in which we stand,**
>   **and we boast in hope of the glory of God.**
Not only that, but we even boast of our afflictions,
>   **knowing that affliction produces endurance,**
>   **and endurance, proven character,**
>   **and proven character, hope,**
>   **and hope does not disappoint,**
>   **because the love of God has been poured out into**
>   **our hearts**
>   **through the Holy Spirit that has been given to us.**

The word of the Lord. All: **Thanks be to God.**

Gospel (John 16:12-15)
Alleluia (*See* Revelation 1:8)
℣. Alleluia, alleluia. ℟. **Alleluia, alleluia.**
℣. Glory to the Father, the Son, and the Holy Spirit;
>   to God who is, who was, and who is to come. ℟.

✠ **A reading from the holy Gospel according to John**

All: **Glory to you, Lord.**

Everything that the Father has is mine; the Spirit will take from what is mine and declare it to you.

Jesus said to his disciples:
>   **"I have much more to tell you, but you cannot bear it**
>   **now.**

But when he comes, the Spirit of truth,
    he will guide you to all truth.
He will not speak on his own,
    but he will speak what he hears,
    and will declare to you the things that are coming.
He will glorify me,
    because he will take from what is mine and declare it
        to you.
Everything that the Father has is mine;
    for this reason I told you that he will take from what
        is mine
    and declare it to you."

The Gospel of the Lord. All: **Praise to you, Lord Jesus Christ.**

Prayer over the Gifts
Lord our God,
make these gifts holy,
and through them
make us a perfect offering to you.
We ask this in the name of Jesus the Lord. All: **Amen.**

Communion Antiphon (Galatians 4:6)
You are the sons of God, so God has given you the Spirit
of his Son to form your hearts and make you cry out:
Abba, Father.

Prayer after Communion
Lord God,
we worship you, a Trinity of Persons, one eternal God.
May our faith and the sacrament we receive
bring us health of mind and body.
We ask this through Christ our Lord. All: **Amen.**

The Most Holy Body and Blood of Christ

June 6, 2010

Reflection on the Gospel

Jesus' gospel command is clear: we are to feed others. We give to others not from the "deserted place" of our own hearts but from the "leftover fragments" of God's blessings. God's abundant nourishment is most startlingly given in the handing over of Jesus' life—on the cross, in the bread and wine. As Jesus' followers we are to be God's abundant nourishment for others by our own self-gift of life. God's abundant giving continues in our own self-giving lives.

- *What is most important to me about the Eucharist is . . .*

—Living Liturgy™, *Body and Blood of Christ 2010*

Entrance Antiphon (Psalm 80:17)
The Lord fed his people with the finest wheat and honey; their hunger was satisfied.

Opening Prayer
Lord Jesus Christ,
you gave us the eucharist
as the memorial of your suffering and death.
May our worship of this sacrament of your body and blood
help us to experience the salvation you won
for us and the peace of the kingdom
where you live with the Father and the Holy Spirit,
one God, for ever and ever. All: **Amen.**

Reading I (L 169-C) (Genesis 14:18-20)
A reading from the Book of Genesis

Melchizedek brought out bread and wine.

**In those days, Melchizedek, king of Salem, brought out bread and wine,
and being a priest of God Most High,**

he blessed Abram with these words:
"Blessed be Abram by God Most High,
 the creator of heaven and earth;
and blessed be God Most High,
 who delivered your foes into your hand."
Then Abram gave him a tenth of everything.

The word of the Lord. All: Thanks be to God.

Responsorial Psalm 110

You are a priest for-ev-er, in the line of Mel-chi-ze-dek.

Music: Jay F. Hunstiger, © 1990, administered by Liturgical Press. All rights reserved.

Psalm 110:1, 2, 3, 4

℟. (4b) **You are a priest forever, in the line of Melchizedek.**

The LORD said to my Lord: "Sit at my right hand
 till I make your enemies your footstool." ℟.

The scepter of your power the LORD will stretch forth
  from Zion:
 "Rule in the midst of your enemies." ℟.

"Yours is princely power in the day of your birth, in holy
  splendor;
 before the daystar, like the dew, I have begotten you." ℟.

The LORD has sworn, and he will not repent:
 "You are a priest forever, according to the order of
  Melchizedek." ℟.

Reading II (1 Corinthians 11:23-26)

A reading from the first Letter of Saint Paul to the Corinthians

For as often as you eat and drink, you proclaim the death of the Lord.

Brothers and sisters:
I received from the Lord what I also handed on to you,
    that the Lord Jesus, on the night he was handed over,
    took bread, and, after he had given thanks,
    broke it and said, "This is my body that is for you.
Do this in remembrance of me."
In the same way also the cup, after supper, saying,
    "This cup is the new covenant in my blood.
Do this, as often as you drink it, in remembrance of me."
For as often as you eat this bread and drink the cup,
    you proclaim the death of the Lord until he comes.

The word of the Lord. All: Thanks be to God.

Sequence
Lauda Sion

The sequence *Laud, O Zion (Lauda Sion),* or the shorter form beginning with the verse *Lo! the angel's food is given,* may be sung optionally before the Alleluia.

Laud, O Zion, your salvation,
Laud with hymns of exultation,
    Christ, your king and shepherd true:

Bring him all the praise you know,
He is more than you bestow.
    Never can you reach his due.

Special theme for glad thanksgiving
Is the quick'ning and the living
    Bread today before you set:

From his hands of old partaken,
As we know, by faith unshaken,
    Where the Twelve at supper met.

Full and clear ring out your chanting,
Joy nor sweetest grace be wanting,
    From your heart let praises burst:

For today the feast is holden,
When the institution olden
    Of that supper was rehearsed.

Here the new law's new oblation,
By the new king's revelation,
   Ends the form of ancient rite:

Now the new the old effaces,
Truth away the shadow chases,
   Light dispels the gloom of night.

What he did at supper seated,
Christ ordained to be repeated,
   His memorial ne'er to cease:

And his rule for guidance taking,
Bread and wine we hallow, making
   Thus our sacrifice of peace.

This the truth each Christian learns,
Bread into his flesh he turns,
   To his precious blood the wine:

Sight has fail'd, nor thought conceives,
But a dauntless faith believes,
   Resting on a pow'r divine.

Here beneath these signs are hidden
Priceless things to sense forbidden;
   Signs, not things are all we see:

Blood is poured and flesh is broken,
Yet in either wondrous token
   Christ entire we know to be.

Whoso of this food partakes,
Does not rend the Lord nor breaks;
   Christ is whole to all that taste:

Thousands are, as one, receivers,
One, as thousands of believers,
   Eats of him who cannot waste.

Bad and good the feast are sharing,
Of what divers dooms preparing,
   Endless death, or endless life.

Life to these, to those damnation,
See how like participation
   Is with unlike issues rife.

When the sacrament is broken,
Doubt not, but believe 'tis spoken,
   That each sever'd outward token
      doth the very whole contain.

Nought the precious gift divides,
Breaking but the sign betides
   Jesus still the same abides,
      still unbroken does remain.

The shorter form of the sequence begins here.

Lo! the angel's food is given
To the pilgrim who has striven;
   See the children's bread from heaven,
      which on dogs may not be spent.

Truth the ancient types fulfilling,
Isaac bound, a victim willing,
   Paschal lamb, its lifeblood spilling,
      manna to the fathers sent.

Very bread, good shepherd, tend us,
Jesu, of your love befriend us,
   You refresh us, you defend us,
   Your eternal goodness send us
In the land of life to see.

You who all things can and know,
Who on earth such food bestow,
   Grant us with your saints, though lowest,
   Where the heav'nly feast you show,
Fellow heirs and guests to be. Amen. Alleluia.

Gospel (Luke 9:11b-17)
Alleluia (John 6:51)
℣. Alleluia, alleluia. ℟. **Alleluia, alleluia.**
℣. I am the living bread that came down from heaven,
says the Lord; whoever eats this bread will live forever. ℟.

✠ **A reading from the holy Gospel according to Luke**

All: **Glory to you, Lord.**

They all ate and were satisfied.

**Jesus spoke to the crowds about the kingdom of God,
and he healed those who needed to be cured.
As the day was drawing to a close,
the Twelve approached him and said,
"Dismiss the crowd
so that they can go to the surrounding villages and farms
and find lodging and provisions;
for we are in a deserted place here."
He said to them, "Give them some food yourselves."
They replied, "Five loaves and two fish are all we have,
unless we ourselves go and buy food for all these people."
Now the men there numbered about five thousand.
Then he said to his disciples,
"Have them sit down in groups of about fifty."
They did so and made them all sit down.
Then taking the five loaves and the two fish,
and looking up to heaven,
he said the blessing over them, broke them,
and gave them to the disciples to set before the crowd.
They all ate and were satisfied.
And when the leftover fragments were picked up,
they filled twelve wicker baskets.**

The Gospel of the Lord. All: **Praise to you, Lord Jesus Christ.**

Prayer over the Gifts

Lord,
may the bread and cup we offer
bring your Church the unity and peace they signify.
We ask this in the name of Jesus the Lord. All: **Amen.**

Communion Antiphon (John 6:57)

Whoever eats my flesh and drinks my blood will live in me and I in him, says the Lord.

Prayer after Communion

Lord Jesus Christ,
you give us your body and blood in the eucharist
as a sign that even now we share your life.
May we come to possess it completely in the kingdom
where you live for ever and ever. All: **Amen.**

Eleventh Sunday in Ordinary Time

June 13, 2010

Reflection on the Gospel

Jesus asks, "Do you see this woman?" The Pharisee looks at her and sees only a sinner. Jesus looks at her and sees a sinner who repents. He sees her tremendous humility, her great sorrow, her desire to minister to him in his need, her "great love," her saving faith. The woman sees Jesus as One whom she can love and who loves her in return. This relationship brings her salvation and peace. Our loving relationship with Jesus can bring us the same gifts.

- *I see family members, closest friends, colleagues at work as . . .*

—Living Liturgy™, *Eleventh Sunday in Ordinary Time 2010*

Entrance Antiphon (Psalm 27:7, 9)

Lord, hear my voice when I call to you. You are my help; do not cast me off, do not desert me, my Savior God.

June 13

Opening Prayer
Almighty God,
our hope and our strength,
without you we falter.
Help us to follow Christ
and to live according to your will.
We ask this through our Lord Jesus Christ, your Son,
who lives and reigns with you and the Holy Spirit,
one God, for ever and ever. All: **Amen.**

Reading I (L 93-C) (2 Samuel 12:7-10, 13)
A reading from the second Book of Samuel

The Lord has forgiven your sin; you shall not die.

**Nathan said to David:
"Thus says the Lord God of Israel:
   'I anointed you king of Israel.
I rescued you from the hand of Saul.
I gave you your lord's house and your lord's wives for
      your own.
I gave you the house of Israel and of Judah.
And if this were not enough, I could count up for you
      still more.
Why have you spurned the Lord and done evil in
      his sight?
You have cut down Uriah the Hittite with the sword;
   you took his wife as your own,
   and him you killed with the sword of the Ammonites.
Now, therefore, the sword shall never depart from your
      house,
   because you have despised me
   and have taken the wife of Uriah to be your wife.'"
Then David said to Nathan,
   "I have sinned against the Lord."
Nathan answered David:
   "The Lord on his part has forgiven your sin:
   you shall not die."**

The word of the Lord. All: **Thanks be to God.**

Responsorial Psalm 32

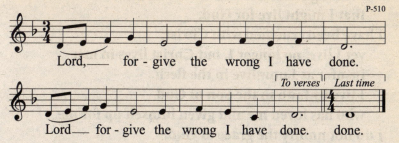

Music: Jay F. Hunstiger, © 1991, administered by Liturgical Press. All rights reserved.

Psalm 32:1-2, 5, 7, 11

℟. *(See 5c)* **Lord, forgive the wrong I have done.**

Blessed is the one whose fault is taken away,
    whose sin is covered.
Blessed the man to whom the Lord imputes not guilt,
    in whose spirit there is no guile. ℟.

I acknowledged my sin to you,
    my guilt I covered not.
I said, "I confess my faults to the Lord,"
    and you took away the guilt of my sin. ℟.

You are my shelter; from distress you will preserve me;
    with glad cries of freedom you will ring me round. ℟.

Be glad in the Lord and rejoice, you just;
    exult, all you upright of heart. ℟.

Reading II (Galatians 2:16, 19-21)
A reading from the Letter of Saint Paul to the Galatians

I live, no longer I, but Christ lives in me.

Brothers and sisters:
We who know that a person is not justified by works of
        the law
    but through faith in Jesus Christ,
    even we have believed in Christ Jesus
    that we may be justified by faith in Christ
    and not by works of the law,
    because by works of the law no one will be justified.

For through the law I died to the law,
> that I might live for God.
I have been crucified with Christ;
> yet I live, no longer I, but Christ lives in me;
> insofar as I now live in the flesh,
> I live by faith in the Son of God
> who has loved me and given himself up for me.
I do not nullify the grace of God;
> for if justification comes through the law,
> then Christ died for nothing.

The word of the Lord. All: **Thanks be to God.**

Gospel (Luke 7:36—8:3) *or* Shorter Form [ ] (Luke 7:36-50)
Alleluia (1 John 4:10b)

℣. Alleluia, alleluia. ℟. **Alleluia, alleluia.**
℣. God loved us and sent his Son
   as expiation for our sins. ℟.

✛ A reading from the holy Gospel according to Luke

All: **Glory to you, Lord.**

Her many sins have been forgiven, because she has shown great love.

[A Pharisee invited Jesus to dine with him,
> and he entered the Pharisee's house and reclined at table.
Now there was a sinful woman in the city
> who learned that he was at table in the house of the Pharisee.
Bringing an alabaster flask of ointment,
> she stood behind him at his feet weeping
> and began to bathe his feet with her tears.
Then she wiped them with her hair,
> kissed them, and anointed them with the ointment.
When the Pharisee who had invited him saw this he said to himself,
> "If this man were a prophet,

he would know who and what sort of woman this is
> who is touching him,
> that she is a sinner."

Jesus said to him in reply,
> "Simon, I have something to say to you."

"Tell me, teacher," he said.

"Two people were in debt to a certain creditor;
> one owed five hundred days' wages and the other
> owed fifty.

Since they were unable to repay the debt, he forgave it
> for both.

Which of them will love him more?"

Simon said in reply,
> "The one, I suppose, whose larger debt was forgiven."

He said to him, "You have judged rightly."

Then he turned to the woman and said to Simon,
> "Do you see this woman?

When I entered your house, you did not give me water
> for my feet,
> but she has bathed them with her tears
> and wiped them with her hair.

You did not give me a kiss,
> but she has not ceased kissing my feet since the time
> I entered.

You did not anoint my head with oil,
> but she anointed my feet with ointment.

So I tell you, her many sins have been forgiven
> because she has shown great love.

But the one to whom little is forgiven, loves little."

He said to her, "Your sins are forgiven."

The others at table said to themselves,
> "Who is this who even forgives sins?"

But he said to the woman,
> "Your faith has saved you; go in peace."]

Afterward he journeyed from one town and village to another,
> preaching and proclaiming the good news of the kingdom of God.

Accompanying him were the Twelve
> and some women who had been cured of evil spirits and infirmities,

Mary, called Magdalene, from whom seven demons had gone out,
> Joanna, the wife of Herod's steward Chuza,

Susanna, and many others who provided for them out of their resources.

The Gospel of the Lord. **All: Praise to you, Lord Jesus Christ.**

Prayer over the Gifts
Lord God,
in this bread and wine
you give us food for body and spirit.
May the eucharist renew our strength
and bring us health of mind and body.
We ask this in the name of Jesus the Lord. **All: Amen.**

Communion Antiphon (Psalm 27:4)
One thing I seek: to dwell in the house of the Lord all the days of my life.

Prayer after Communion
Lord,
may this eucharist
accomplish in your Church
the unity and peace it signifies.
Grant this through Christ our Lord. **All: Amen.**

Twelfth Sunday in Ordinary Time

June 20, 2010

Reflection on the Gospel

Jesus asks again a pretty simple question about his identity. Jesus clarifies the meaning of "the Christ": he is to "suffer greatly," "be rejected," "be killed." This is the way Jesus becomes who he really is—the risen One. To realize our own truest identity, we must daily die to ourselves. This is the way we become who we truly are to be—followers of Jesus who daily die to ourselves and daily share more and more in the life of the risen Lord.

- *The cross that I face in my life is . . . What I must "deny" in order to take it up is . . .*

—Living Liturgy™, *Twelfth Sunday in Ordinary Time 2010*

Entrance Antiphon (Psalm 28:8-9)

God is the strength of his people. In him, we his chosen live in safety. Save us, Lord, who share in your life, and give us your blessing; be our shepherd for ever.

Opening Prayer

Father,
guide and protector of your people,
grant us an unfailing respect for your name,
and keep us always in your love.
Grant this through our Lord Jesus Christ, your Son,
who lives and reigns with you and the Holy Spirit,
one God, for ever and ever. All: **Amen.**

Reading I (L 96-C) (Zechariah 12:10-11; 13:1)

A reading from the Book of the Prophet Zechariah

They shall look on him whom they have pierced.

**Thus says the Lord:
I will pour out on the house of David
and on the inhabitants of Jerusalem
a spirit of grace and petition;**

and they shall look on him whom they have pierced,
and they shall mourn for him as one mourns for an
only son,
and they shall grieve over him as one grieves over a
firstborn.

On that day the mourning in Jerusalem shall be as great
as the mourning of Hadadrimmon in the plain of
Megiddo.

On that day there shall be open to the house of David
and to the inhabitants of Jerusalem,
a fountain to purify from sin and uncleanness.

The word of the Lord. All: Thanks be to God.

Responsorial Psalm 63

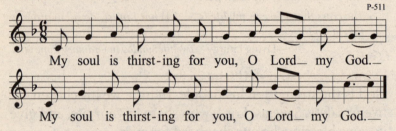

Music: Jay F. Hunstiger, © 1993, administered by Liturgical Press. All rights reserved.

Psalm 63:2, 3-4, 5-6, 8-9

℟. (2b) **My soul is thirsting for you, O Lord my God.**

O God, you are my God whom I seek;
 for you my flesh pines and my soul thirsts
 like the earth, parched, lifeless and without water. ℟.

Thus have I gazed toward you in the sanctuary
 to see your power and your glory,
for your kindness is a greater good than life;
 my lips shall glorify you. ℟.

Thus will I bless you while I live;
 lifting up my hands, I will call upon your name.
As with the riches of a banquet shall my soul be satisfied,
 and with exultant lips my mouth shall praise you. ℟.

You are my help,
>   and in the shadow of your wings I shout for joy.
My soul clings fast to you;
>   your right hand upholds me. ℟.

Reading II (Galatians 3:26-29)
A reading from the Letter of Saint Paul to the Galatians

All of you who were baptized have clothed yourselves with Christ.

**Brothers and sisters:
Through faith you are all children of God in Christ Jesus.
For all of you who were baptized into Christ
>   have clothed yourselves with Christ.
There is neither Jew nor Greek,
>   there is neither slave nor free person,
>   there is not male and female;
>   for you are all one in Christ Jesus.
And if you belong to Christ,
>   then you are Abraham's descendant,
>   heirs according to the promise.

The word of the Lord.** All: **Thanks be to God.**

Gospel (Luke 9:18-24)
Alleluia (John 10:27)
℣. Alleluia, alleluia.   ℟. **Alleluia, alleluia.**
℣. My sheep hear my voice, says the Lord;
I know them, and they follow me. ℟.

✠ **A reading from the holy Gospel according to Luke**

All: **Glory to you, Lord.**

You are the Christ of God. The Son of Man must suffer greatly.

**Once when Jesus was praying in solitude,
>   and the disciples were with him,
>   he asked them, "Who do the crowds say that I am?"
They said in reply, "John the Baptist;
>   others, Elijah;
>   still others, 'One of the ancient prophets has arisen.'"**

Then he said to them, "But who do you say that I am?"
Peter said in reply, "The Christ of God."
He rebuked them
    and directed them not to tell this to anyone.

He said, "The Son of Man must suffer greatly
    and be rejected by the elders, the chief priests, and the
        scribes,
    and be killed and on the third day be raised."

Then he said to all,
    "If anyone wishes to come after me, he must deny
        himself
    and take up his cross daily and follow me.
For whoever wishes to save his life will lose it,
    but whoever loses his life for my sake will save it."

The Gospel of the Lord. All: **Praise to you, Lord Jesus Christ.**

Prayer over the Gifts
Lord,
receive our offering,
and may this sacrifice of praise
purify us in mind and heart
and make us always eager to serve you.
We ask this in the name of Jesus the Lord. All: **Amen.**

Communion Antiphon (Psalm 145:15)
The eyes of all look to you, O Lord, and you give them food in due season.

Prayer after Communion
Lord,
you give us the body and blood of your Son
to renew your life within us.
In your mercy, assure our redemption
and bring us to the eternal life
we celebrate in this eucharist.
We ask this through Christ our Lord. All: **Amen.**

Thirteenth Sunday in Ordinary Time

June 27, 2010

Reflection on the Gospel

This gospel depicts various responses to Jesus: some refuse him entrance into their village, some naively swear to follow wherever he leads, some put the exigencies of life ahead of following him. Each response suggests that people have some sense of the cost of following Jesus. Those who follow him must separate themselves from anything that hinders their resolutely journeying with him through death to new life. The price is high but so are the stakes and so is the reward.

- *One thing I could alter in order to journey to Jerusalem with Jesus more faithfully is . . .*

—Living Liturgy™, *Thirteenth Sunday in Ordinary Time 2010*

ENTRANCE ANTIPHON (Psalm 47:2)

All nations, clap your hands. Shout with a voice of joy to God.

OPENING PRAYER

Father,
you call your children
to walk in the light of Christ.
Free us from darkness
and keep us in the radiance of your truth.
We ask this through our Lord Jesus Christ, your Son,
who lives and reigns with you and the Holy Spirit,
one God, for ever and ever. All: **Amen.**

READING I (L 99-C) (1 Kings 19:16b, 19-21)

A reading from the first Book of Kings

Then Elisha left and followed Elijah as his attendant.

The LORD said to Elijah:
  "You shall anoint Elisha, son of Shaphat of
      Abel-meholah,
    as prophet to succeed you."

Elijah set out and came upon Elisha, son of Shaphat,
  as he was plowing with twelve yoke of oxen;
  he was following the twelfth.
Elijah went over to him and threw his cloak over him.
Elisha left the oxen, ran after Elijah, and said,
  "Please, let me kiss my father and mother goodbye,
  and I will follow you."
Elijah answered, "Go back!
Have I done anything to you?"
Elisha left him and, taking the yoke of oxen, slaughtered them;
  he used the plowing equipment for fuel to boil their flesh,
  and gave it to his people to eat.
Then Elisha left and followed Elijah as his attendant.

The word of the Lord. All: Thanks be to God.

Responsorial Psalm 16

P-512

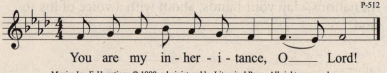

You are my in-her-i-tance, O—— Lord!

Music: Jay F. Hunstiger, © 1990, administered by Liturgical Press. All rights reserved.

Psalm 16:1-2, 5, 7-8, 9-10, 11

℟. (See 5a) **You are my inheritance, O Lord.**

Keep me, O God, for in you I take refuge;
  I say to the Lord, "My Lord are you.
O Lord, my allotted portion and my cup,
  you it is who hold fast my lot." ℟.

I bless the Lord who counsels me;
  even in the night my heart exhorts me.
I set the Lord ever before me;
  with him at my right hand I shall not be disturbed. ℟.

Therefore my heart is glad and my soul rejoices,
  my body, too, abides in confidence

because you will not abandon my soul to the
    netherworld,
  nor will you suffer your faithful one to undergo
    corruption. ℟.

You will show me the path to life,
  fullness of joys in your presence,
  the delights at your right hand forever. ℟.

Reading II (Galatians 5:1, 13-18)
A reading from the Letter of Saint Paul to the Galatians
You were called for freedom.

Brothers and sisters:
For freedom Christ set us free;
  so stand firm and do not submit again to the yoke of
    slavery.

For you were called for freedom, brothers and sisters.
But do not use this freedom
  as an opportunity for the flesh;
  rather, serve one another through love.
For the whole law is fulfilled in one statement,
  namely, *You shall love your neighbor as yourself.*
But if you go on biting and devouring one another,
  beware that you are not consumed by one another.

I say, then: live by the Spirit
  and you will certainly not gratify the desire of the flesh.
For the flesh has desires against the Spirit,
  and the Spirit against the flesh;
  these are opposed to each other,
  so that you may not do what you want.
But if you are guided by the Spirit, you are not under
  the law.

The word of the Lord. All: **Thanks be to God.**

Gospel (Luke 9:51-62)

Alleluia (1 Samuel 3:9; John 6:68c)

℣. Alleluia, alleluia. ℟. **Alleluia, alleluia.**
℣. Speak, Lord, your servant is listening;
you have the words of everlasting life. ℟.

✢ **A reading from the holy Gospel according to Luke**

All: **Glory to you, Lord.**

He resolutely determined to journey to Jerusalem. I will follow you wherever you go.

**When the days for Jesus' being taken up were fulfilled,
he resolutely determined to journey to Jerusalem,
and he sent messengers ahead of him.
On the way they entered a Samaritan village
to prepare for his reception there,
but they would not welcome him
because the destination of his journey was Jerusalem.
When the disciples James and John saw this they asked,
"Lord, do you want us to call down fire from heaven
to consume them?"
Jesus turned and rebuked them, and they journeyed to
another village.
As they were proceeding on their journey someone said
to him,
"I will follow you wherever you go."
Jesus answered him,
"Foxes have dens and birds of the sky have nests,
but the Son of Man has nowhere to rest his head."
And to another he said, "Follow me."
But he replied, "Lord, let me go first and bury my father."
But he answered him, "Let the dead bury their dead.
But you, go and proclaim the kingdom of God."
And another said, "I will follow you, Lord,
but first let me say farewell to my family at home."**

To him Jesus said, "No one who sets a hand to the plow and looks to what was left behind is fit for the kingdom of God."

The Gospel of the Lord. All: **Praise to you, Lord Jesus Christ.**

PRAYER OVER THE GIFTS
Lord God,
through your sacraments
you give us the power of your grace.
May this eucharist
help us to serve you faithfully.
We ask this in the name of Jesus the Lord. All: **Amen.**

COMMUNION ANTIPHON (John 17:20-21)
Father, I pray for them; may they be one in us, so that the world may believe it was you who sent me.

PRAYER AFTER COMMUNION
Lord,
may this sacrifice and communion
give us a share in your life
and help us bring your love to the world.
Grant this through Christ our Lord. All: **Amen.**

Fourteenth Sunday in Ordinary Time

July 4, 2010

Reflection on the Gospel

In this Sunday's gospel Jesus refers three times to an abundant harvest. The nature of this harvest is evident through the ministry of the disciples Jesus sends forth: peace, stability, nourishment, healing, rejoicing. This is no ordinary harvest of the fruits of the earth. This harvest is the fruit of God's kingdom "at hand" through the very ministry of Jesus and his disciples. Moreover, the harvest is being reaped today through us who continue to go forth in Jesus' name.

- *The abundance of "the kingdom of God is at hand" for me when . . .*

—Living Liturgy™, *Fourteenth Sunday in Ordinary Time 2010*

July 4

Entrance Antiphon (Psalm 47:10-11)
Within your temple, we ponder your loving kindness, O God. As your name, so also your praise reaches to the ends of the earth; your right hand is filled with justice.

Opening Prayer
Father,
through the obedience of Jesus,
your servant and your Son,
you raised a fallen world.
Free us from sin
and bring us the joy that lasts for ever.
We ask this through our Lord Jesus Christ, your Son,
who lives and reigns with you and the Holy Spirit,
one God, for ever and ever. All: **Amen.**

Reading I (L 102-C) (Isaiah 66:10-14c)
A reading from the Book of the Prophet Isaiah

Behold, I will spread prosperity over her like a river.

**Thus says the Lord:
Rejoice with Jerusalem and be glad because of her,
 all you who love her;
exult, exult with her,
 all you who were mourning over her!
Oh, that you may suck fully
 of the milk of her comfort,
that you may nurse with delight
 at her abundant breasts!
 For thus says the Lord:
Lo, I will spread prosperity over Jerusalem like a river,
 and the wealth of the nations like an overflowing
  torrent.
As nurslings, you shall be carried in her arms,
 and fondled in her lap;
as a mother comforts her child,
 so will I comfort you;
 in Jerusalem you shall find your comfort.**

When you see this, your heart shall rejoice
  and your bodies flourish like the grass;
the LORD's power shall be known to his servants.

The word of the Lord. All: **Thanks be to God.**

RESPONSORIAL PSALM 66

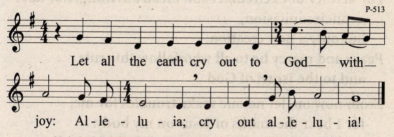

Music: Jay F. Hunstiger, © 1991, administered by Liturgical Press. All rights reserved.

Psalm 66:1-3, 4-5, 6-7, 16, 20

℟. (1) **Let all the earth cry out to God with joy.**

> Shout joyfully to God, all the earth,
>   sing praise to the glory of his name;
>   proclaim his glorious praise.
> Say to God, "How tremendous are your deeds!" ℟.

> "Let all on earth worship and sing praise to you,
>   sing praise to your name!"
> Come and see the works of God,
>   his tremendous deeds among the children of Adam. ℟.

> He has changed the sea into dry land;
>   through the river they passed on foot.
> Therefore let us rejoice in him.
> He rules by his might forever. ℟.

> Hear now, all you who fear God,
>   while I declare what he has done for me.
> Blessed be God who refused me not
>   my prayer or his kindness! ℟.

READING II (Galatians 6:14-18)

A reading from the Letter of Saint Paul to the Galatians

I bear the marks of Jesus on my body.

Brothers and sisters:
May I never boast except in the cross of our Lord Jesus
    Christ,
  through which the world has been crucified to me,
  and I to the world.
For neither does circumcision mean anything, nor does
    uncircumcision,
  but only a new creation.
Peace and mercy be to all who follow this rule
  and to the Israel of God.

From now on, let no one make troubles for me;
  for I bear the marks of Jesus on my body.

The grace of our Lord Jesus Christ be with your spirit,
  brothers and sisters. Amen.

The word of the Lord. All: Thanks be to God.

GOSPEL (Luke 10:1-12, 17-20) or Shorter Form [ ] (Luke 10:1-9)
ALLELUIA (Colossians 3:15a, 16a)
℣. Alleluia, alleluia. ℟. **Alleluia, alleluia.**
℣. Let the peace of Christ control your hearts;
  let the word of Christ dwell in you richly. ℟.

☩ A reading from the holy Gospel according to Luke

All: **Glory to you, Lord.**

Your peace will rest on that person.

[At that time the Lord appointed seventy-two others
  whom he sent ahead of him in pairs
  to every town and place he intended to visit.
He said to them,
  "The harvest is abundant but the laborers are few;
  so ask the master of the harvest
  to send out laborers for his harvest.
Go on your way;
  behold, I am sending you like lambs among wolves.
Carry no money bag, no sack, no sandals;
  and greet no one along the way.

Into whatever house you enter, first say,
>   'Peace to this household.'

If a peaceful person lives there,
>   your peace will rest on him;
>   but if not, it will return to you.

Stay in the same house and eat and drink what is offered to you,
>   for the laborer deserves his payment.

Do not move about from one house to another.

Whatever town you enter and they welcome you,
>   eat what is set before you,
>   cure the sick in it and say to them,
>   'The kingdom of God is at hand for you.']

Whatever town you enter and they do not receive you,
>   go out into the streets and say,
>   'The dust of your town that clings to our feet,
>   even that we shake off against you.'

Yet know this: the kingdom of God is at hand.

I tell you,
>   it will be more tolerable for Sodom on that day than for that town."

The seventy-two returned rejoicing, and said,
>   "Lord, even the demons are subject to us because of your name."

Jesus said, "I have observed Satan fall like lightning from the sky.

Behold, I have given you the power to 'tread upon serpents' and scorpions
>   and upon the full force of the enemy and nothing will harm you.

Nevertheless, do not rejoice because the spirits are subject to you,
>   but rejoice because your names are written in heaven."

The Gospel of the Lord. All: **Praise to you, Lord Jesus Christ.**

PRAYER OVER THE GIFTS

Lord,
let this offering to the glory of your name
purify us and bring us closer to eternal life.
We ask this in the name of Jesus the Lord. All: **Amen.**

COMMUNION ANTIPHON (Psalm 33:9)

Taste and see the goodness of the Lord; blessed is he who hopes in God.

PRAYER AFTER COMMUNION

Lord,
may we never fail to praise you
for the fullness of life and salvation
you give us in this eucharist.
We ask this through Christ our Lord. All: **Amen.**

Fifteenth Sunday in Ordinary Time

July 11, 2010

Reflection on the Gospel

The lawyer put an important question to Jesus, but it is insincere because he is really posing the question "to test" him. Jesus takes his question at face value and gives a right and all-embracing answer about how we "inherit eternal life." We must make love of God and neighbor the guiding focus of our lives here and now. The Good Samaritan parable admirably and clearly illustrates this kind of love. Our challenge: to go this far in our loving.

- *In loving God, I have gone this far . . . In loving my neighbor I have gone this far . . .*

—*Living Liturgy™, Fifteenth Sunday in Ordinary Time 2010*

ENTRANCE ANTIPHON (Psalm 16:15)

In my justice I shall see your face, O Lord; when your glory appears, my joy will be full.

July 11   315

Opening Prayer
God our Father,
your light of truth
guides us to the way of Christ.
May all who follow him
reject what is contrary to the gospel.
We ask this through our Lord Jesus Christ, your Son,
who lives and reigns with you and the Holy Spirit,
one God, for ever and ever. All: **Amen.**

Reading I (L 105-C) (Deuteronomy 30:10-14)
A reading from the Book of Deuteronomy

The word is very near to you: you have only to carry it out.

Moses said to the people:
   "If only you would heed the voice of the L ORD,
         your God,
   and keep his commandments and statutes
   that are written in this book of the law,
   when you return to the L ORD, your God,
   with all your heart and all your soul.

"For this command that I enjoin on you today
   is not too mysterious and remote for you.
It is not up in the sky, that you should say,
   'Who will go up in the sky to get it for us
   and tell us of it, that we may carry it out?'
Nor is it across the sea, that you should say,
   'Who will cross the sea to get it for us
   and tell us of it, that we may carry it out?'
No, it is something very near to you,
   already in your mouths and in your hearts;
   you have only to carry it out."

The word of the Lord. All: Thanks be to God.

Responsorial Psalm 69 or 19

P-514

Turn to the Lord in your need, and you will live.

Music: Jay F. Hunstiger, © 1991, administered by Liturgical Press. All rights reserved.

1. Psalm 69:14, 17, 30-31, 33-34, 36, 37

℟. (*See* 33) **Turn to the Lord in your need, and you will live.**

> I pray to you, O Lord,
> > for the time of your favor, O God!
> In your great kindness answer me
> > with your constant help.
> Answer me, O Lord, for bounteous is your kindness:
> > in your great mercy turn toward me. ℟.
>
> I am afflicted and in pain;
> > let your saving help, O God, protect me.
> I will praise the name of God in song,
> > and I will glorify him with thanksgiving. ℟.
>
> "See, you lowly ones, and be glad;
> > you who seek God, may your hearts revive!
> For the Lord hears the poor,
> > and his own who are in bonds he spurns not." ℟.
>
> For God will save Zion
> > and rebuild the cities of Judah.
> The descendants of his servants shall inherit it,
> > and those who love his name shall inhabit it. ℟.

or:

Music: Jay F. Hunstiger, © 1991, administered by Liturgical Press. All rights reserved.

2. Psalm 19:8, 9, 10, 11

℟. (9a) **Your words, Lord, are Spirit and life.**

> The law of the Lord is perfect,
> > refreshing the soul;
> the decree of the Lord is trustworthy,
> > giving wisdom to the simple. ℟.

The precepts of the Lord are right,
   rejoicing the heart;
the command of the Lord is clear,
   enlightening the eye. ℟.

The fear of the Lord is pure,
   enduring forever;
the ordinances of the Lord are true,
   all of them just. ℟.

They are more precious than gold,
   than a heap of purest gold;
sweeter also than syrup
   or honey from the comb. ℟.

Reading II (Colossians 1:15-20)

A reading from the Letter of Saint Paul to the Colossians

All things were created through him and for him.

**Christ Jesus is the image of the invisible God,
   the firstborn of all creation.
For in him were created all things in heaven and on earth,
   the visible and the invisible,
      whether thrones or dominions or principalities or powers;
   all things were created through him and for him.
He is before all things,
   and in him all things hold together.
He is the head of the body, the church.
He is the beginning, the firstborn from the dead,
   that in all things he himself might be preeminent.
For in him all the fullness was pleased to dwell,
   and through him to reconcile all things for him,
   making peace by the blood of his cross
      through him, whether those on earth or those in heaven.

The word of the Lord.** All: **Thanks be to God.**

Gospel (Luke 10:25-37)
Alleluia (See John 6:63c, 68c)

℣. Alleluia, alleluia. ℟. **Alleluia, alleluia.**
℣. Your words, Lord, are Spirit and life;
you have the words of everlasting life. ℟.

✠ A reading from the holy Gospel according to Luke

All: **Glory to you, Lord.**

Who is my neighbor?

There was a scholar of the law who stood up to test Jesus and said,
 "Teacher, what must I do to inherit eternal life?"
Jesus said to him, "What is written in the law?
How do you read it?"
He said in reply,
 "You shall love the Lord, your God,
 with all your heart,
 with all your being,
 with all your strength,
 and with all your mind,
 and your neighbor as yourself."
He replied to him, "You have answered correctly;
 do this and you will live."
But because he wished to justify himself, he said to Jesus,
 "And who is my neighbor?"
Jesus replied,
 "A man fell victim to robbers
 as he went down from Jerusalem to Jericho.
They stripped and beat him and went off leaving him half-dead.
A priest happened to be going down that road,
 but when he saw him, he passed by on the opposite side.
Likewise a Levite came to the place,
 and when he saw him, he passed by on the opposite side.
But a Samaritan traveler who came upon him
 was moved with compassion at the sight.

He approached the victim,
>   poured oil and wine over his wounds and bandaged them.
Then he lifted him up on his own animal,
>   took him to an inn, and cared for him.
The next day he took out two silver coins
>   and gave them to the innkeeper with the instruction,
>   'Take care of him.
If you spend more than what I have given you,
>   I shall repay you on my way back.'
Which of these three, in your opinion,
>   was neighbor to the robbers' victim?"
He answered, "The one who treated him with mercy."
Jesus said to him, "Go and do likewise."

The Gospel of the Lord. All: **Praise to you, Lord Jesus Christ.**

Prayer over the Gifts
Lord,
accept the gifts of your Church.
May this eucharist
help us grow in holiness and faith.
We ask this in the name of Jesus the Lord. All: **Amen.**

Communion Antiphon (Psalm 83:4-5)
The sparrow even finds a home, the swallow finds a nest wherein to place her young, near to your altars, Lord of hosts, my King, my God! How happy they who dwell in your house! For ever they are praising you.

Prayer after Communion
Lord,
by our sharing in the mystery of this eucharist,
let your saving love grow within us.
Grant this through Christ our Lord. All: **Amen.**

Sixteenth Sunday in Ordinary Time

July 18, 2010

Reflection on the Gospel

What is each of the people in the gospel story doing? Martha is serving; Mary is listening; Jesus is teaching. While Jesus says that Mary has the "better part," this doesn't necessarily mean that listening to Jesus is either the only or the easier part. Listening to Jesus with a heart truly able to hear is difficult, indeed. Listening to Jesus is the "better part" only when it leads us to serve and teach as Jesus himself did.

- *I understand the "better part" chosen by Mary to mean . . . For me to embrace this teaching of Jesus more deeply I need to . . .*

—Living Liturgy™, *Sixteenth Sunday in Ordinary Time 2010*

ENTRANCE ANTIPHON (Psalm 53:6, 8)

God himself is my help. The Lord upholds my life. I will offer you a willing sacrifice; I will praise your name, O Lord, for its goodness.

OPENING PRAYER

Lord,
be merciful to your people.
Fill us with your gifts
and make us always eager to serve you
in faith, hope, and love.
Grant this through our Lord Jesus Christ, your Son,
who lives and reigns with you and the Holy Spirit,
one God, for ever and ever. All: **Amen.**

READING I (L 108-C) (Genesis 18:1-10a)

A reading from the Book of Genesis

Lord, do not go on past your servant.

**The LORD appeared to Abraham by the terebinth of Mamre,
  as he sat in the entrance of his tent,
  while the day was growing hot.**

Looking up, Abraham saw three men standing nearby.
When he saw them, he ran from the entrance of the tent
 to greet them;
 and bowing to the ground, he said:
 "Sir, if I may ask you this favor,
 please do not go on past your servant.
Let some water be brought, that you may bathe your feet,
 and then rest yourselves under the tree.
Now that you have come this close to your servant,
 let me bring you a little food, that you may refresh
 yourselves;
 and afterward you may go on your way."
The men replied, "Very well, do as you have said."

Abraham hastened into the tent and told Sarah,
 "Quick, three measures of fine flour! Knead it and
 make rolls."
He ran to the herd, picked out a tender, choice steer,
 and gave it to a servant, who quickly prepared it.
Then Abraham got some curds and milk,
 as well as the steer that had been prepared,
 and set these before the three men;
 and he waited on them under the tree while they ate.

They asked Abraham, "Where is your wife Sarah?"
He replied, "There in the tent."
One of them said, "I will surely return to you about this
 time next year,
 and Sarah will then have a son."

The word of the Lord. All: Thanks be to God.

Responsorial Psalm 15

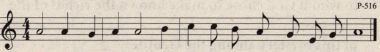

He who does jus-tice will live in the pres-ence of the Lord.

Music: Jay F. Hunstiger, © 1990, administered by Liturgical Press. All rights reserved.

Psalm 15:2-3, 3-4, 5

℟. (1a) **He who does justice will live in the presence of the Lord.**

One who walks blamelessly and does justice;
 who thinks the truth in his heart
 and slanders not with his tongue. ℟.

Who harms not his fellow man,
 nor takes up a reproach against his neighbor;
by whom the reprobate is despised,
 while he honors those who fear the Lord. ℟.

Who lends not his money at usury
 and accepts no bribe against the innocent.
One who does these things
 shall never be disturbed. ℟.

Reading II (Colossians 1:24-28)
A reading from the Letter of Saint Paul to the Colossians

The mystery hidden from ages has now been manifested to his holy ones.

**Brothers and sisters:
Now I rejoice in my sufferings for your sake,
 and in my flesh I am filling up
 what is lacking in the afflictions of Christ
 on behalf of his body, which is the church,
 of which I am a minister
 in accordance with God's stewardship given to me
 to bring to completion for you the word of God,
 the mystery hidden from ages and from generations past.
But now it has been manifested to his holy ones,
 to whom God chose to make known the riches of the glory
 of this mystery among the Gentiles;
 it is Christ in you, the hope for glory.**

It is he whom we proclaim,
> admonishing everyone and teaching everyone with all wisdom,
> that we may present everyone perfect in Christ.

The word of the Lord. All: **Thanks be to God.**

Gospel (Luke 10:38-42)
Alleluia (*See* Luke 8:15)

℣. Alleluia, alleluia. ℟. **Alleluia, alleluia.**
℣. Blessed are they who have kept the word with a generous heart
> and yield a harvest through perseverance. ℟.

✠ **A reading from the holy Gospel according to Luke**

All: **Glory to you, Lord.**

Martha welcomed him. Mary has chosen the better part.

Jesus entered a village
> where a woman whose name was Martha welcomed him.

She had a sister named Mary
> who sat beside the Lord at his feet listening to him speak.

Martha, burdened with much serving, came to him and said,
> "Lord, do you not care
> that my sister has left me by myself to do the serving?

Tell her to help me."

The Lord said to her in reply,
> "Martha, Martha, you are anxious and worried about many things.

There is need of only one thing.

Mary has chosen the better part
> and it will not be taken from her."

The Gospel of the Lord. All: **Praise to you, Lord Jesus Christ.**

July 18

Prayer over the Gifts
Lord,
bring us closer to salvation
through these gifts which we bring in your honor.
Accept the perfect sacrifice you have given us,
bless it as you blessed the gifts of Abel.
We ask this through Christ our Lord. All: **Amen.**

Communion Antiphon (Psalm 110:4-5)
The Lord keeps in our minds the wonderful things he has done. He is compassion and love; he always provides for his faithful.

Prayer after Communion
Merciful Father,
may these mysteries
give us new purpose
and bring us to a new life in you.
We ask this in the name of Jesus the Lord. All: **Amen.**

Seventeenth Sunday in Ordinary Time

July 25, 2010

Reflection on the Gospel

In this gospel Jesus teaches us to whom we pray: God who is a generous and caring Father. He also teaches us for what we should pray: not just for our "daily bread" but, more important, for ultimate needs: the furthering of God's kingdom, the gift of forgiveness, and protection from anything that would take us from God. It is persistence in prayer that brings us deeper into our relationship with God and that assures us of the ultimate goal of life: eternal happiness with our divine Lover.

• *What is most comforting about praying is . . . most difficult is . . .*

—Living Liturgy™, *Seventeenth Sunday in Ordinary Time 2010*

Entrance Antiphon (Psalm 67:6-7, 36)
God is in his holy dwelling; he will give a home to the lonely, he gives power and strength to his people.

Opening Prayer

God our Father and protector,
without you nothing is holy,
nothing has value.
Guide us to everlasting life
by helping us to use wisely
the blessings you have given to the world.
We ask this through our Lord Jesus Christ, your Son,
who lives and reigns with you and the Holy Spirit,
one God, for ever and ever. All: **Amen.**

Reading I (L 111-C) (Genesis 18:20-32)
A reading from the Book of Genesis

Let not my Lord grow angry if I speak.

**In those days, the LORD said: "The outcry against Sodom
    and Gomorrah is so great,
    and their sin so grave,
    that I must go down and see whether or not their
        actions
    fully correspond to the cry against them that comes
        to me.
I mean to find out."**

**While Abraham's visitors walked on farther toward
    Sodom,
    the LORD remained standing before Abraham.
Then Abraham drew nearer and said:
    "Will you sweep away the innocent with the guilty?
Suppose there were fifty innocent people in the city;
    would you wipe out the place, rather than spare it
    for the sake of the fifty innocent people within it?
Far be it from you to do such a thing,
    to make the innocent die with the guilty
        so that the innocent and the guilty would be treated
            alike!
Should not the judge of all the world act with justice?"**

The LORD replied,
  "If I find fifty innocent people in the city of Sodom,
  I will spare the whole place for their sake."
Abraham spoke up again:
  "See how I am presuming to speak to my Lord,
  though I am but dust and ashes!
What if there are five less than fifty innocent people?
Will you destroy the whole city because of those five?"
He answered, "I will not destroy it, if I find forty-five
  there."
But Abraham persisted, saying, "What if only forty are
  found there?"
He replied, "I will forbear doing it for the sake of the forty."
Then Abraham said, "Let not my Lord grow impatient if
  I go on.
What if only thirty are found there?"
He replied, "I will forbear doing it if I can find but thirty
  there."
Still Abraham went on,
  "Since I have thus dared to speak to my Lord,
  what if there are no more than twenty?"
The LORD answered, "I will not destroy it, for the sake of
  the twenty."
But he still persisted:
  "Please, let not my Lord grow angry if I speak up this
  last time.
What if there are at least ten there?"
He replied, "For the sake of those ten, I will not destroy it."

The word of the Lord. All: Thanks be to God.

RESPONSORIAL PSALM 138

P-517

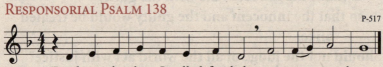

Lord, on the day I called for help, you an-swered me.

Music: Jay F. Hunstiger, © 1991, administered by Liturgical Press. All rights reserved.

Psalm 138:1-2, 2-3, 6-7, 7-8

℟. (3a) **Lord, on the day I called for help, you answered me.**

I will give thanks to you, O Lord, with all my heart,
   for you have heard the words of my mouth;
   in the presence of the angels I will sing your praise;
I will worship at your holy temple
   and give thanks to your name. ℟.

Because of your kindness and your truth;
   for you have made great above all things
   your name and your promise.
When I called you answered me;
   you built up strength within me. ℟.

The Lord is exalted, yet the lowly he sees,
   and the proud he knows from afar.
Though I walk amid distress, you preserve me;
   against the anger of my enemies you raise your hand. ℟.

Your right hand saves me.
   The Lord will complete what he has done for me;
your kindness, O Lord, endures forever;
   forsake not the work of your hands. ℟.

Reading II (Colossians 2:12-14)

A reading from the Letter of Saint Paul to the Colossians

God has brought you to life along with Christ, having forgiven us all our transgressions.

**Brothers and sisters:
You were buried with him in baptism,
   in which you were also raised with him
   through faith in the power of God,
   who raised him from the dead.
And even when you were dead
   in transgressions and the uncircumcision of your flesh,
   he brought you to life along with him,
   having forgiven us all our transgressions;
   obliterating the bond against us, with its legal claims,
   which was opposed to us,**

he also removed it from our midst, nailing it to the
cross.

The word of the Lord. All: **Thanks be to God.**

GOSPEL (Luke 11:1-13)
ALLELUIA (Romans 8:15bc)
℣. Alleluia, alleluia. ℟. **Alleluia, alleluia.**
℣. You have received a Spirit of adoption,
through which we cry, Abba, Father. ℟.

✠ **A reading from the holy Gospel according to Luke**

All: **Glory to you, Lord.**

Ask and you will receive.

**Jesus was praying in a certain place, and when he had finished,
one of his disciples said to him,
"Lord, teach us to pray just as John taught his disciples."
He said to them, "When you pray, say:
Father, hallowed be your name,
your kingdom come.
Give us each day our daily bread
and forgive us our sins
for we ourselves forgive everyone in debt to us,
and do not subject us to the final test."
And he said to them, "Suppose one of you has a friend
to whom he goes at midnight and says,
'Friend, lend me three loaves of bread,
for a friend of mine has arrived at my house from a journey
and I have nothing to offer him,'
and he says in reply from within,
'Do not bother me; the door has already been locked
and my children and I are already in bed.
I cannot get up to give you anything.'
I tell you,
if he does not get up to give the visitor the loaves**

> because of their friendship,
> he will get up to give him whatever he needs
> because of his persistence.

"And I tell you, ask and you will receive;
   seek and you will find;
   knock and the door will be opened to you.
For everyone who asks, receives;
   and the one who seeks, finds;
   and to the one who knocks, the door will be opened.
What father among you would hand his son a snake
   when he asks for a fish?
Or hand him a scorpion when he asks for an egg?
If you then, who are wicked,
   know how to give good gifts to your children,
   how much more will the Father in heaven
   give the Holy Spirit to those who ask him?"

The Gospel of the Lord. All: **Praise to you, Lord Jesus Christ.**

Prayer over the Gifts

Lord,
receive these offerings
chosen from your many gifts.
May these mysteries make us holy
and lead us to eternal joy.
Grant this through Christ our Lord. All: **Amen.**

Communion Antiphon (Psalm 102:2)

O bless the Lord, my soul, and remember all his kindness.

Prayer after Communion

Lord,
we receive the sacrament
which celebrates the memory
of the death and resurrection of Christ your Son.
May this gift bring us closer to our eternal salvation.
We ask this through Christ our Lord. All: **Amen.**

Eighteenth Sunday in Ordinary Time

August 1, 2010

Reflection on the Gospel

The rich man in the gospel is a fool because he mistakenly thinks his future happiness is guaranteed by his possessions. Even had his life not been demanded of him, those possessions could not have bought him happiness. Jesus cautions us to "guard against" such greed and turn our attention to where our real inheritance lies: in the fullness of life God wishes to give us. How mistaken the rich man is to identify good living with material things and miss "[W]hat matters to God"!

- *For me being "rich in what matters to God" means . . . My richness (or poverty) in what matters to God is revealed by . . .*

—Living Liturgy™, *Eighteenth Sunday in Ordinary Time 2010*

Entrance Antiphon (Psalm 70:2, 6)

God, come to my help. Lord, quickly give me assistance. You are the one who helps me and sets me free: Lord, do not be long in coming.

Opening Prayer

Father of everlasting goodness,
our origin and guide,
be close to us
and hear the prayers of all who praise you.
Forgive our sins and restore us to life.
Keep us safe in your love.
Grant this through our Lord Jesus Christ, your Son,
who lives and reigns with you and the Holy Spirit,
one God, for ever and ever. All: **Amen.**

Reading I (L 114-C) (Ecclesiastes 1:2; 2:21-23)

A reading from the Book of Ecclesiastes

What profit comes to a man from all his toil?

Vanity of vanities, says Qoheleth,
   vanity of vanities! All things are vanity!

Here is one who has labored with wisdom and knowledge and skill,
   and yet to another who has not labored over it,
   he must leave property.
This also is vanity and a great misfortune.
For what profit comes to man from all the toil and anxiety of heart
   with which he has labored under the sun?
All his days sorrow and grief is his occupation;
   even at night his mind is not at rest.
This also is vanity.

The word of the Lord. All: **Thanks be to God.**

Responsorial Psalm 90

If to-day you hear his voice, hard-en not your hearts.

If to-day you hear his voice, hard-en not your hearts.

_{Music: Jay F. Hunstiger, © 1993, administered by Liturgical Press. All rights reserved.}

Psalm 90:3-4, 5-6, 12-13, 14 and 17

℟. (8) **If today you hear his voice, harden not your hearts.**

You turn man back to dust,
   saying, "Return, O children of men."
For a thousand years in your sight
   are as yesterday, now that it is past,
   or as a watch of the night. ℟.

You make an end of them in their sleep;
   the next morning they are like the changing grass,
which at dawn springs up anew,
   but by evening wilts and fades. ℟.

(continued)

Teach us to number our days aright,
> that we may gain wisdom of heart.
Return, O Lord! How long?
> Have pity on your servants! ℟.

Fill us at daybreak with your kindness,
> that we may shout for joy and gladness all our days.
And may the gracious care of the Lord our God be ours;
> prosper the work of our hands for us!
> Prosper the work of our hands! ℟.

Reading II (Colossians 3:1-5, 9-11)
A reading from the Letter of Saint Paul to the Colossians

Seek what is above, where Christ is.

Brothers and sisters:
If you were raised with Christ, seek what is above,
> **where Christ is seated at the right hand of God.**
Think of what is above, not of what is on earth.
For you have died,
> **and your life is hidden with Christ in God.**
When Christ your life appears,
> **then you too will appear with him in glory.**

Put to death, then, the parts of you that are earthly:
> **immorality, impurity, passion, evil desire,**
> **and the greed that is idolatry.**
Stop lying to one another,
> **since you have taken off the old self with its practices**
> **and have put on the new self,**
> **which is being renewed, for knowledge,**
> **in the image of its creator.**
Here there is not Greek and Jew,
> **circumcision and uncircumcision,**
> **barbarian, Scythian, slave, free;**
> **but Christ is all and in all.**

The word of the Lord. All: **Thanks be to God.**

Gospel (Luke 12:13-21)
Alleluia (Matthew 5:3)
℣. Alleluia, alleluia. ℟. **Alleluia, alleluia.**
℣. Blessed are the poor in spirit,
for theirs is the kingdom of heaven. ℟.

✠ **A reading from the holy Gospel according to Luke**

All: **Glory to you, Lord.**

The things you have prepared, to whom will they belong?

Someone in the crowd said to Jesus,
   "Teacher, tell my brother to share the inheritance
      with me."
He replied to him,
   "Friend, who appointed me as your judge and
      arbitrator?"
Then he said to the crowd,
   "Take care to guard against all greed,
   for though one may be rich,
   one's life does not consist of possessions."
Then he told them a parable.
"There was a rich man whose land produced a bountiful
      harvest.
He asked himself, 'What shall I do,
   for I do not have space to store my harvest?'
And he said, 'This is what I shall do:
   I shall tear down my barns and build larger ones.
There I shall store all my grain and other goods
   and I shall say to myself, "Now as for you,
   you have so many good things stored up for many
      years,
   rest, eat, drink, be merry!"'
But God said to him,
   'You fool, this night your life will be demanded of you;
   and the things you have prepared, to whom will they
      belong?'

Thus will it be for all who store up treasure for themselves but are not rich in what matters to God."

The Gospel of the Lord. All: **Praise to you, Lord Jesus Christ.**

Prayer over the Gifts
Merciful Lord,
make holy these gifts,
and let our spiritual sacrifice
make us an everlasting gift to you.
We ask this in the name of Jesus the Lord. All: **Amen.**

Communion Antiphon (John 6:35)
The Lord says: I am the bread of life. A man who comes to me will not go away hungry, and no one who believes in me will thirst.

Prayer after Communion
Lord,
you give us the strength of new life
by the gift of the eucharist.
Protect us with your love
and prepare us for eternal redemption.
We ask this through Christ our Lord. All: **Amen.**

Nineteenth Sunday in Ordinary Time

August 8, 2010

Reflection on the Gospel

In the gospel Jesus makes clear that the blessed servant is the one who does the master's will even when the master is absent. Being prepared for the master's presence is not a matter of calculating time; it is a matter of faithfulness. In the master's absence, the faithful servant acts as the master himself would—caring for others, giving them all they need. Doing the master's will and remaining faithful is being the master in his absence. Of such is discipleship.

• *In the Master's absence, I continue his work by . . .*

—Living Liturgy™, *Nineteenth Sunday in Ordinary Time 2010*

Entrance Antiphon (Psalm 73:20, 19, 22, 23)
Lord, be true to your covenant, forget not the life of your poor ones for ever. Rise up, O God, and defend your cause; do not ignore the shouts of your enemies.

Opening Prayer
Almighty and ever-living God,
your Spirit made us your children,
confident to call you Father.
Increase your Spirit within us
and bring us to our promised inheritance.
Grant this through our Lord Jesus Christ, your Son,
who lives and reigns with you and the Holy Spirit,
one God, for ever and ever. All: **Amen.**

Reading I (L 117-C) (Wisdom 18:6-9)
A reading from the Book of Wisdom

Just as you punished our adversaries, you glorified us whom you had summoned.

**The night of the passover was known beforehand to our fathers,
    that, with sure knowledge of the oaths in which they put their faith,
    they might have courage.
Your people awaited the salvation of the just
    and the destruction of their foes.
For when you punished our adversaries,
    in this you glorified us whom you had summoned.
For in secret the holy children of the good were offering sacrifice
    and putting into effect with one accord the divine institution.**

The word of the Lord. All: **Thanks be to God.**

Responsorial Psalm 33

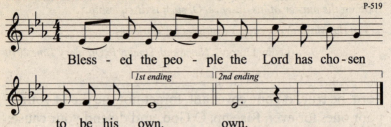

Music: Jay F. Hunstiger, © 1991, administered by Liturgical Press. All rights reserved.

Psalm 33:1, 12, 18-19, 20-22

℟. (12b) **Blessed the people the Lord has chosen to be his own.**

Exult, you just, in the LORD;
 praise from the upright is fitting.
Blessed the nation whose God is the LORD,
 the people he has chosen for his own inheritance. ℟.

See, the eyes of the LORD are upon those who fear him,
 upon those who hope for his kindness,
to deliver them from death
 and preserve them in spite of famine. ℟.

Our soul waits for the LORD,
 who is our help and our shield.
May your kindness, O LORD, be upon us
 who have put our hope in you. ℟.

Reading II (Hebrews 11:1-2, 8-19) *or* Shorter Form [ ] (Hebrews 11:1-2, 8-12)

A reading from the Letter to the Hebrews

Abraham looked forward to the city whose architect and maker is God.

**[Brothers and sisters:
Faith is the realization of what is hoped for
 and evidence of things not seen.
Because of it the ancients were well attested.

By faith Abraham obeyed when he was called to go out
 to a place**

that he was to receive as an inheritance;
    he went out, not knowing where he was to go.
By faith he sojourned in the promised land as in a
      foreign country,
    dwelling in tents with Isaac and Jacob, heirs of the
      same promise;
    for he was looking forward to the city with foundations,
    whose architect and maker is God.
By faith he received power to generate,
    even though he was past the normal age
    —and Sarah herself was sterile—
    for he thought that the one who had made the promise
      was trustworthy.
So it was that there came forth from one man,
    himself as good as dead,
      descendants as numerous as the stars in the sky
      and as countless as the sands on the seashore.]

All these died in faith.
They did not receive what had been promised
    but saw it and greeted it from afar
    and acknowledged themselves to be strangers and
      aliens on earth,
    for those who speak thus show that they are seeking a
      homeland.
If they had been thinking of the land from which they
      had come,
    they would have had opportunity to return.
But now they desire a better homeland, a heavenly one.
Therefore, God is not ashamed to be called their God,
    for he has prepared a city for them.

By faith Abraham, when put to the test, offered up Isaac,
    and he who had received the promises was ready to
      offer his only son,
    of whom it was said,
    "Through Isaac descendants shall bear your name."

He reasoned that God was able to raise even from the
    dead,
  and he received Isaac back as a symbol.

The word of the Lord. All: **Thanks be to God.**

Gospel (Luke 12:32-48) *or* Shorter Form [ ] (Luke 12:35-40)
Alleluia (Matthew 24:42a, 44)
℣. Alleluia, alleluia. ℟. **Alleluia, alleluia.**
℣. Stay awake and be ready!
  For you do not know on what day the Son of Man will
    come. ℟.

✠ **A reading from the holy Gospel according to Luke**

All: **Glory to you, Lord.**

You also must be prepared.

[Jesus said to his disciples:]
  "Do not be afraid any longer, little flock,
  for your Father is pleased to give you the kingdom.
Sell your belongings and give alms.
Provide money bags for yourselves that do not wear out,
  an inexhaustible treasure in heaven
  that no thief can reach nor moth destroy.
For where your treasure is, there also will your heart be.

["Gird your loins and light your lamps
  and be like servants who await their master's return
    from a wedding,
  ready to open immediately when he comes and knocks.
Blessed are those servants
  whom the master finds vigilant on his arrival.
Amen, I say to you, he will gird himself,
  have them recline at table, and proceed to wait on them.
And should he come in the second or third watch
  and find them prepared in this way,
  blessed are those servants.
Be sure of this:
  if the master of the house had known the hour

when the thief was coming,
he would not have let his house be broken into.
You also must be prepared, for at an hour you do not expect,
the Son of Man will come."]

Then Peter said,
"Lord, is this parable meant for us or for everyone?"
And the Lord replied,
"Who, then, is the faithful and prudent steward
whom the master will put in charge of his servants
to distribute the food allowance at the proper time?
Blessed is that servant whom his master on arrival finds doing so.
Truly, I say to you, the master will put the servant
in charge of all his property.
But if that servant says to himself,
'My master is delayed in coming,'
and begins to beat the menservants and the maidservants,
to eat and drink and get drunk,
then that servant's master will come
on an unexpected day and at an unknown hour
and will punish the servant severely
and assign him a place with the unfaithful.
That servant who knew his master's will
but did not make preparations nor act in accord with his will
shall be beaten severely;
and the servant who was ignorant of his master's will
but acted in a way deserving of a severe beating
shall be beaten only lightly.
Much will be required of the person entrusted with much,
and still more will be demanded of the person entrusted with more."

The Gospel of the Lord. All: **Praise to you, Lord Jesus Christ.**

Prayer over the Gifts
God of power,
giver of the gifts we bring,
accept the offering of your Church
and make it the sacrament of our salvation.
We ask this through Christ our Lord. All: **Amen.**

Communion Antiphon (Psalm 147:12, 14)
Praise the Lord, Jerusalem; he feeds you with the finest wheat.

Prayer after Communion
Lord,
may the eucharist you give us
bring us to salvation
and keep us faithful to the light of your truth.
We ask this in the name of Jesus the Lord. All: **Amen.**

Assumption of the Blessed Virgin Mary

VIGIL MASS

August 14, 2010

The Mass of the Vigil of the Assumption is to be used at evening Masses.

Reflection on the Gospel

This solemnity celebrates the "great things" God has done for Mary. Mary's assumption of body and soul into heaven celebrates the mercy of God and the promise to us of a share in that same mercy. It is God who does great things because God has promised mercy. The great thing Mary does is say yes to being an instrument of God's promise. The great thing God does for us is invite us to share in that same promise—everlasting life.

- The "great things" God did for Mary are . . . God does for me are . . .

—*Living Liturgy*™, *Assumption 2010*

Entrance Antiphon
All honor to you, Mary! Today you were raised above the choirs of angels to lasting glory with Christ.

Opening Prayer
Almighty God,
you gave a humble virgin
the privilege of being the mother of your Son,
and crowned her with the glory of heaven.
May the prayers of the Virgin Mary
bring us to the salvation of Christ
and raise us up to eternal life.
We ask this through our Lord Jesus Christ, your Son,
who lives and reigns with you and the Holy Spirit,
one God, for ever and ever. All: **Amen.**

Reading I (L 621) (1 Chronicles 15:3-4, 15-16; 16:1-2)
A reading from the first Book of Chronicles

They brought in the ark of God and set it within the tent which David had pitched for it.

David assembled all Israel in Jerusalem to bring the ark of the Lord
    to the place which he had prepared for it.
David also called together the sons of Aaron and the Levites.

The Levites bore the ark of God on their shoulders with poles,
    as Moses had ordained according to the word of the Lord.

David commanded the chiefs of the Levites
    to appoint their kinsmen as chanters,
    to play on musical instruments, harps, lyres, and cymbals,
    to make a loud sound of rejoicing.

They brought in the ark of God and set it within the tent which David had pitched for it.
Then they offered up burnt offerings and peace offerings to God.

When David had finished offering up the burnt offerings and peace offerings,
he blessed the people in the name of the Lord.

The word of the Lord. All: **Thanks be to God.**

Responsorial Psalm 132

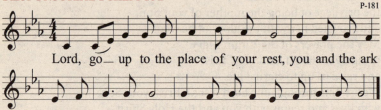

Lord, go up to the place of your rest, you and the ark of your ho-li-ness, you and the ark of your ho-li-ness.

Music: Jay F. Hunstiger, © 1990, administered by Liturgical Press. All rights reserved.

Psalm 132:6-7, 9-10, 13-14

℟. (8) **Lord, go up to the place of your rest, you and the ark of your holiness.**

Behold, we heard of it in Ephrathah;
  we found it in the fields of Jaar.
Let us enter into his dwelling,
  let us worship at his footstool. ℟.

May your priests be clothed with justice;
  let your faithful ones shout merrily for joy.
For the sake of David your servant,
  reject not the plea of your anointed. ℟.

For the Lord has chosen Zion;
  he prefers her for his dwelling.
"Zion is my resting place forever;
  in her will I dwell, for I prefer her." ℟.

Reading II (1 Corinthians 15:54b-57)
A reading from the first Letter of Saint Paul to the Corinthians

God gave us victory through Jesus Christ.

Brothers and sisters:
When that which is mortal clothes itself with immortality,
   then the word that is written shall come about:

> *Death is swallowed up in victory.*
> *Where, O death, is your victory?*
> *Where, O death, is your sting?*

The sting of death is sin,
   and the power of sin is the law.
But thanks be to God who gives us the victory
   through our Lord Jesus Christ.

The word of the Lord. All: Thanks be to God.

Gospel (Luke 11:27-28)
Alleluia (Luke 11:28)
℣. Alleluia, alleluia. ℟. **Alleluia, alleluia.**
℣. Blessed are they who hear the word of God
   and observe it. ℟.

✠ **A reading from the holy Gospel according to Luke**

All: **Glory to you, Lord.**

Blessed is the womb that carried you!

**While Jesus was speaking,
   a woman from the crowd called out and said to him,
   "Blessed is the womb that carried you
   and the breasts at which you nursed."
He replied,
   "Rather, blessed are those
   who hear the word of God and observe it."**

The Gospel of the Lord. All: **Praise to you, Lord Jesus Christ.**

Prayer over the Gifts
Lord,
receive this sacrifice of praise and peace
in honor of the assumption of the Mother of God.
May our offering bring us pardon
and make our lives a thanksgiving to you.
We ask this in the name of Jesus the Lord. All: **Amen.**

August 14

Communion Antiphon (*See* Luke 11:27)
Blessed is the womb of the Virgin Mary; she carried the Son of the eternal Father.

Prayer after Communion
God of mercy,
we rejoice because Mary, the mother of our Lord,
was taken into the glory of heaven.
May the holy food we receive at this table
free us from evil.
We ask this through Christ our Lord. All: **Amen.**

Sunday, August 15

MASS DURING THE DAY

Entrance Antiphon (Revelation 12:1)
A great sign appeared in heaven: a woman clothed with the sun, the moon beneath her feet, and a crown of twelve stars on her head.

Opening Prayer
All-powerful and ever-living God,
you raised the sinless Virgin Mary, mother of your Son,
body and soul to the glory of heaven.
May we see heaven as our final goal
and come to share her glory.
We ask this through our Lord Jesus Christ, your Son,
who lives and reigns with you and the Holy Spirit,
one God, for ever and ever. All: **Amen.**

Reading I (L 622) (Revelation 11:19a; 12:1-6a, 10ab)
A reading from the Book of Revelation

A woman clothed with the sun, with the moon beneath her feet.

**God's temple in heaven was opened,
   and the ark of his covenant could be seen in the temple.**

**A great sign appeared in the sky, a woman clothed with the sun,
   with the moon under her feet,
   and on her head a crown of twelve stars.**

She was with child and wailed aloud in pain as she
 labored to give birth.
Then another sign appeared in the sky;
 it was a huge red dragon, with seven heads and
  ten horns,
 and on its heads were seven diadems.
Its tail swept away a third of the stars in the sky
 and hurled them down to the earth.
Then the dragon stood before the woman about to
  give birth,
 to devour her child when she gave birth.
She gave birth to a son, a male child,
 destined to rule all the nations with an iron rod.
Her child was caught up to God and his throne.
The woman herself fled into the desert
 where she had a place prepared by God.

Then I heard a loud voice in heaven say:
 "Now have salvation and power come,
  and the Kingdom of our God
  and the authority of his Anointed One."

The word of the Lord. All: Thanks be to God.

Responsorial Psalm 45

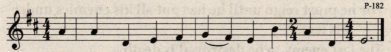

The queen stands at your right hand, arrayed in gold.

Music: Jay F. Hunstiger, © 1990, administered by Liturgical Press. All rights reserved.

Psalm 45:10bc, 11, 12ab, 16

℟. (10bc) **The queen stands at your right hand, arrayed
 in gold.**

 The queen takes her place at your right hand in gold of
  Ophir. ℟.

 Hear, O daughter, and see; turn your ear,
  forget your people and your father's house. ℟.

So shall the king desire your beauty;
> for he is your lord. ℟.

They are borne in with gladness and joy;
> they enter the palace of the king. ℟.

Reading II (1 Corinthians 15:20-27)

A reading from the first Letter of Saint Paul to the Corinthians

Christ, the firstfruits; then those who belong to him.

Brothers and sisters:
Christ has been raised from the dead,
> the firstfruits of those who have fallen asleep.

For since death came through man,
> the resurrection of the dead came also through man.

For just as in Adam all die,
> so too in Christ shall all be brought to life,
> but each one in proper order:
> Christ the firstfruits;
> then, at his coming, those who belong to Christ;
> then comes the end,
> when he hands over the Kingdom to his God and Father,
> when he has destroyed every sovereignty
> and every authority and power.

For he must reign until he has put all his enemies under his feet.

The last enemy to be destroyed is death,
> for "he subjected everything under his feet."

The word of the Lord. All: **Thanks be to God.**

Gospel (Luke 1:39-56)

Alleluia

℣. Alleluia, alleluia. ℟. **Alleluia, alleluia.**
℣. Mary is taken up to heaven;
> a chorus of angels exults. ℟.

✣ **A reading from the holy Gospel according to Luke**

All: **Glory to you, Lord.**

The Almighty has done great things for me; he has raised up the lowly.

**Mary set out
and traveled to the hill country in haste
to a town of Judah,
where she entered the house of Zechariah
and greeted Elizabeth.
When Elizabeth heard Mary's greeting,
the infant leaped in her womb,
and Elizabeth, filled with the Holy Spirit,
cried out in a loud voice and said,
"Blessed are you among women,
and blessed is the fruit of your womb.
And how does this happen to me,
that the mother of my Lord should come to me?
For at the moment the sound of your greeting reached my ears,
the infant in my womb leaped for joy.
Blessed are you who believed
that what was spoken to you by the Lord
would be fulfilled."
And Mary said:
"My soul proclaims the greatness of the Lord;
my spirit rejoices in God my Savior
for he has looked with favor on his lowly servant.
From this day all generations will call me blessed:
the Almighty has done great things for me
and holy is his Name.
He has mercy on those who fear him
in every generation.
He has shown the strength of his arm,
and has scattered the proud in their conceit.**

> **He has cast down the mighty from their thrones,**
>   **and has lifted up the lowly.**
> **He has filled the hungry with good things,**
>   **and the rich he has sent away empty.**
> **He has come to the help of his servant Israel**
>   **for he has remembered his promise of mercy,**
>   **the promise he made to our fathers,**
>   **to Abraham and his children forever."**

Mary remained with her about three months
  and then returned to her home.

The Gospel of the Lord. All: **Praise to you, Lord Jesus Christ.**

Prayer over the Gifts
Lord,
receive this offering of our service.
You raised the Virgin Mary to the glory of heaven.
By her prayers, help us to seek you
and to live in your love.
Grant this through Christ our Lord. All: **Amen.**

Communion Antiphon (Luke 1:48-49)
All generations will call me blessed, for the Almighty has done great things for me.

Prayer after Communion
Lord,
may we who receive this sacrament of salvation
be led to the glory of heaven
by the prayers of the Virgin Mary.
We ask this in the name of Jesus the Lord. All: **Amen.**

Twenty-first Sunday in Ordinary Time

August 22, 2010

Reflection on the Gospel

The issue in the gospel is not really about how many would be saved, but who would be saved. The saved are those who don't merely accompany Jesus but who freely choose to follow him through the "narrow gate" of self-surrender. Why would anyone choose this journey? Because the immediate destination (Jerusalem, with its promised death) is the way to a greater destination (new and eternal life).

- *The people and/or practices that enable me to "strive to enter through the narrow gate" are . . .*

—Living Liturgy™, *Twenty-first Sunday in Ordinary Time 2010*

Entrance Antiphon (Psalm 85:1-3)

Listen, Lord, and answer me. Save your servant who trusts in you. I call to you all day long, have mercy on me, O Lord.

Opening Prayer

Father,
help us to seek the values
that will bring us lasting joy in this changing world.
In our desire for what you promise
make us one in mind and heart.
Grant this through our Lord Jesus Christ, your Son,
who lives and reigns with you and the Holy Spirit,
one God, for ever and ever. All: **Amen.**

Reading I (L 123-C) (Isaiah 66:18-21)

A reading from the Book of the Prophet Isaiah

They shall bring all your brothers and sisters from all the nations.

Thus says the Lord:
I know their works and their thoughts,
and I come to gather nations of every language;
    they shall come and see my glory.

I will set a sign among them;
   from them I will send fugitives to the nations:
   to Tarshish, Put and Lud, Mosoch, Tubal and Javan,
   to the distant coastlands
   that have never heard of my fame, or seen my glory;
   and they shall proclaim my glory among the nations.
They shall bring all your brothers and sisters from all the nations
   as an offering to the Lord,
   on horses and in chariots, in carts, upon mules and dromedaries,
   to Jerusalem, my holy mountain, says the Lord,
   just as the Israelites bring their offering
   to the house of the Lord in clean vessels.
Some of these I will take as priests and Levites,
   says the Lord.

The word of the Lord. All: **Thanks be to God.**

Responsorial Psalm 117

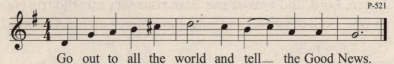

Go out to all the world and tell the Good News.

Music: Jay F. Hunstiger, © 1991, administered by Liturgical Press. All rights reserved.

Psalm 117:1, 2

℟. (Mark 16:15) **Go out to all the world and tell the good news.** *or:* ℟. **Alleluia.**

Praise the Lord, all you nations;
   glorify him, all you peoples! ℟.

For steadfast is his kindness toward us,
   and the fidelity of the Lord endures forever. ℟.

Reading II (Hebrews 12:5-7, 11-13)
A reading from the Letter to the Hebrews

Those whom the Lord loves, he disciplines.

Brothers and sisters,
You have forgotten the exhortation addressed to you as
    children:
    "My son, do not disdain the discipline of the Lord
        or lose heart when reproved by him;
    for whom the Lord loves, he disciplines;
        he scourges every son he acknowledges."
Endure your trials as "discipline";
    God treats you as sons.
For what "son" is there whom his father does not
    discipline?
At the time,
    all discipline seems a cause not for joy but for pain,
    yet later it brings the peaceful fruit of righteousness
    to those who are trained by it.

So strengthen your drooping hands and your weak knees.
Make straight paths for your feet,
    that what is lame may not be disjointed but healed.

The word of the Lord. All: Thanks be to God.

Gospel (Luke 13:22-30)
Alleluia (John 14:6)
℣. Alleluia, alleluia.   ℟. **Alleluia, alleluia.**
℣. I am the way, the truth and the life, says the Lord;
    no one comes to the Father, except through me. ℟.

✢ **A reading from the holy Gospel according to Luke**

All: **Glory to you, Lord.**

They will come from east and west and recline at table in the kingdom of God.

Jesus passed through towns and villages,
    teaching as he went and making his way to Jerusalem.
Someone asked him,
    "Lord, will only a few people be saved?"
He answered them,
    "Strive to enter through the narrow gate,

> for many, I tell you, will attempt to enter
> but will not be strong enough.
> After the master of the house has arisen and locked the door,
> then will you stand outside knocking and saying,
> 'Lord, open the door for us.'
> He will say to you in reply,
> 'I do not know where you are from.'
> And you will say,
> 'We ate and drank in your company and you taught in our streets.'
> Then he will say to you,
> 'I do not know where you are from.
> Depart from me, all you evildoers!'
> And there will be wailing and grinding of teeth
> when you see Abraham, Isaac, and Jacob
> and all the prophets in the kingdom of God
> and you yourselves cast out.
> And people will come from the east and the west
> and from the north and the south
> and will recline at table in the kingdom of God.
> For behold, some are last who will be first,
> and some are first who will be last."

The Gospel of the Lord. All: **Praise to you, Lord Jesus Christ.**

Prayer over the Gifts
Merciful God,
the perfect sacrifice of Jesus Christ
made us your people.
In your love,
grant peace and unity to your Church.
We ask this through Christ our Lord. All: **Amen.**

Communion Antiphon (Psalm 103:13-15)
Lord, the earth is filled with your gift from heaven; man grows bread from earth, and wine to cheer his heart.

Prayer after Communion
Lord,
may this eucharist increase within us
the healing power of your love.
May it guide and direct our efforts
to please you in all things.
We ask this in the name of Jesus the Lord. *All:* **Amen.**

Twenty-second Sunday in Ordinary Time

August 29, 2010

Reflection on the Gospel
In the gospel the people dining with Jesus were "observing him carefully." What Jesus says turns the tables by inviting the guests to look at themselves. Jesus challenges them to choose not a "higher position" but a "lower place," teaching us who we are to be before God and each other. Jesus calls us to true humility: to know the truth about ourselves, to sit in right relationship with one another, and to allow ourselves to be lifted up by God.

- *To be humble means to me . . . A time when I acted/lived humbly was . . .*

—*Living Liturgy*™, *Twenty-second Sunday in Ordinary Time 2010*

Entrance Antiphon (Psalm 85:3, 5)
I call to you all day long, have mercy on me, O Lord. You are good and forgiving, full of love for all who call to you.

Opening Prayer
Almighty God,
every good thing comes from you.
Fill our hearts with love for you,
increase our faith,
and by your constant care

protect the good you have given us.
We ask this through our Lord Jesus Christ, your Son,
who lives and reigns with you and the Holy Spirit,
one God, for ever and ever. All: **Amen.**

READING I (L 126-C) (Sirach 3:17-18, 20, 28-29)
A reading from the Book of Sirach

Humble yourself and you will find favor with God.

**My child, conduct your affairs with humility,
   and you will be loved more than a giver of gifts.
Humble yourself the more, the greater you are,
   and you will find favor with God.
What is too sublime for you, seek not,
   into things beyond your strength search not.
The mind of a sage appreciates proverbs,
   and an attentive ear is the joy of the wise.
Water quenches a flaming fire,
   and alms atone for sins.**

The word of the Lord. All: **Thanks be to God.**

RESPONSORIAL PSALM 68

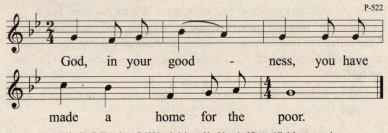

Music: Jay F. Hunstiger, © 1991, administered by Liturgical Press. All rights reserved.

Psalm 68:4-5, 6-7, 10-11

℟. (*See* 11b) **God, in your goodness, you have made a home for the poor.**

   The just rejoice and exult before God;
      they are glad and rejoice.
   Sing to God, chant praise to his name;
      whose name is the LORD. ℟.

The father of orphans and the defender of widows
   is God in his holy dwelling.
God gives a home to the forsaken;
   he leads forth prisoners to prosperity. ℟.

A bountiful rain you showered down, O God, upon
   your inheritance;
  you restored the land when it languished;
your flock settled in it;
   in your goodness, O God, you provided it for the
     needy. ℟.

READING II (Hebrews 12:18-19, 22-24a)

A reading from the Letter to the Hebrews

You have approached Mount Zion and the city of the living God.

Brothers and sisters:
You have not approached that which could be touched
  and a blazing fire and gloomy darkness
  and storm and a trumpet blast
  and a voice speaking words such that those who heard
  begged that no message be further addressed to them.
No, you have approached Mount Zion
  and the city of the living God, the heavenly Jerusalem,
  and countless angels in festal gathering,
  and the assembly of the firstborn enrolled in heaven,
  and God the judge of all,
  and the spirits of the just made perfect,
  and Jesus, the mediator of a new covenant,
  and the sprinkled blood that speaks more eloquently
    than that of Abel.

The word of the Lord. All: **Thanks be to God.**

GOSPEL (Luke 14:1, 7-14)
ALLELUIA (Matthew 11:29ab)
℣. Alleluia, alleluia. ℟. **Alleluia, alleluia.**
℣. Take my yoke upon you, says the Lord,
  and learn from me, for I am meek and humble of heart. ℟.

✠ **A reading from the holy Gospel according to Luke**

All: **Glory to you, Lord.**

Everyone who exalts himself will be humbled, everyone who humbles himself will be exalted.

**On a sabbath Jesus went to dine
    at the home of one of the leading Pharisees,
    and the people there were observing him carefully.
He told a parable to those who had been invited,
    noticing how they were choosing the places of honor
        at the table.
"When you are invited by someone to a wedding banquet,
    do not recline at table in the place of honor.
A more distinguished guest than you may have been
        invited by him,
    and the host who invited both of you may approach
        you and say,
    'Give your place to this man,'
    and then you would proceed with embarrassment
    to take the lowest place.
Rather, when you are invited,
    go and take the lowest place
    so that when the host comes to you he may say,
    'My friend, move up to a higher position.'
Then you will enjoy the esteem of your companions at
        the table.
For everyone who exalts himself will be humbled,
    but the one who humbles himself will be exalted."
Then he said to the host who invited him,
    "When you hold a lunch or a dinner,
    do not invite your friends or your brothers
    or your relatives or your wealthy neighbors,
    in case they may invite you back and you have
        repayment.
Rather, when you hold a banquet,
    invite the poor, the crippled, the lame, the blind;**

blessed indeed will you be because of their inability
to repay you.
For you will be repaid at the resurrection of the righteous."
The Gospel of the Lord. All: Praise to you, Lord Jesus Christ.

Prayer over the Gifts
Lord,
may this holy offering
bring us your blessing
and accomplish within us
its promise of salvation.
Grant this through Christ our Lord. All: **Amen.**

Communion Antiphon (Psalm 30:20)
O Lord, how great is the depth of the kindness which you have shown to those who love you.

Prayer after Communion
Lord,
you renew us at your table with the bread of life.
May this food strengthen us in love
and help us to serve you in each other.
We ask this in the name of Jesus the Lord. All: **Amen.**

Twenty-third Sunday in Ordinary Time

September 5, 2010

Reflection on the Gospel
Jesus bluntly challenges the crowd to take up the demands of discipleship with eyes wide open. Jesus clearly spells out the fine print in large, large letters: disciples must put Jesus ahead of their families and even their own lives, carry their cross, and renounce all they have. Why would anyone make such a choice to be his follower? Because Jesus has shown us by his own choices that this is the only way to the fullness of life.

- *I am willing to pay the high cost of discipleship because . . . I am unwilling when . . .*

—Living Liturgy™, *Twenty-third Sunday in Ordinary Time 2010*

Entrance Antiphon (Psalm 118:137, 124)

Lord, you are just, and the judgments you make are right.
Show mercy when you judge me, your servant.

Opening Prayer

God our Father,
you redeem us
and make us your children in Christ.
Look upon us,
give us true freedom
and bring us to the inheritance you promised.
Grant this through our Lord Jesus Christ, your Son,
who lives and reigns with you and the Holy Spirit,
one God, for ever and ever. All: **Amen.**

Reading I (L 129-C) (Wisdom 9:13-18a)

A reading from the Book of Wisdom

Who can conceive what the Lord intends?

**Who can know God's counsel,
   or who can conceive what the Lord intends?
For the deliberations of mortals are timid,
   and unsure are our plans.
For the corruptible body burdens the soul
   and the earthen shelter weighs down the mind that
      has many concerns.
And scarce do we guess the things on earth,
   and what is within our grasp we find with difficulty;
   but when things are in heaven, who can search them
      out?
Or who ever knew your counsel, except you had given
      wisdom
   and sent your holy spirit from on high?
And thus were the paths of those on earth made straight.

The word of the Lord.** All: **Thanks be to God.**

Responsorial Psalm 90

In every age, O Lord, you have been our refuge, you have been our refuge.

Music: Jay F. Hunstiger, © 1991, administered by Liturgical Press. All rights reserved.

Psalm 90:3-4, 5-6, 12-13, 14-17

℟. (1) **In every age, O Lord, you have been our refuge.**

You turn man back to dust,
   saying, "Return, O children of men."
For a thousand years in your sight
   are as yesterday, now that it is past,
   or as a watch of the night. ℟.

You make an end of them in their sleep;
   the next morning they are like the changing grass,
which at dawn springs up anew,
   but by evening wilts and fades. ℟.

Teach us to number our days aright,
   that we may gain wisdom of heart.
Return, O Lord! How long?
   Have pity on your servants! ℟.

Fill us at daybreak with your kindness,
   that we may shout for joy and gladness all our days.
And may the gracious care of the Lord our God be ours;
   prosper the work of our hands for us!
   Prosper the work of our hands! ℟.

Reading II (Philemon 9-10, 12-17)

A reading from the Letter of Saint Paul to Philemon

Receive him no longer as a slave but as a beloved brother.

**I, Paul, an old man,
   and now also a prisoner for Christ Jesus,
   urge you on behalf of my child Onesimus,**

whose father I have become in my imprisonment;
 I am sending him, that is, my own heart, back to you.
I should have liked to retain him for myself,
 so that he might serve me on your behalf
 in my imprisonment for the gospel,
 but I did not want to do anything without your consent,
 so that the good you do might not be forced but
  voluntary.
Perhaps this is why he was away from you for a while,
 that you might have him back forever,
 no longer as a slave
 but more than a slave, a brother,
 beloved especially to me, but even more so to you,
 as a man and in the Lord.
So if you regard me as a partner, welcome him as you
  would me.

The word of the Lord. All: Thanks be to God.

Gospel (Luke 14:25-33)
Alleluia (Psalm 119:135)
℣. Alleluia, alleluia. ℟. **Alleluia, alleluia.**
℣. Let your face shine upon your servant;
 and teach me your laws. ℟.

✠ **A reading from the holy Gospel according to Luke**

All: **Glory to you, Lord.**

Anyone of you who does not renounce all possessions cannot be my disciple.

**Great crowds were traveling with Jesus,
 and he turned and addressed them,
  "If anyone comes to me without hating his father and
   mother,
 wife and children, brothers and sisters,
 and even his own life,
 he cannot be my disciple.
Whoever does not carry his own cross and come after me
 cannot be my disciple.**

Which of you wishing to construct a tower
>> does not first sit down and calculate the cost
>> to see if there is enough for its completion?
> Otherwise, after laying the foundation
>> and finding himself unable to finish the work
>> the onlookers should laugh at him and say,
>>> 'This one began to build but did not have the resources
>>>> to finish.'
> Or what king marching into battle would not first sit down
>> and decide whether with ten thousand troops
>> he can successfully oppose another king
>> advancing upon him with twenty thousand troops?
> But if not, while he is still far away,
>> he will send a delegation to ask for peace terms.
> In the same way,
>> anyone of you who does not renounce all his possessions
>> cannot be my disciple."

The Gospel of the Lord. All: **Praise to you, Lord Jesus Christ.**

Prayer over the Gifts
God of peace and love,
may our offering bring you true worship
and make us one with you.
Grant this through Christ our Lord. All: **Amen.**

Communion Antiphon (Psalm 41:2-3)
Like a deer that longs for running streams, my soul longs for you, my God. My soul is thirsting for the living God.

Prayer after Communion
Lord,
your word and your sacrament
give us food and life.
May this gift of your Son
lead us to share his life for ever.
We ask this through Christ our Lord. All: **Amen.**

Twenty-fourth Sunday in Ordinary Time

September 12, 2010

Reflection on the Gospel

Jesus uses three situations (a lost sheep, a lost coin, a lost son) to dramatize that whenever we stray from God's steadfast compassion and love (become lost), God always seeks to find us and show us divine mercy. For our part, we must realize we are lost, recognize our need for God, and begin the journey home to be embraced by divine mercy. When God's offer of mercy is met by our repentance, all in heaven rejoice.

- *I am most in need of God's steadfast compassion and love when . . .*

—*Living Liturgy™, Twenty-fourth Sunday in Ordinary Time 2010*

ENTRANCE ANTIPHON (*See* Sirach 36:18)

Give peace, Lord, to those who wait for you and your prophets will proclaim you as you deserve. Hear the prayers of your servant and of your people Israel.

OPENING PRAYER

Almighty God,
our creator and guide,
may we serve you with all our heart
and know your forgiveness in our lives.
We ask this through our Lord Jesus Christ, your Son,
who lives and reigns with you and the Holy Spirit,
one God, for ever and ever. All: **Amen.**

READING I (L 132-C) (Exodus 32:7-11, 13-14)

A reading from the Book of Exodus

The Lord relented in the punishment he had threatened to inflict on his people.

The Lord said to Moses,
    "Go down at once to your people,
    whom you brought out of the land of Egypt,
    for they have become depraved.
They have soon turned aside from the way I pointed out to them,
    making for themselves a molten calf and worshiping it,
    sacrificing to it and crying out,
    'This is your God, O Israel,
    who brought you out of the land of Egypt!'
I see how stiff-necked this people is," continued the Lord to Moses.
"Let me alone, then,
    that my wrath may blaze up against them to consume them.
Then I will make of you a great nation."

But Moses implored the Lord, his God, saying,
    "Why, O Lord, should your wrath blaze up against your own people,
    whom you brought out of the land of Egypt
    with such great power and with so strong a hand?
Remember your servants Abraham, Isaac, and Israel,
    and how you swore to them by your own self, saying,
    'I will make your descendants as numerous as the stars in the sky;
    and all this land that I promised,
    I will give your descendants as their perpetual heritage.'"
So the Lord relented in the punishment
    he had threatened to inflict on his people.

The word of the Lord. All: Thanks be to God.

Responsorial Psalm 51

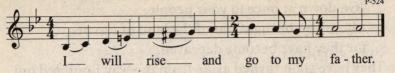

I will rise and go to my father.

Music: Jay F. Hunstiger, © 1991, administered by Liturgical Press. All rights reserved.

Psalm 51:3-4, 12-13, 17, 19

℟. (Luke 15:18) **I will rise and go to my father.**

> Have mercy on me, O God, in your goodness;
> > in the greatness of your compassion wipe out my offense.
> Thoroughly wash me from my guilt
> > and of my sin cleanse me. ℟.
>
> A clean heart create for me, O God,
> > and a steadfast spirit renew within me.
> Cast me not out from your presence,
> > and your holy spirit take not from me. ℟.
>
> O Lord, open my lips,
> > and my mouth shall proclaim your praise.
> My sacrifice, O God, is a contrite spirit;
> > a heart contrite and humbled, O God, you will not spurn. ℟.

Reading II (1 Timothy 1:12-17)

A reading from the first Letter of Saint Paul to Timothy

Christ came to save sinners.

**Beloved:
I am grateful to him who has strengthened me, Christ Jesus our Lord,
> because he considered me trustworthy
> in appointing me to the ministry.
I was once a blasphemer and a persecutor and arrogant,
> but I have been mercifully treated
> because I acted out of ignorance in my unbelief.
Indeed, the grace of our Lord has been abundant,
> along with the faith and love that are in Christ Jesus.**

This saying is trustworthy and deserves full acceptance:
> Christ Jesus came into the world to save sinners.

Of these I am the foremost.
But for that reason I was mercifully treated,
> so that in me, as the foremost,
> > Christ Jesus might display all his patience as an example
> > for those who would come to believe in him for
> > > everlasting life.

To the king of ages, incorruptible, invisible, the only God,
> honor and glory forever and ever. Amen.

The word of the Lord. **All: Thanks be to God.**

GOSPEL (Luke 15:1-32) *or* Shorter Form [ ] (Luke 15:1-10)
ALLELUIA (2 Corinthians 5:19)
℣. Alleluia, alleluia. ℟. **Alleluia, alleluia.**
℣. God was reconciling the world to himself in Christ
and entrusting to us the message of reconciliation. ℟.

✠ **A reading from the holy Gospel according to Luke**

All: **Glory to you, Lord.**

There will be great joy in heaven over one sinner who repents.

[Tax collectors and sinners were all drawing near to
> listen to Jesus,
> > but the Pharisees and scribes began to complain,
> > > saying,
> > "This man welcomes sinners and eats with them."

So to them he addressed this parable.
"What man among you having a hundred sheep and
> losing one of them
> > would not leave the ninety-nine in the desert
> > and go after the lost one until he finds it?

And when he does find it,
> he sets it on his shoulders with great joy
> and, upon his arrival home,
> he calls together his friends and neighbors and says
> > to them,
> > > 'Rejoice with me because I have found my lost sheep.'

I tell you, in just the same way
>   there will be more joy in heaven over one sinner who repents
>   than over ninety-nine righteous people
>   who have no need of repentance.

"Or what woman having ten coins and losing one
>   would not light a lamp and sweep the house,
>   searching carefully until she finds it?

And when she does find it,
>   she calls together her friends and neighbors
>   and says to them,
>   'Rejoice with me because I have found the coin that I lost.'

In just the same way, I tell you,
>   there will be rejoicing among the angels of God
>   over one sinner who repents."]

Then he said,
>   "A man had two sons, and the younger son said to his father,
>   'Father give me the share of your estate that should come to me.'

So the father divided the property between them.
After a few days, the younger son collected all his belongings
>   and set off to a distant country
>   where he squandered his inheritance on a life of dissipation.

When he had freely spent everything,
>   a severe famine struck that country,
>   and he found himself in dire need.

So he hired himself out to one of the local citizens
>   who sent him to his farm to tend the swine.

And he longed to eat his fill of the pods on which the swine fed,
>   but nobody gave him any.

Coming to his senses he thought,
    'How many of my father's hired workers
    have more than enough food to eat,
    but here am I, dying from hunger.
I shall get up and go to my father and I shall say to him,
    "Father, I have sinned against heaven and against you.
I no longer deserve to be called your son;
    treat me as you would treat one of your hired workers."'
So he got up and went back to his father.
While he was still a long way off,
    his father caught sight of him,
    and was filled with compassion.
He ran to his son, embraced him and kissed him.
His son said to him,
    'Father, I have sinned against heaven and against you;
    I no longer deserve to be called your son.'
But his father ordered his servants,
    'Quickly bring the finest robe and put it on him;
    put a ring on his finger and sandals on his feet.
Take the fattened calf and slaughter it.
Then let us celebrate with a feast,
    because this son of mine was dead, and has come to
        life again;
    he was lost, and has been found.'
Then the celebration began.
Now the older son had been out in the field
    and, on his way back, as he neared the house,
    he heard the sound of music and dancing.
He called one of the servants and asked what this might
    mean.
The servant said to him,
    'Your brother has returned
    and your father has slaughtered the fattened calf
    because he has him back safe and sound.'

He became angry,
>   and when he refused to enter the house,
>   his father came out and pleaded with him.
> He said to his father in reply,
>   'Look, all these years I served you
>   and not once did I disobey your orders;
>   yet you never gave me even a young goat to feast on
>   with my friends.
> But when your son returns,
>   who swallowed up your property with prostitutes,
>   for him you slaughter the fattened calf.'
> He said to him,
>   'My son, you are here with me always;
>   everything I have is yours.
> But now we must celebrate and rejoice,
>   because your brother was dead and has come to life again;
>   he was lost and has been found.'"

The Gospel of the Lord. All: **Praise to you, Lord Jesus Christ.**

Prayer over the Gifts
Lord,
hear the prayers of your people
and receive our gifts.
May the worship of each one here
bring salvation to all.
Grant this through Christ our Lord. All: **Amen.**

Communion Antiphon (Psalm 35:8)
O God, how much we value your mercy! All mankind can gather under your protection.

Prayer after Communion
Lord,
may the eucharist you have given us
influence our thoughts and actions.
May your Spirit guide and direct us in your way.
We ask this in the name of Jesus the Lord. All: **Amen.**

Twenty-fifth Sunday in Ordinary Time

September 19, 2010

Reflection on the Gospel

Jesus does not commend the steward's dishonesty; he does commend his shrewdness in cleverly ensuring a secure future for himself. Disciples must be equally shrewd but make very different choices: choosing trustworthy service over dishonesty for personal gain, choosing concern for others over personal needs, choosing eternal happiness above security in this world at any cost. In these very choices, disciples serve God and God alone. Thus can we secure for ourselves a sure future: being "welcomed into eternal dwellings."

- *If Jesus were to say to me "Prepare a full account of your stewardship," my response would be . . .*

—Living Liturgy™, *Twenty-fifth Sunday in Ordinary Time 2010*

Entrance Antiphon

I am the Savior of all people, says the Lord. Whatever their troubles, I will answer their cry, and I will always be their Lord.

Opening Prayer

Father,
guide us, as you guide creation
according to your law of love.
May we love one another
and come to perfection
in the eternal life prepared for us.
Grant this through our Lord Jesus Christ, your Son,
who lives and reigns with you and the Holy Spirit,
one God, for ever and ever. All: **Amen.**

Reading I (L 135-C) (Amos 8:4-7)
A reading from the Book of the Prophet Amos

Against those who buy the poor for money.

Hear this, you who trample upon the needy
  and destroy the poor of the land!
"When will the new moon be over," you ask,
  "that we may sell our grain,
  and the sabbath, that we may display the wheat?
We will diminish the ephah,
  add to the shekel,
  and fix our scales for cheating!
We will buy the lowly for silver,
  and the poor for a pair of sandals;
  even the refuse of the wheat we will sell!"
The LORD has sworn by the pride of Jacob:
  Never will I forget a thing they have done!

The word of the Lord. All: Thanks be to God.

Responsorial Psalm 113

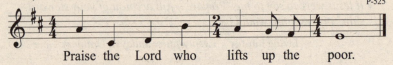

Praise the Lord who lifts up the poor.

Music: Jay F. Hunstiger, © 1991, administered by Liturgical Press. All rights reserved.

Psalm 113:1-2, 4-6, 7-8

℟. (*See* 1a, 7b) **Praise the Lord, who lifts up the poor.**
  or: ℟. **Alleluia.**

Praise, you servants of the LORD,
  praise the name of the LORD.
Blessed be the name of the LORD
  both now and forever. ℟.

High above all nations is the LORD;
  above the heavens is his glory.
Who is like the LORD, our God, who is enthroned on high
  and looks upon the heavens and the earth below? ℟.

He raises up the lowly from the dust;
  from the dunghill he lifts up the poor
to seat them with princes,
  with the princes of his own people. ℟.

Reading II (1 Timothy 2:1-8)

A reading from the first Letter of Saint Paul to Timothy

Let prayers be offered for everyone to God who wills everyone to be saved.

**Beloved:
First of all, I ask that supplications, prayers,
   petitions, and thanksgivings be offered for everyone,
   for kings and for all in authority,
   that we may lead a quiet and tranquil life
   in all devotion and dignity.
This is good and pleasing to God our savior,
   who wills everyone to be saved
   and to come to knowledge of the truth.
      For there is one God.
      There is also one mediator between God and men,
         the man Christ Jesus,
      who gave himself as ransom for all.
This was the testimony at the proper time.
For this I was appointed preacher and apostle
   —I am speaking the truth, I am not lying—,
   teacher of the Gentiles in faith and truth.
It is my wish, then, that in every place the men should pray,
   lifting up holy hands, without anger or argument.
The word of the Lord.** All: **Thanks be to God.**

Gospel (Luke 16:1-13) or Shorter Form [ ] (Luke 16:10-13)

Alleluia (*See* 2 Corinthians 8:9)

℣. Alleluia, alleluia. ℟. **Alleluia, alleluia.**
℣. Though our Lord Jesus Christ was rich, he became poor, so that by his poverty you might become rich. ℟.

✠ **A reading from the holy Gospel according to Luke**

All: **Glory to you, Lord.**

You cannot serve both God and mammon.

[Jesus said to his disciples:]
   "A rich man had a steward
      who was reported to him for squandering his property.
He summoned him and said,
   'What is this I hear about you?
Prepare a full account of your stewardship,
   because you can no longer be my steward.'
The steward said to himself, 'What shall I do,
      now that my master is taking the position of steward
         away from me?
I am not strong enough to dig and I am ashamed to beg.
I know what I shall do so that,
   when I am removed from the stewardship,
   they may welcome me into their homes.'
He called in his master's debtors one by one.
To the first he said,
   'How much do you owe my master?'
He replied, 'One hundred measures of olive oil.'
He said to him, 'Here is your promissory note.
Sit down and quickly write one for fifty.'
Then to another the steward said, 'And you, how much
      do you owe?'
He replied, 'One hundred kors of wheat.'
The steward said to him, 'Here is your promissory note;
   write one for eighty.'
And the master commended that dishonest steward for
      acting prudently.

"For the children of this world
   are more prudent in dealing with their own generation
   than are the children of light.
I tell you, make friends for yourselves with dishonest
      wealth,
   so that when it fails, you will be welcomed into eternal
      dwellings.

[The person who is trustworthy in very small matters
  is also trustworthy in great ones;
 and the person who is dishonest in very small matters
  is also dishonest in great ones.
If, therefore, you are not trustworthy with dishonest wealth,
  who will trust you with true wealth?
If you are not trustworthy with what belongs to another,
  who will give you what is yours?
No servant can serve two masters.
He will either hate one and love the other,
  or be devoted to one and despise the other.
You cannot serve both God and mammon."]

The Gospel of the Lord. All: **Praise to you, Lord Jesus Christ.**

Prayer over the Gifts
Lord,
may these gifts which we now offer
to show our belief and our love
be pleasing to you.
May they become for us
the eucharist of Jesus Christ your Son,
who is Lord for ever and ever. All: **Amen.**

Communion Antiphon (Psalm 118:4-5)
You have laid down your precepts to be faithfully kept.
May my footsteps be firm in keeping your commands.

Prayer after Communion
Lord,
help us with your kindness.
Make us strong through the eucharist.
May we put into action
the saving mystery we celebrate.
We ask this in the name of Jesus the Lord. All: **Amen.**

Twenty-sixth Sunday in Ordinary Time

September 26, 2010

Reflection on the Gospel

Jesus makes clear at the end of this gospel parable that we are given everything we need to set our values and relationships right. We have the words of "Moses and the prophets." Even more, unlike the rich man in the parable, we do *have Someone among us who has "rise[n] from the dead." We need only listen. This is how we gain the insight to see those in need at our own door and choose how to respond.*

- *I listen to the risen Jesus when . . . This changes my relationships to others by . . .*

—Living Liturgy™, *Twenty-sixth Sunday in Ordinary Time 2010*

Entrance Antiphon (Daniel 3:31, 29, 30, 43, 42)

O Lord, you had just cause to judge men as you did:
because we sinned against you and disobeyed your will.
But now show us your greatness of heart, and treat us with
your unbounded kindness.

Opening Prayer

Father,
you show your almighty power
in your mercy and forgiveness.
Continue to fill us with your gifts of love.
Help us to hurry toward the eternal life you promise
and come to share in the joys of your kingdom.
Grant this through our Lord Jesus Christ, your Son,
who lives and reigns with you and the Holy Spirit,
one God, for ever and ever. All: **Amen.**

Reading I (L 138-C) (Amos 6:1a, 4-7)

A reading from the Book of the Prophet Amos

Their wanton revelry shall be done away with.

Thus says the Lord, the God of hosts:
>Woe to the complacent in Zion!
>Lying upon beds of ivory,
>>stretched comfortably on their couches,
>
>they eat lambs taken from the flock,
>>and calves from the stall!
>
>Improvising to the music of the harp,
>>like David, they devise their own accompaniment.
>
>They drink wine from bowls
>>and anoint themselves with the best oils;
>>yet they are not made ill by the collapse of Joseph!
>
>Therefore, now they shall be the first to go into exile,
>>and their wanton revelry shall be done away with.

The word of the Lord. All: Thanks be to God.

Responsorial Psalm 146

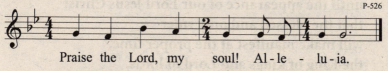

Praise the Lord, my soul! Al-le-lu-ia.

Music: Jay F. Hunstiger, © 1990, administered by Liturgical Press. All rights reserved.

Psalm 146:7, 8-9, 9-10

℟. (1b) **Praise the Lord, my soul!** *or:* ℟. **Alleluia.**

Blessed is he who keeps faith forever,
>secures justice for the oppressed,
>gives food to the hungry.

The Lord sets captives free. ℟.

The Lord gives sight to the blind.
>The Lord raises up those who were bowed down;

the Lord loves the just.
>The Lord protects strangers. ℟.

The fatherless and the widow he sustains,
>but the way of the wicked he thwarts.

The Lord shall reign forever;
>your God, O Zion, through all generations. Alleluia. ℟.

September 26

READING II (1 Timothy 6:11-16)

A reading from the first Letter of Saint Paul to Timothy

Keep the commandment until the appearance of the Lord Jesus Christ.

**But you, man of God, pursue righteousness,
devotion, faith, love, patience, and gentleness.
Compete well for the faith.
Lay hold of eternal life, to which you were called
when you made the noble confession in the presence
of many witnesses.
I charge you before God, who gives life to all things,
and before Christ Jesus,
who gave testimony under Pontius Pilate for the
noble confession,
to keep the commandment without stain or reproach
until the appearance of our Lord Jesus Christ
that the blessed and only ruler
will make manifest at the proper time,
the King of kings and Lord of lords,
who alone has immortality, who dwells in
unapproachable light,
and whom no human being has seen or can see.
To him be honor and eternal power. Amen.**

The word of the Lord. All: **Thanks be to God.**

GOSPEL (Luke 16:19-31)

ALLELUIA (*See* 2 Corinthians 8:9)

℣. Alleluia, alleluia. ℟. **Alleluia, alleluia.**
℣. Though our Lord Jesus Christ was rich, he became poor, so that by his poverty you might become rich. ℟.

✠ **A reading from the holy Gospel according to Luke**

All: **Glory to you, Lord.**

You received what was good, Lazarus what was bad; now he is comforted, whereas you are tormented.

Jesus said to the Pharisees:
"There was a rich man who dressed in purple garments
and fine linen
and dined sumptuously each day.
And lying at his door was a poor man named Lazarus,
covered with sores,
who would gladly have eaten his fill of the scraps
that fell from the rich man's table.
Dogs even used to come and lick his sores.
When the poor man died,
he was carried away by angels to the bosom of Abraham.
The rich man also died and was buried,
and from the netherworld, where he was in torment,
he raised his eyes and saw Abraham far off
and Lazarus at his side.
And he cried out, 'Father Abraham, have pity on me.
Send Lazarus to dip the tip of his finger in water and
cool my tongue,
for I am suffering torment in these flames.'
Abraham replied,
'My child, remember that you received
what was good during your lifetime
while Lazarus likewise received what was bad;
but now he is comforted here, whereas you are
tormented.
Moreover, between us and you a great chasm is
established
to prevent anyone from crossing who might wish to go
from our side to yours or from your side to ours.'
He said, 'Then I beg you, father,
send him to my father's house, for I have five brothers,
so that he may warn them,
lest they too come to this place of torment.'
But Abraham replied, 'They have Moses and the prophets.
Let them listen to them.'

He said, 'Oh no, father Abraham,
  but if someone from the dead goes to them, they will repent.'
Then Abraham said, 'If they will not listen to Moses and the prophets,
  neither will they be persuaded if someone should rise from the dead.'"

The Gospel of the Lord. All: **Praise to you, Lord Jesus Christ.**

Prayer over the Gifts
God of mercy,
accept our offering
and make it a source of blessing for us.
We ask this in the name of Jesus the Lord. All: **Amen.**

Communion Antiphon (Psalm 118:49-50)
O Lord, remember the words you spoke to me, your servant, which made me live in hope and consoled me when I was downcast.

Prayer after Communion
Lord,
may this eucharist
in which we proclaim the death of Christ
bring us salvation
and make us one with him in glory,
for he is Lord for ever and ever. All: **Amen.**

Twenty-seventh Sunday in Ordinary Time

October 3, 2010

Reflection on the Gospel

In this Sunday's gospel the apostles ask Jesus to "increase [their] faith." What he gives them instead is greater confidence in the power of the faith they already have. What is this faith? It is obedience to responsibility, a matter of willingness to undertake decisive action for the sake of God's kingdom. Even faith that "feels" small possesses great power. Faithfulness is doing all we have been commanded. "Faith-filledness" is acting decisively.

- *I have experienced the power of faith when . . .*

—Living Liturgy™, *Twenty-seventh Sunday in Ordinary Time 2010*

Entrance Antiphon (Esther 13:9, 10-11)

O Lord, you have given everything its place in the world, and no one can make it otherwise. For it is your creation, the heavens and the earth and the stars: you are the Lord of all.

Opening Prayer

Father,
your love for us
surpasses all our hopes and desires.
Forgive our failings,
keep us in your peace
and lead us in the way of salvation.
We ask this through our Lord Jesus Christ, your Son,
who lives and reigns with you and the Holy Spirit,
one God, for ever and ever. All: **Amen.**

Reading I (L 141-C) (Habakkuk 1:2-3; 2:2-4)

A reading from the Book of the Prophet Habakkuk

The just one, because of his faith, shall live.

How long, O Lord? I cry for help
   but you do not listen!
I cry out to you, "Violence!"
   but you do not intervene.
Why do you let me see ruin;
   why must I look at misery?
Destruction and violence are before me;
   there is strife, and clamorous discord.
Then the Lord answered me and said:
   Write down the vision clearly upon the tablets,
   so that one can read it readily.
For the vision still has its time,
   presses on to fulfillment, and will not disappoint;
if it delays, wait for it,
   it will surely come, it will not be late.
The rash one has no integrity;
   but the just one, because of his faith, shall live.

The word of the Lord. All: Thanks be to God.

Responsorial Psalm 95

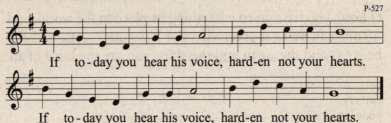

Music: Jay F. Hunstiger, © 1993, administered by Liturgical Press. All rights reserved.

Psalm 95:1-2, 6-7, 8-9

℟. (8) **If today you hear his voice, harden not your hearts.**

Come, let us sing joyfully to the Lord;
   let us acclaim the Rock of our salvation.
Let us come into his presence with thanksgiving;
   let us joyfully sing psalms to him. ℟.

Come, let us bow down in worship;
   let us kneel before the Lord who made us.

For he is our God,
> and we are the people he shepherds, the flock he
>> guides. ℟.

Oh, that today you would hear his voice:
> "Harden not your hearts as at Meribah,
> as in the day of Massah in the desert,
> where your fathers tempted me;
>> they tested me though they had seen my works." ℟.

Reading II (2 Timothy 1:6-8, 13-14)
A reading from the second Letter of Saint Paul to Timothy

Do not be ashamed of your testimony to our Lord.

Beloved:
I remind you to stir into flame
> **the gift of God that you have through the imposition**
>> **of my hands.**

For God did not give us a spirit of cowardice
> **but rather of power and love and self-control.**

So do not be ashamed of your testimony to our Lord,
> **nor of me, a prisoner for his sake;**
> **but bear your share of hardship for the gospel**
>> **with the strength that comes from God.**

Take as your norm the sound words that you heard
>> **from me,**
> **in the faith and love that are in Christ Jesus.**

Guard this rich trust with the help of the Holy Spirit
> **that dwells within us.**

The word of the Lord. All: **Thanks be to God.**

Gospel (Luke 17:5-10)
Alleluia (1 Peter 1:25)
℣. Alleluia, alleluia. ℟. **Alleluia, alleluia.**
℣. The word of the Lord remains forever.
> This is the word that has been proclaimed to you. ℟.

✢ **A reading from the holy Gospel according to Luke**

All: **Glory to you, Lord.**

If you have faith!

**The apostles said to the Lord, "Increase our faith."
The Lord replied,
    "If you have faith the size of a mustard seed,
    you would say to this mulberry tree,
    'Be uprooted and planted in the sea,' and it would
        obey you.
"Who among you would say to your servant
    who has just come in from plowing or tending sheep
        in the field,
    'Come here immediately and take your place at table'?
Would he not rather say to him,
    'Prepare something for me to eat.
Put on your apron and wait on me while I eat and drink.
You may eat and drink when I am finished'?
Is he grateful to that servant because he did what was
        commanded?
So should it be with you.
When you have done all you have been commanded,
    say, 'We are unprofitable servants;
    we have done what we were obliged to do.'"**

The Gospel of the Lord. All: **Praise to you, Lord Jesus Christ.**

Prayer over the Gifts
Father,
receive these gifts
which our Lord Jesus Christ
has asked us to offer in his memory.
May our obedient service
bring us to the fullness of your redemption.
We ask this in the name of Jesus the Lord. All: **Amen.**

Communion Antiphon (Lamentations 3:25)
The Lord is good to those who hope in him, to those who are searching for his love.

Prayer after Communion
Almighty God,
let the eucharist we share
fill us with your life.
May the love of Christ
which we celebrate here
touch our lives and lead us to you.
We ask this in the name of Jesus the Lord. All: **Amen.**

Twenty-eighth Sunday in Ordinary Time

October 10, 2010

Reflection on the Gospel

One leper is very different from the other nine—he alone returned to the Source of his healing to give thanks. Jesus is not only the One who healed him of his leprosy but, more important, he is the One who drew him to act on the faith that assured him of the new life of restoration and salvation. Faith is discovering who Jesus is; salvation is the lifelong journey of returning to and encountering him.

- *Times when my faith has brought me to encounter Jesus are . . .*

—Living Liturgy™, *Twenty-eighth Sunday in Ordinary Time 2010*

Entrance Antiphon (Psalm 129:3-4)
If you, O Lord, laid bare our guilt, who could endure it?
But you are forgiving, God of Israel.

Opening Prayer
Lord,
our help and guide,
make your love the foundation of our lives.
May our love for you express itself
in our eagerness to do good for others.
Grant this through our Lord Jesus Christ, your Son,
who lives and reigns with you and the Holy Spirit,
one God, for ever and ever. All: **Amen.**

October 10

Reading I (L 144-C) (2 Kings 5:14-17)
A reading from the second Book of Kings
Naaman returned to the man of God and acknowledged the Lord.

**Naaman went down and plunged into the Jordan seven times
at the word of Elisha, the man of God.
His flesh became again like the flesh of a little child,
and he was clean of his leprosy.**

**Naaman returned with his whole retinue to the man of God.
On his arrival he stood before Elisha and said,
"Now I know that there is no God in all the earth,
except in Israel.
Please accept a gift from your servant."**

**Elisha replied, "As the Lord lives whom I serve, I will not take it";
and despite Naaman's urging, he still refused.
Naaman said: "If you will not accept,
please let me, your servant, have two mule-loads of earth,
for I will no longer offer holocaust or sacrifice
to any other god except to the Lord."**

The word of the Lord. All: **Thanks be to God.**

Responsorial Psalm 98

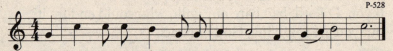

The Lord has re-vealed to the na-tions his sav-ing pow'r.

_{Music: Jay F. Hunstiger, © 1990, administered by Liturgical Press. All rights reserved.}

Psalm 98:1, 2-3, 3-4

℟. (*See* 2b) **The Lord has revealed to the nations his saving power.**

Sing to the Lord a new song,
  for he has done wondrous deeds;

> his right hand has won victory for him,
> his holy arm. ℟.
>
> The LORD has made his salvation known:
> in the sight of the nations he has revealed his justice.
> He has remembered his kindness and his faithfulness
> toward the house of Israel. ℟.
>
> All the ends of the earth have seen
> the salvation by our God.
> Sing joyfully to the LORD, all you lands:
> break into song; sing praise. ℟.

READING II (2 Timothy 2:8-13)
A reading from the second Letter of Saint Paul to Timothy

If we persevere we shall also reign with Christ.

**Beloved:
Remember Jesus Christ, raised from the dead, a descendant of David:
such is my gospel, for which I am suffering,
even to the point of chains, like a criminal.
But the word of God is not chained.
Therefore, I bear with everything for the sake of those who are chosen,
so that they too may obtain the salvation that is in Christ Jesus,
together with eternal glory.
This saying is trustworthy:
If we have died with him
we shall also live with him;
if we persevere
we shall also reign with him.
But if we deny him
he will deny us.
If we are unfaithful
he remains faithful,
for he cannot deny himself.
The word of the Lord.** All: **Thanks be to God.**

Gospel (Luke 17:11-19)
Alleluia (1 Thessalonians 5:18)

℣. Alleluia, alleluia. ℟. **Alleluia, alleluia.**
℣. In all circumstances, give thanks,
for this is the will of God for you in Christ Jesus. ℟.

✠ **A reading from the holy Gospel according to Luke**

All: **Glory to you, Lord.**

None but this foreigner has returned to give thanks to God.

As Jesus continued his journey to Jerusalem,
he traveled through Samaria and Galilee.
As he was entering a village, ten lepers met him.
They stood at a distance from him and raised their voices,
saying,
"Jesus, Master! Have pity on us!"
And when he saw them, he said,
"Go show yourselves to the priests."
As they were going they were cleansed.

And one of them, realizing he had been healed,
returned, glorifying God in a loud voice;
and he fell at the feet of Jesus and thanked him.
He was a Samaritan.
Jesus said in reply,
"Ten were cleansed, were they not?
Where are the other nine?
Has none but this foreigner returned to give thanks to
God?"
Then he said to him, "Stand up and go;
your faith has saved you."

The Gospel of the Lord. All: **Praise to you, Lord Jesus Christ.**

Prayer over the Gifts

Lord,
accept the prayers and gifts
we offer in faith and love.
May this eucharist bring us to your glory.
We ask this in the name of Jesus the Lord. All: **Amen.**

Communion Antiphon (Psalm 33:11)

The rich suffer want and go hungry, but nothing shall be lacking to those who fear the Lord.

Prayer after Communion

Almighty Father,
may the body and blood of your Son
give us a share in his life,
for he is Lord for ever and ever. All: **Amen.**

Twenty-ninth Sunday in Ordinary Time

October 17, 2010

Reflection on the Gospel

In this gospel Jesus relates persistence in prayer and faith to his second coming ("when the Son of Man comes"). Persistence in prayer is not only about asking for what we need now but is also about maintaining hope that God will persist in bringing about final justice. Moreover, there is no real prayer without faith. Faith gives prayer a longer view and a broader vision—the view and vision of Jesus himself.

- *The longer view and broader vision faith and prayer bring me are . . .*

—Living Liturgy™, *Twenty-ninth Sunday in Ordinary Time 2010*

Entrance Antiphon (Psalm 16:6, 8)

I call upon you, God, for you will answer me; bend your ear and hear my prayer. Guard me as the pupil of your eye; hide me in the shade of your wings.

Opening Prayer

Almighty and ever-living God,
our source of power and inspiration,
give us strength and joy
in serving you as followers of Christ,

who lives and reigns with you and the Holy Spirit,
one God, for ever and ever. All: **Amen.**

READING I (L 147-C) (Exodus 17:8-13)
A reading from the Book of Exodus

As long as Moses kept his hands raised up, Israel had the better of the fight.

**In those days, Amalek came and waged war against Israel.
Moses, therefore, said to Joshua,
   "Pick out certain men,
   and tomorrow go out and engage Amalek in battle.
I will be standing on top of the hill
   with the staff of God in my hand."
So Joshua did as Moses told him:
   he engaged Amalek in battle
      after Moses had climbed to the top of the hill with
         Aaron and Hur.**

**As long as Moses kept his hands raised up,
   Israel had the better of the fight,
   but when he let his hands rest,
   Amalek had the better of the fight.
Moses' hands, however, grew tired;
   so they put a rock in place for him to sit on.
Meanwhile Aaron and Hur supported his hands,
   one on one side and one on the other,
   so that his hands remained steady till sunset.
And Joshua mowed down Amalek and his people
   with the edge of the sword.**

The word of the Lord. All: **Thanks be to God.**

RESPONSORIAL PSALM 121

Our help is from the Lord who made heaven and earth.

_{Music: Jay F. Hunstiger, © 1991, administered by Liturgical Press. All rights reserved.}

Psalm 121:1-2, 3-4, 5-6, 7-8

℟. (*See* 2) **Our help is from the Lord, who made heaven and earth.**

I lift up my eyes toward the mountains;
  whence shall help come to me?
My help is from the L<small>ORD</small>,
  who made heaven and earth. ℟.

May he not suffer your foot to slip;
  may he slumber not who guards you:
indeed he neither slumbers nor sleeps,
  the guardian of Israel. ℟.

The L<small>ORD</small> is your guardian; the L<small>ORD</small> is your shade;
  he is beside you at your right hand.
The sun shall not harm you by day,
  nor the moon by night. ℟.

The L<small>ORD</small> will guard you from all evil;
  he will guard your life.
The L<small>ORD</small> will guard your coming and your going,
  both now and forever. ℟.

R<small>EADING</small> II (2 Timothy 3:14—4:2)
A reading from the second Letter of Saint Paul to Timothy

One who belongs to God may be competent, equipped for every good work.

**Beloved:
Remain faithful to what you have learned and believed,
  because you know from whom you learned it,
    and that from infancy you have known the sacred
      Scriptures,
    which are capable of giving you wisdom for salvation
    through faith in Christ Jesus.
All Scripture is inspired by God
  and is useful for teaching, for refutation, for correction,
  and for training in righteousness,
  so that one who belongs to God may be competent,
  equipped for every good work.**

I charge you in the presence of God and of Christ Jesus,
   who will judge the living and the dead,
   and by his appearing and his kingly power:
   proclaim the word;
   be persistent whether it is convenient or inconvenient;
   convince, reprimand, encourage through all patience
      and teaching.

The word of the Lord. All: **Thanks be to God.**

Gospel (Luke 18:1-8)
Alleluia (Hebrews 4:12)

℣. Alleluia, alleluia. ℟. **Alleluia, alleluia.**
℣. The word of God is living and effective,
   discerning reflections and thoughts of the heart. ℟.

✠ **A reading from the holy Gospel according to Luke**

All: **Glory to you, Lord.**

God will secure the rights of his chosen ones who call out to him.

**Jesus told his disciples a parable
   about the necessity for them to pray always without
      becoming weary.
He said, "There was a judge in a certain town
   who neither feared God nor respected any human being.
And a widow in that town used to come to him and say,
   'Render a just decision for me against my adversary.'
For a long time the judge was unwilling, but eventually
   he thought,
   'While it is true that I neither fear God nor respect
      any human being,
   because this widow keeps bothering me
   I shall deliver a just decision for her
   lest she finally come and strike me.'"
The Lord said, "Pay attention to what the dishonest
   judge says.
Will not God then secure the rights of his chosen ones
   who call out to him day and night?**

Will he be slow to answer them?
I tell you, he will see to it that justice is done for them
  speedily.
But when the Son of Man comes, will he find faith on
  earth?"

The Gospel of the Lord. All: **Praise to you, Lord Jesus Christ.**

Prayer over the Gifts
Lord God,
may the gifts we offer
bring us your love and forgiveness
and give us freedom to serve you with our lives.
We ask this in the name of Jesus the Lord. All: **Amen.**

Communion Antiphon (Psalm 32:18-19)
See how the eyes of the Lord are on those who fear him,
on those who hope in his love, that he may rescue them
from death and feed them in time of famine.

Prayer after Communion
Lord,
may this eucharist help us to remain faithful.
May it teach us the way to eternal life.
Grant this through Christ our Lord. All: **Amen.**

Thirtieth Sunday in Ordinary Time

October 24, 2010

(World Mission Sunday)

Reflection on the Gospel

In the parable the Pharisee's prayer is praise for himself that he is "not like the rest of humanity." The tax collector, on the other hand, identifies himself with all of humanity as a sinner in need of God's mercy.

The former is taken up with what he does for God (fasts, pays tithes). The latter is overcome by awareness of what he needs from God (mercy). The Pharisee justified himself; the tax collector "went home justified" by God.

- *What I most need from God is . . .*

—Living Liturgy™, *Thirtieth Sunday in Ordinary Time 2010*

Entrance Antiphon (Psalm 104:3-4)

Let hearts rejoice who search for the Lord. Seek the Lord and his strength, seek always the face of the Lord.

Opening Prayer

Almighty and ever-living God,
strengthen our faith, hope, and love.
May we do with loving hearts
what you ask of us
and come to share the life you promise.
We ask this through our Lord Jesus Christ, your Son,
who lives and reigns with you and the Holy Spirit,
one God, for ever and ever. All: **Amen.**

Reading I (L 150-C) (Sirach 35:12-14, 16-18)

A reading from the Book of Sirach

The prayer of the lowly pierces the clouds.

**The Lord is a God of justice,
   who knows no favorites.
Though not unduly partial toward the weak,
   yet he hears the cry of the oppressed.
The Lord is not deaf to the wail of the orphan,
   nor to the widow when she pours out her complaint.
The one who serves God willingly is heard;
   his petition reaches the heavens.
The prayer of the lowly pierces the clouds;
   it does not rest till it reaches its goal,
nor will it withdraw till the Most High responds,
   judges justly and affirms the right,
and the Lord will not delay.**

The word of the Lord. All: **Thanks be to God.**

Responsorial Psalm 34

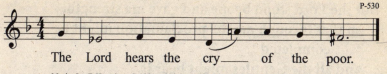

The Lord hears the cry of the poor.

Music: Jay F. Hunstiger, © 1991, administered by Liturgical Press. All rights reserved.

Psalm 34:2-3, 17-18, 19, 23

℟. (7a) **The Lord hears the cry of the poor.**

> I will bless the LORD at all times;
>> his praise shall be ever in my mouth.
>
> Let my soul glory in the LORD;
>> the lowly will hear me and be glad. ℟.
>
> The LORD confronts the evildoers,
>> to destroy remembrance of them from the earth.
>
> When the just cry out, the LORD hears them,
>> and from all their distress he rescues them. ℟.
>
> The LORD is close to the brokenhearted;
>> and those who are crushed in spirit he saves.
>
> The LORD redeems the lives of his servants;
>> no one incurs guilt who takes refuge in him. ℟.

Reading II (2 Timothy 4:6-8, 16-18)

A reading from the second Letter of Saint Paul to Timothy

From now on, the crown of righteousness awaits me.

**Beloved:
I am already being poured out like a libation,
 and the time of my departure is at hand.
I have competed well; I have finished the race;
 I have kept the faith.
From now on the crown of righteousness awaits me,
 which the Lord, the just judge,
  will award to me on that day, and not only to me,
  but to all who have longed for his appearance.
At my first defense no one appeared on my behalf,
 but everyone deserted me.**

May it not be held against them!
But the Lord stood by me and gave me strength,
> so that through me the proclamation might be completed
> and all the Gentiles might hear it.
And I was rescued from the lion's mouth.
The Lord will rescue me from every evil threat
> and will bring me safe to his heavenly kingdom.
To him be glory forever and ever. Amen.

The word of the Lord. All: **Thanks be to God.**

Gospel (Luke 18:9-14)
Alleluia (2 Corinthians 5:19)
℣. Alleluia, alleluia. ℟. **Alleluia, alleluia.**
℣. God was reconciling the world to himself in Christ,
> and entrusting to us the message of salvation. ℟.

✠ **A reading from the holy Gospel according to Luke**

All: **Glory to you, Lord.**

The tax collector, not the Pharisee, went home justified.

Jesus addressed this parable
> to those who were convinced of their own righteousness
> and despised everyone else.
"Two people went up to the temple area to pray;
> one was a Pharisee and the other was a tax collector.
The Pharisee took up his position and spoke this prayer to himself,
> 'O God, I thank you that I am not like the rest of humanity—greedy, dishonest, adulterous—or even like this tax collector.
I fast twice a week, and I pay tithes on my whole income.'
But the tax collector stood off at a distance
> and would not even raise his eyes to heaven
> but beat his breast and prayed,
> 'O God, be merciful to me a sinner.'

I tell you, the latter went home justified, not the former;
for whoever exalts himself will be humbled,
and the one who humbles himself will be exalted."

The Gospel of the Lord. All: Praise to you, Lord Jesus Christ.

Prayer over the Gifts
Lord God of power and might,
receive the gifts we offer
and let our service give you glory.
Grant this through Christ our Lord. All: **Amen.**

Communion Antiphon (Psalm 19:6)
We will rejoice at the victory of God and make our boast in his great name.

Prayer after Communion
Lord,
bring to perfection within us
the communion we share in this sacrament.
May our celebration have an effect in our lives.
We ask this in the name of Jesus the Lord. All: **Amen.**

Thirty-first Sunday in Ordinary Time

October 31, 2010

Reflection on the Gospel
Encountering Jesus does not depend upon goodness of life, but encountering him can bring about conversion of life: Zacchaeus undergoes dramatic change (he sets his affairs right and gives to the poor). His newfound concern for others is a sign of encounter with Jesus who brings salvation. Our own encounters with Jesus can bring about just as dramatic a change in our lives. We need only be willing to go to ever greater heights to "see him."

- *A change in me that encountering Jesus needs to bring about is . . .*

—Living Liturgy™, *Thirty-first Sunday in Ordinary Time 2010*

Entrance Antiphon (Psalm 38:22-23)
Do not abandon me, Lord. My God, do not go away from me! Hurry to help me, Lord, my Savior.

Opening Prayer
God of power and mercy,
only with your help
can we offer you fitting service and praise.
May we live the faith we profess
and trust your promise of eternal life.
Grant this through our Lord Jesus Christ, your Son,
who lives and reigns with you and the Holy Spirit,
one God, for ever and ever. All: **Amen.**

Reading I (L 153-C) (Wisdom 11:22—12:2)
A reading from the Book of Wisdom

You have mercy on all because you love all things that are.

**Before the Lord the whole universe is as a grain
   from a balance
      or a drop of morning dew come down upon the earth.
But you have mercy on all, because you can do all things;
   and you overlook people's sins that they may repent.
For you love all things that are
   and loathe nothing that you have made;
      for what you hated, you would not have fashioned.
And how could a thing remain, unless you willed it;
   or be preserved, had it not been called forth by you?
But you spare all things, because they are yours,
   O Lord and lover of souls,
      for your imperishable spirit is in all things!
Therefore you rebuke offenders little by little,
   warn them and remind them of the sins
      they are committing,
   that they may abandon their wickedness
      and believe in you, O Lord!**

The word of the Lord. All: **Thanks be to God.**

Responsorial Psalm 145

I will praise your name for-ev-er, my king and my God.

Music: Jay F. Hunstiger, © 1991, administered by Liturgical Press. All rights reserved.

Psalm 145:1-2, 8-9, 10-11, 13, 14

℟. (*See* 1) **I will praise your name forever, my king and my God.**

I will extol you, O my God and King,
   and I will bless your name forever and ever.
Every day will I bless you,
   and I will praise your name forever and ever. ℟.

The Lord is gracious and merciful,
   slow to anger and of great kindness.
The Lord is good to all
   and compassionate toward all his works. ℟.

Let all your works give you thanks, O Lord,
   and let your faithful ones bless you.
Let them discourse of the glory of your kingdom
   and speak of your might. ℟.

The Lord is faithful in all his words
   and holy in all his works.
The Lord lifts up all who are falling
   and raises up all who are bowed down. ℟.

Reading II (2 Thessalonians 1:11—2:2)

A reading from the second Letter of Saint Paul to the Thessalonians

May the name of Christ be glorified in you and you in him.

Brothers and sisters:
We always pray for you,
   that our God may make you worthy of his calling
   and powerfully bring to fulfillment every good purpose
   and every effort of faith,
   that the name of our Lord Jesus may be glorified in you,

and you in him,
in accord with the grace of our God and Lord Jesus Christ.

We ask you, brothers and sisters,
with regard to the coming of our Lord Jesus Christ
and our assembling with him,
not to be shaken out of your minds suddenly, or to be alarmed
either by a "spirit," or by an oral statement,
or by a letter allegedly from us
to the effect that the day of the Lord is at hand.

The word of the Lord. All: **Thanks be to God.**

Gospel (Luke 19:1-10)
Alleluia (John 3:16)

℣. Alleluia, alleluia.   ℟. **Alleluia, alleluia.**
℣. God so loved the world that he gave his only Son, so that everyone who believes in him might have eternal life. ℟.

✠ A reading from the holy Gospel according to Luke

All: **Glory to you, Lord.**

The Son of Man has come to seek and to save what was lost.

At that time, Jesus came to Jericho and intended to pass through the town.
Now a man there named Zacchaeus,
who was a chief tax collector and also a wealthy man,
was seeking to see who Jesus was;
but he could not see him because of the crowd,
for he was short in stature.
So he ran ahead and climbed a sycamore tree in order to see Jesus,
who was about to pass that way.
When he reached the place, Jesus looked up and said,
"Zacchaeus, come down quickly,
for today I must stay at your house."

And he came down quickly and received him with joy.
When they all saw this, they began to grumble, saying,
> "He has gone to stay at the house of a sinner."

But Zacchaeus stood there and said to the Lord,
> "Behold, half of my possessions, Lord, I shall give to the poor,
> and if I have extorted anything from anyone
> I shall repay it four times over."

And Jesus said to him,
> "Today salvation has come to this house
> because this man too is a descendant of Abraham.

For the Son of Man has come to seek
> and to save what was lost."

The Gospel of the Lord. All: **Praise to you, Lord Jesus Christ.**

Prayer over the Gifts
God of mercy,
may we offer a pure sacrifice
for the forgiveness of our sins.
We ask this through Christ our Lord. All: **Amen.**

Communion Antiphon (Psalm 16:11)
Lord, you will show me the path of life and fill me with joy in your presence.

Prayer after Communion
Lord,
you give us new hope in this eucharist.
May the power of your love
continue its saving work among us
and bring us to the joy you promise.
We ask this in the name of Jesus the Lord. All: **Amen.**

Thirty-second Sunday in Ordinary Time

November 7, 2010

Reflection on the Gospel

The Sadducees in this gospel suggest a preposterous example to ridicule belief in the resurrection. With supreme confidence Jesus counters that God "is not God of the dead, but of the living." We do indeed live forever. Like the brothers in the first reading, like Jesus himself, we believe in God's promise of resurrection. It is the bedrock of our hope and the inspiration for our fidelity to the living God.

- *I show my fidelity to the God of the living when . . .*

—*Living Liturgy™, Thirty-second Sunday in Ordinary Time 2010*

Entrance Antiphon (Psalm 88:3)

Let my prayer come before you, Lord; listen, and answer me.

Opening Prayer

God of power and mercy,
protect us from all harm.
Give us freedom of spirit
and health in mind and body
to do your work on earth.
We ask this through our Lord Jesus Christ, your Son,
who lives and reigns with you and the Holy Spirit,
one God, for ever and ever. All: **Amen.**

Reading I (L 156-C) (2 Maccabees 7:1-2, 9-14)

A reading from the second Book of Maccabees

The King of the world will raise us up to live again forever.

It happened that seven brothers with their mother were arrested
   and tortured with whips and scourges by the king,
   to force them to eat pork in violation of God's law.
One of the brothers, speaking for the others, said:
   "What do you expect to achieve by questioning us?
We are ready to die rather than transgress the laws of our ancestors."

At the point of death he said:
   "You accursed fiend, you are depriving us of this present life,
   but the King of the world will raise us up to live again forever.
It is for his laws that we are dying."

After him the third suffered their cruel sport.
He put out his tongue at once when told to do so,
   and bravely held out his hands, as he spoke these noble words:
   "It was from Heaven that I received these;
   for the sake of his laws I disdain them;
   from him I hope to receive them again."
Even the king and his attendants marveled at the young man's courage,
   because he regarded his sufferings as nothing.

After he had died,
   they tortured and maltreated the fourth brother in the same way.
When he was near death, he said,
   "It is my choice to die at the hands of men
   with the hope God gives of being raised up by him;
   but for you, there will be no resurrection to life."

The word of the Lord. All: Thanks be to God.

Responsorial Psalm 17

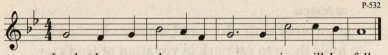

Lord, when your glory appears, my joy will be full.

Music: Jay F. Hunstiger, © 1991, administered by Liturgical Press. All rights reserved.

Psalm 17:1, 5-6, 8, 15

℟. (15b) **Lord, when your glory appears, my joy will be full.**

Hear, O L‍ord, a just suit;
  attend to my outcry;
  hearken to my prayer from lips without deceit. ℟.

My steps have been steadfast in your paths,
  my feet have not faltered.
I call upon you, for you will answer me, O God;
  incline your ear to me; hear my word. ℟.

Keep me as the apple of your eye,
  hide me in the shadow of your wings.
But I in justice shall behold your face;
  on waking I shall be content in your presence. ℟.

Reading II (2 Thessalonians 2:16—3:5)

A reading from the second Letter of Saint Paul to the Thessalonians

May the Lord encourage your hearts and strengthen them in every good deed and word.

**Brothers and sisters:
May our Lord Jesus Christ himself and God our Father,
  who has loved us and given us everlasting encouragement
  and good hope through his grace,
  encourage your hearts and strengthen them in every good deed and word.

Finally, brothers and sisters, pray for us,
  so that the word of the Lord may speed forward and be glorified,**

as it did among you,
and that we may be delivered from perverse and
    wicked people,
for not all have faith.
But the Lord is faithful;
he will strengthen you and guard you from the evil one.
We are confident of you in the Lord that what we instruct
    you,
you are doing and will continue to do.
May the Lord direct your hearts to the love of God
    and to the endurance of Christ.

The word of the Lord. All: **Thanks be to God.**

GOSPEL (Luke 20:27-38) *or* Shorter Form [ ] (Luke 20:27, 34-38)
ALLELUIA (Revelation 1:5a, 6b)
℣. Alleluia, alleluia.   ℟. **Alleluia, alleluia.**
℣. Jesus Christ is the firstborn of the dead;
to him be glory and power, forever and ever. ℟.

✠ **A reading from the holy Gospel according to Luke**

All: **Glory to you, Lord.**

He is not God of the dead, but of the living.

**[Some Sadducees, those who deny that there is a
    resurrection,
came forward]** **and put this question to Jesus, saying,
"Teacher, Moses wrote for us,
*If someone's brother dies leaving a wife but no child,
his brother must take the wife
and raise up descendants for his brother.*
Now there were seven brothers;
the first married a woman but died childless.
Then the second and the third married her,
and likewise all the seven died childless.
Finally the woman also died.
Now at the resurrection whose wife will that woman be?
For all seven had been married to her."**

[Jesus said to them,
"The children of this age marry and remarry;
but those who are deemed worthy to attain to the coming age
and to the resurrection of the dead
neither marry nor are given in marriage.
They can no longer die,
for they are like angels;
and they are the children of God
because they are the ones who will rise.
That the dead will rise
even Moses made known in the passage about the bush,
when he called out 'Lord,'
the God of Abraham, the God of Isaac, and the God of Jacob;
and he is not God of the dead, but of the living,
for to him all are alive."]

The Gospel of the Lord. All: **Praise to you, Lord Jesus Christ.**

Prayer over the Gifts
God of mercy,
in this eucharist we proclaim the death of the Lord.
Accept the gifts we present
and help us follow him with love,
for he is Lord for ever and ever. All: **Amen.**

Communion Antiphon (Psalm 23:1-2)
The Lord is my shepherd; there is nothing I shall want.
In green pastures he gives me rest, he leads me beside the waters of peace.

Prayer after Communion
Lord,
we thank you for the nourishment you give us
through your holy gift.
Pour out your Spirit upon us
and in the strength of this food from heaven
keep us single-minded in your service.
We ask this in the name of Jesus the Lord. All: **Amen.**

Thirty-third Sunday in Ordinary Time

November 14, 2010

Reflection on the Gospel

The signs of the end times that Jesus names in the gospel describe human history as it has always been. Jesus assures us that the end is not immediate. The challenge for us as faithful followers is to face persecution with courage now, testify to Jesus' name now, open ourselves now to the wisdom given us by Jesus. Embracing this way of living gives us hope and confidence that, no matter when the end times come, our lives are secure.

- *I need courage to live and proclaim the gospel when . . .*

—Living Liturgy™, *Thirty-third Sunday in Ordinary Time 2010*

ENTRANCE ANTIPHON (Jeremiah 29:11, 12, 14)

The Lord says: my plans for you are peace and not disaster; when you call to me, I will listen to you, and I will bring you back to the place from which I exiled you.

OPENING PRAYER

Father of all that is good,
keep us faithful in serving you,
for to serve you is our lasting joy.
We ask this through our Lord Jesus Christ, your Son,
who lives and reigns with you and the Holy Spirit,
one God, for ever and ever. All: **Amen.**

READING I (L 159-C) (Malachi 3:19-20a)

A reading from the Book of the Prophet Malachi

The sun of justice will shine on you.

**Lo, the day is coming, blazing like an oven,
    when all the proud and all evildoers will be stubble,
and the day that is coming will set them on fire,
    leaving them neither root nor branch,
    says the LORD of hosts.**

But for you who fear my name, there will arise
    the sun of justice with its healing rays.

The word of the Lord. All: Thanks be to God.

Responsorial Psalm 98

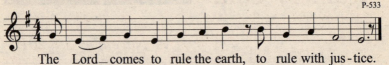

The Lord comes to rule the earth, to rule with justice.

Music: Jay F. Hunstiger, © 1991, administered by Liturgical Press. All rights reserved.

Psalm 98:5-6, 7-8, 9

℟. (See 9) **The Lord comes to rule the earth with justice.**

Sing praise to the LORD with the harp,
    with the harp and melodious song.
With trumpets and the sound of the horn
    sing joyfully before the King, the LORD. ℟.

Let the sea and what fills it resound,
    the world and those who dwell in it;
let the rivers clap their hands,
    the mountains shout with them for joy. ℟.

Before the LORD, for he comes,
    for he comes to rule the earth;
he will rule the world with justice
    and the peoples with equity. ℟.

Reading II (2 Thessalonians 3:7-12)

A reading from the second Letter of Saint Paul to the Thessalonians

If anyone is unwilling to work, neither should that one eat.

Brothers and sisters:
You know how one must imitate us.
For we did not act in a disorderly way among you,
    nor did we eat food received free from anyone.
On the contrary, in toil and drudgery, night and day
    we worked, so as not to burden any of you.
Not that we do not have the right.

Rather, we wanted to present ourselves as a model for you,
> so that you might imitate us.
In fact, when we were with you,
> we instructed you that if anyone was unwilling to work,
> neither should that one eat.
We hear that some are conducting themselves among
> you in a disorderly way,
> by not keeping busy but minding the business of others.
Such people we instruct and urge in the Lord Jesus Christ
> to work quietly
> and to eat their own food.

The word of the Lord. All: **Thanks be to God.**

Gospel (Luke 21:5-19)
Alleluia (Luke 21:28)
℣. Alleluia, alleluia. ℟. **Alleluia, alleluia.**
℣. Stand erect and raise your heads
> because your redemption is at hand. ℟.

✛ **A reading from the holy Gospel according to Luke**

All: **Glory to you, Lord.**

By your perseverance you will secure your lives.

**While some people were speaking about
> how the temple was adorned with costly stones and
>> votive offerings,
> Jesus said, "All that you see here—
> the days will come when there will not be left
> a stone upon another stone that will not be thrown
>> down."
Then they asked him,
> "Teacher, when will this happen?
And what sign will there be when all these things are
> about to happen?"
He answered,**

"See that you not be deceived,
 for many will come in my name, saying,
 'I am he,' and 'The time has come.'
Do not follow them!
When you hear of wars and insurrections,
 do not be terrified; for such things must happen first,
 but it will not immediately be the end."
Then he said to them,
 "Nation will rise against nation, and kingdom against kingdom.
There will be powerful earthquakes, famines, and plagues
 from place to place;
 and awesome sights and mighty signs will come from the sky.
"Before all this happens, however,
 they will seize and persecute you,
 they will hand you over to the synagogues and to prisons,
 and they will have you led before kings and governors
 because of my name.
It will lead to your giving testimony.
Remember, you are not to prepare your defense beforehand,
 for I myself shall give you a wisdom in speaking
 that all your adversaries will be powerless to resist or refute.
You will even be handed over by parents, brothers, relatives, and friends,
 and they will put some of you to death.
You will be hated by all because of my name,
 but not a hair on your head will be destroyed.
By your perseverance you will secure your lives."

The Gospel of the Lord. All: **Praise to you, Lord Jesus Christ.**

Prayer over the Gifts
Lord God,
may the gifts we offer
increase our love for you
and bring us to eternal life.
We ask this in the name of Jesus the Lord. All: **Amen.**

Communion Antiphon (Mark 11:23, 24)
I tell you solemnly, whatever you ask for in prayer, believe that you have received it, and it will be yours, says the Lord.

Prayer after Communion
Father,
may we grow in love
by the eucharist we have celebrated
in memory of the Lord Jesus,
who is Lord for ever and ever. All: **Amen.**

Christ the King

November 21, 2010

Reflection on the Gospel

By naming Christ the "king" we acknowledge him and his way of living as the wellspring of our goodness and salvation. We acknowledge our status as his "subjects" called to relate to others as he did. We acknowledge our shared inheritance as those who receive life through him. By naming Christ our King we identify him as the One who offers us the fullness of life in his kingdom both now and forever.

- *What this gospel teaches me about Jesus as king is . . . What this gospel teaches me about being Jesus' "subject" is . . .*

—Living Liturgy™, *Christ the King 2010*

Entrance Antiphon (Revelation 5:12; 1:6)
The Lamb who was slain is worthy to receive strength and divinity, wisdom and power and honor: to him be glory and power for ever.

November 21

Opening Prayer

Almighty and merciful God,
you break the power of evil
and make all things new
in your Son Jesus Christ, the King of the universe.
May all in heaven and earth acclaim your glory
and never cease to praise you.
We ask this through our Lord Jesus Christ, your Son,
who lives and reigns with you and the Holy Spirit,
one God, for ever and ever. All: **Amen.**

Reading I (L 162-C) (2 Samuel 5:1-3)

A reading from the second Book of Samuel

They anointed David king of Israel.

**In those days, all the tribes of Israel came to David in Hebron and said:
"Here we are, your bone and your flesh.
In days past, when Saul was our king,
it was you who led the Israelites out and brought them back.
And the Lord said to you,
'You shall shepherd my people Israel
and shall be commander of Israel.'"
When all the elders of Israel came to David in Hebron,
King David made an agreement with them there before the Lord,
and they anointed him king of Israel.
The word of the Lord.** All: **Thanks be to God.**

Responsorial Psalm 122

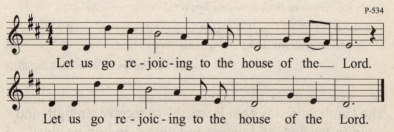

Let us go rejoicing to the house of the Lord.
Let us go rejoicing to the house of the Lord.

Music: Jay F. Hunstiger, © 2004, administered by Liturgical Press. All rights reserved.

Psalm 122:1-2, 3-4, 4-5

℟. (*See 1*) **Let us go rejoicing to the house of the Lord.**

> I rejoiced because they said to me,
>> "We will go up to the house of the Lord."
>
> And now we have set foot
>> within your gates, O Jerusalem. ℟.
>
> Jerusalem, built as a city
>> with compact unity.
>
> To it the tribes go up,
>> the tribes of the Lord. ℟.
>
> According to the decree for Israel,
>> to give thanks to the name of the Lord.
>
> In it are set up judgment seats,
>> seats for the house of David. ℟.

Reading II (Colossians 1:12-20)

A reading from the Letter of Saint Paul to the Colossians

He transferred us to the kingdom of his beloved Son.

**Brothers and sisters:
Let us give thanks to the Father,
   who has made you fit to share
   in the inheritance of the holy ones in light.
He delivered us from the power of darkness
   and transferred us to the kingdom of his beloved Son,
   in whom we have redemption, the forgiveness of sins.
      He is the image of the invisible God,
         the firstborn of all creation.
      For in him were created all things in heaven and on earth,
         the visible and the invisible,
         whether thrones or dominions or principalities
            or powers;
         all things were created through him and for him.
      He is before all things,
         and in him all things hold together.**

He is the head of the body, the church.
He is the beginning, the firstborn from the dead,
   that in all things he himself might be preeminent.
For in him all the fullness was pleased to dwell,
   and through him to reconcile all things for him,
   making peace by the blood of his cross
   through him, whether those on earth or those in heaven.

The word of the Lord. All: **Thanks be to God.**

Gospel (Luke 23:35-43)
Alleluia (Mark 11:9, 10)
℣. Alleluia, alleluia. ℟. **Alleluia, alleluia.**
℣. Blessed is he who comes in the name of the Lord!
   Blessed is the kingdom of our father David that is to come! ℟.

✠ **A reading from the holy Gospel according to Luke**

All: **Glory to you, Lord.**

Lord, remember me when you come into your kingdom.

The rulers sneered at Jesus and said,
   "He saved others, let him save himself
   if he is the chosen one, the Christ of God."
Even the soldiers jeered at him.
As they approached to offer him wine they called out,
   "If you are King of the Jews, save yourself."
Above him there was an inscription that read,
   "This is the King of the Jews."
Now one of the criminals hanging there reviled Jesus, saying,
   "Are you not the Christ?
Save yourself and us."
The other, however, rebuking him, said in reply,
   "Have you no fear of God,
   for you are subject to the same condemnation?

And indeed, we have been condemned justly,
> for the sentence we received corresponds to our crimes,
> but this man has done nothing criminal."

Then he said,
> "Jesus, remember me when you come into your
> > kingdom."

He replied to him,
> "Amen, I say to you,
> today you will be with me in Paradise."

The Gospel of the Lord. All: **Praise to you, Lord Jesus Christ.**

Prayer over the Gifts
Lord,
we offer you the sacrifice
by which your Son reconciles mankind.
May it bring unity and peace to the world.
We ask this through Christ our Lord. All: **Amen.**

Communion Antiphon (Psalm 29:10-11)
The Lord will reign for ever and will give his people the gift of peace.

Prayer after Communion
Lord,
you give us Christ, the King of all creation,
as food for everlasting life.
Help us to live by his gospel
and bring us to the joy of his kingdom,
where he lives and reigns for ever and ever. All: **Amen.**

GUIDELINES FOR RECEIVING COMMUNION

For Catholics

As Catholics, we fully participate in the celebration of the Eucharist when we receive Holy Communion. We are encouraged to receive Communion devoutly and frequently. In order to be properly disposed to receive Communion, participants should not be conscious of grave sin and normally should have fasted for one hour. A person who is conscious of grave sin is not to receive the Body and Blood of the Lord without prior sacramental confession except for a grave reason where there is no opportunity for confession. In this case, the person is to be mindful of the obligation to make an act of perfect contrition, including the intention of confessing as soon as possible (Code of Canon Law, canon 916). A frequent reception of the Sacrament of Penance is encouraged for all.

For our fellow Christians

We welcome our fellow Christians to this celebration of the Eucharist as our brothers and sisters. We pray that our common baptism and the action of the Holy Spirit in this Eucharist will draw us closer to one another and begin to dispel the sad divisions which separate us. We pray that these will lessen and finally disappear, in keeping with Christ's prayer for us "that they may all be one" (Jn 17:21).

Because Catholics believe that the celebration of the Eucharist is a sign of the reality of the oneness of faith, life, and worship, members of those churches with whom we are not yet fully united are ordinarily not admitted to Holy Communion. Eucharistic sharing in exceptional circumstances by other Christians requires permission according to the directives of the diocesan bishop and the provisions of canon law (canon 844 § 4). Members of the Orthodox Churches, the Assyrian Church of the East, and the Polish National Catholic Church are urged to respect the discipline of their own Churches. According to Roman Catholic discipline, the Code of Canon Law does not object to the reception of Communion by Christians of these Churches (canon 844 § 3).

For those not receiving Holy Communion

All who are not receiving Holy Communion are encouraged to express in their hearts a prayerful desire for unity with the Lord Jesus and with one another.

For non-Christians

We also welcome to this celebration those who do not share our faith in Jesus Christ. While we cannot admit them to Holy Communion, we ask them to offer their prayers for the peace and unity of the human family.

Copyright © 1997 United States Catholic Conference. All rights reserved.